LET THE CHIPS FALL

My Battles Against Corruption

BY

NEWBOLD MORRIS

in collaboration with

DANA LEE THOMAS

APPLETON - CENTURY - CROFTS, INC.

NEW YORK

Copyright, 1955, by

NEWBOLD MORRIS and DANA LEE THOMAS

Library of Congress Card Number: 55-6071

The excerpt from Harry S. Truman's *Mr. President,* edited by William Hillman with pictures by Alfred Wagg, copyright 1952, is reprinted with the permission of the publishers, Farrar, Straus and Young, Inc.

"Dedication Poem" by Bonaro Overstreet appeared in the first number of *The Program Magazine of the City Center of Music and Drama,* December 11, 1943, by courtesy of the author and *P.M.* Reprinted here with the kind permission of Mrs. Overstreet.

The quotation from Judge Learned Hand's Address to the 86th Convocation of the University of the State of New York in October, 1952, is reprinted from *The Spirit of Liberty,* Alfred A. Knopf, Inc., copyright 1952.

PRINTED IN THE UNITED STATES OF AMERICA

To the hundreds of my fellow citizens
who have joined me
in the fight for good Government
often without hope of victory and
always without hope of material reward,
this book is dedicated.

N.M.

INTRODUCTION

FIFTY YEARS AGO Lincoln Steffens, Ida Tarbell, Ray Stannard Baker opened the eyes of the American people to how the corruptors were exploiting our political system and making a mockery of it. At that time President Theodore Roosevelt pinned a label on the effort of these hard-hitting journalists that has stuck through the ages. He called it "muckraking." Since the days of the early muckrakers, politicians have grown more subtle in their exploitation. Today, many of them have learned to practice graft legally. Nevertheless, despite this refinement, corruption is as harmful to the health of democracy today as in the days of Steffens and company; as a matter of fact, it is even more so. At present our society has been forced by the totalitarians into the open market of competition for millions of uncommitted human beings. The situation we face because of our obligations of leadership was never dreamed of by the early muckrakers. Steffens urged us to clean house for the sake of our national well-being; today, the stakes are for the freedom of the world's billions.

Since Lincoln Steffens' studies, there has been remarkably little work approaching his level in the field of municipal corruption. In particular, there has been no systematic, comprehensive attempt to analyze the New York City reform movement from firsthand political

sources since the Walker scandals. Yet, New York in
many respects has been a fountainhead of political corruption that has reached far beyond its borders. Political
friends had for years been emphasizing to me certain
aspects of the story that should be told. But there was a
major obstacle. Many of the details, especially those involving America's great reform mayor, Fiorello H. La-
Guardia, existed in the private papers and the memories
of the people who had played a leading part in the times.
I realized that there were significant areas of the story
that could be best revealed through the eyes of a political
personality who had dominated the scene.

Newbold Morris occupied a particularly strategic spot.
He was a leader of the fusion movement that kept La-
Guardia in office for three terms. As President of the
City Council, he became LaGuardia's closest political
associate, and when he strove to keep up the momentum
of good government upon LaGuardia's retirement, the
latter supported him vigorously. During two turbulent
mayoralty campaigns, in 1945 as an Independent, and in
1949, as the candidate of the Republican, Liberal and
Fusion parties, Morris hit hard at the revived Tammany
machine and he exposed the scandals of the Democratic
administration that succeeded reform. In fact, so intimately had Morris's name become associated with the
struggle against political corruption that the Truman
Administration, riddled with boss politics, selected him
to come to Washington as "government cleanup man"
to help restore the confidence of the people in their
national government.

And there is another aspect to the Morris story that
interested me. Morris is as far removed, in personality

and background, from the typical politician as can be imagined. A descendant of seventeenth-century Americans, and of Gouverneur Morris, the "penman" of the Constitution, Morris is an aristocrat among bluebloods, born to a life of sheltered comfort. Yet he threw himself into the rough-and-tumble of street-corner politics and championed the cause of the immigrant, the Negro, the sweatshop worker, risking his political career time and again (like Franklin Delano Roosevelt) against the vested interests of his own class. The affectionate and close-knit partnership of LaGuardia, who was born in an East Side tenement house, with this descendant of early colonial stock could have taken place only in America.

As I progressed in my collaboration with Morris (entered into on his part only after modest, emphatic protests that his story was unimportant), I became vividly aware of the scope of the problems faced by that phenomenon in our public life, the honest politician. Morris had refused to play politics according to the rules of patronage. He refused to be blindly loyal to the machine. He spoke out when other politicians would have remained silent. He seemed to have a genius for sponsoring politically unpopular causes. Yet, although Morris has fought bitterly against corruption, he has refused to pass judgment on the individual who plays along with the system. He has often wondered whether he, too, like the corner policeman, might not have succumbed to the taking of graft, if this would have meant more milk for his family. Fortunately he has not had to use politics as a livelihood. And, precisely because he has been able to divorce his political actions from blind economic self-interest, his career has a fascinating clinical value for the student of politics. It may well be that the effective political reformers must inevitably be recruited from an economic class of men who, in entering public life, have nothing at stake but their conscience.

At any rate, here is the book that I believed should be written—a book that substitutes political practice for political theory. Morris pulls no punches. If the reader becomes somewhat pessimistic in reviewing one citizen's frustrated efforts to buck the political machine, let him bear in mind that it was the social "dreamers" of yesterday who set the "impossible" standards that the average American enjoys today.

Once Morris was won over to the idea of the book, he put his heart and soul into the undertaking. As I worked with him from his personal files and the public records, his memory became refreshed. He has labored with me at every step, dictating and redictating to insure painstaking and meticulous accuracy. I am indebted to the numerous people who have helped in the reconstruction of this story—politicians not only on Morris's side of the fence but on the opposite side as well. I am grateful, among others, to Murray Stand, a leader in Democratic party politics since the days of Governor Al Smith; to Adolf Berle, the former Roosevelt "brain truster" and a moving spirit behind Fusion; to Hubert Delany, the brilliant jurist; to Reuben Lazarus, one of the country's leading authorities on municipal government; to Louis I. Gottlieb, an old LaGuardia partisan, who was the earliest to envisage the possibilities of this book; to Morton Baum, taxation expert in the LaGuardia administrations and a long-time associate of Morris in good-government projects. I am grateful

also to associates of Morris in other walks of life—to
John Golden, the Broadway producer and a colleague
of Morris's in that interesting experiment in popular
aesthetics, the City Center of Music and Drama; to Elsa
Maxwell, one of the City Center's most enthusiastic supporters. I want to thank Mr. Robert Hug and the staff
of the New York Public Library for the assistance they
have given me in my researches. I owe a special debt of
gratitude to George White, that truly extraordinary corruption hunter and one of the United States Government's top experts in crime. White has seen politicians
come and go. (In fact, he has helped to put away several
himself.) Perhaps the greatest testimonial to Morris's in-
ability to play political ducks and drakes is the fact that
White has hung Morris's picture on the wall of his study
—the gesture of an admiring fan. I wonder how many
likenesses of other politicians adorn the walls of government crime hunters.

One question raised by the Morris story which is of
particular importance today is this: How can one be a
Republican and remain a liberal? Unfortunately, this
happens to be an American and not a partisan problem,
since the American people are wedded, for good or evil,
to a Republican President and to a Republican Administration whose wisdom or lack of it may determine
the future of the world. In the nineteen-twenties Morris
and other young Republicans joined the party in the belief that it would continue to press forward in the traditions of Abraham Lincoln and Theodore Roosevelt, and
that its Warren Gamaliel Harding phase was simply a
passing madness. Morris joined with LaGuardia, George
Norris, the young La Follette, Wendell Willkie, Bronson

Cutting and other like-minded Republicans to harness the progressive forces of Republicanism to keep pace with the social planning of the New Deal. The systematic deterioration of liberal Republicanism under the counterattack of the conservative party leadership marks the story of Morris's own career and underlines the tragedy of the Republican party at present.

This book was written primarily for those Americans who would be happy to see more eggheads and fewer deadheads in public office today and who harbor the notion that it takes intellectual courage not irresponsible demagoguery to cope with the problems of the world.

DANA LEE THOMAS

Kew Gardens, N.Y.

CONTENTS

xiii

CHAPTER 1 How to Lose Friends in Washington

O N the afternoon of January 28, 1952, I was at work in my law office at 52 Wall Street, when the telephone rang. Washington was calling. Peyton Ford, Deputy Attorney General of the United States, was at the other end of the wire. I had first met Ford through one of my law partners who had become friendly with him during the recent war. Shortly afterward, he had phoned me on behalf of Attorney General McGrath asking me to talk my wife's father, Judge Learned Hand, into accepting the chairmanship of a recently established commission to draw up an internal security code. On another occasion, Peyton had wanted me to try to convince the husband of Judge Hand's eldest daughter, Norris Darrell, a distinguished lawyer, to accept a job as Chief of the Tax Division in the Justice Department.

On this afternoon in January, Ford came quickly to the point.

He was calling at the request of the Attorney General who, he said, would like me to come to Washington to talk over with him an appointment as a special assistant. My duty would be to make a survey of the extent of misconduct in the Federal Government.

This was a tall order to be confronted with unexpectedly on a quiet, bleak January afternoon. Of course, I

1

had been involved for twenty-five years in reform politics in New York. I had been reading in the newspapers that the Truman Administration, rocked to its heels with revelations of bribed tax collectors, influence peddlers and donors of mink coats, realized that there was a public demand for swift action. I knew that efforts were being made to restore confidence in the Administration with the presidential election coming up in the fall. Still, it was incredible that they should want the services of a Republican and—particularly—the services of Newbold Morris who had done his best to put an end to the Tammany spoils system ever since the days of Jimmy Walker. For a minute I kept repeating surely it was one of my relatives that he wanted me to persuade, but Ford insisted that McGrath wanted to talk to me.

I agreed to come to Washington. On Tuesday, January 29th, I took the sleeper at Pennsylvania Station and arrived the following morning in the Capital. At the Department of Justice Peyton Ford took me into the office of Philip Perlman, the Solicitor General of the United States. We talked for a while then drove out to the Attorney General's beautiful house. That was my first meeting with J. Howard McGrath. I had no inkling during that first friendly conversation that two nightmarish months were ahead of me.

The Attorney General wasted no time in preliminaries. It turned out that what he wanted wasn't just a survey. *Mr. McGrath desired a full-scale government investigation.* He pointed out that the whole federal civil service was suffering because of the acts of misconduct of a few. The only way confidence could be restored, he declared, was in a thorough house cleaning.

I was unprepared for this, to put it mildly. A government cleanup man? This conception was certainly a novel one. In fact, it was unprecedented. There had been plenty of investigations of individuals in public office, but never before had anyone been hired to investigate the entire Federal Government—a giant octopus of departments, bureaus and agencies employing two and a half million workers and running on a seventy-billion-dollar annual budget.

"Mr. Attorney General," I said, "if you are looking for a corruption hunter, are you sure you want someone like me poking into your affairs? I'm poison to politicians in both parties in New York. I might break some crockery down here."

McGrath replied that the Administration had reached a point where it was anxious to have accusations investigated by an impartial observer, one who had a reputation for integrity, without any ax to grind. He emphasized the President's desire to prove to the people that the stories of graft in his Administration had been maliciously exaggerated by his enemies.

I told McGrath I would like to think things over for a couple of days, because this would mean my leaving home for a certain period of time. I took the afternoon train back to New York and had four hours of reflection as the Congressional Limited raced through the countryside.

This was the end of January, and whatever I could do had to be accomplished within eight or ten months. The offer seemed fantastic, and looking back on it now, it appears even more so. If I was expected to direct an honest-to-goodness investigation, the President would have to be prepared to obtain from Congress grants of executive power greater than had ever before been given to an individual. And, of course, there were obvious snares involved. I learned that this job had been previously offered to at least two other individuals, Federal Judge Thomas Murphy and Robert Patterson, the former Secretary of War. Both had turned it down. Bob had done a long tour of duty for his country brilliantly and with devotion.

I'm certain that if I had discussed the offer with my political associates, they would have tried to dissuade me. They would have pointed out that the Truman Government desired a "whitewash"; that the Democrats weren't anxious for a bona fide investigation; that I actually wouldn't be permitted to investigate the very people who hired me.

I had never turned away from a challenging situation. I suppose that, deep down in my heart, I felt that whether I succeeded or not, I would at least have one more excursion into the field of government which interested me so greatly. So I accepted. I telephoned Peyton Ford and told him I would be down on Friday to go over details with the Attorney General and meet the President. I severed my connections with my law firm for the duration of the assignment. On my last evening in New York, my wife and I attended the opera with the Adolf Berles and Mrs. August Belmont. As the final curtain came down on *Carmen,* I felt a sudden twinge. This curtain was a symbol of my parting from New York. I felt uneasy about the future.

In my years in the New York City government I had become used to the rough and tumble of politics. I had been up against some mighty case-hardened opponents. I had seen "Dutch" Schultz, the numbers racket king and czar of the bootlegging industry, turn an election into a defeat for a candidate for the State Senate who had refused to be blackjacked into dealing with him. I had seen mobsters in gray fedoras pull up to polling places in limousines and attempt to intimidate voters. I had known on occasion that bosses of both major parties who appeared to be battling one another in so-called "two-party" election contests, met secretly behind the scenes and divided the spoils. I had been kicked in the shins in my office in City Hall by an infuriated councilman. I had been threatened with jail for contempt of court in refusing to obey an injunction that attempted to dictate the parliamentary procedure of the City Council. But never before had I been challenged to enter the high-tension politics of Washington.

I arrived at the Department of Justice on Friday morning and was closeted for a time with the Attorney General, the Solicitor General, and Peyton Ford. At eleven o'clock we arrived at the White House and I was presented to Harry S. Truman. I had met Mr. Truman once before, in the fall of 1944, when, as a candidate for Vice President, he visited New York to make a speech and he arrived at City Hall to call on Mayor LaGuardia.

The mayor often seemed to derive satisfaction in keeping distinguished visitors waiting while he attended to city business with his commissioners. On that occasion, I had come out of the mayor's office and was surprised to find Truman standing shyly alone, his hands thrust into his pockets, staring out of the window toward the cross section of Broadway and Chambers Street. I had introduced myself to the Senator from Missouri and told him a little about the history of City Hall. I spoke about the furniture in my office—the chandelier, the grandfather's clock and the mirror which had been used by John Adams when he was President of the United States and New York was the nation's capital.

And now, eight years later, this pleasant man was the President. And I was a private citizen. He stood up and shook hands with an assurance I had not remembered from our previous meeting. He was so friendly that I almost forgot that I wasn't just sight-seeing in Washington; that he expected me to take on a difficult assignment. I told him something of my background, my hatred of the spoils system. He replied that he knew all about me, that that was the very reason he welcomed my assistance in Washington. He said he would be receptive to any measures I suggested for getting on with the house cleaning. He assured me that I would have complete freedom to operate unhampered. It was decided that I would be sworn in as Special Assistant to McGrath that afternoon.

Before leaving I told the President and the Attorney General that I would like to work quietly, avoiding publicity. But this was an impossible hope. We had entered the Executive Office by one door and we went out by another. There was nothing quiet about this exit. As we descended the stairs of the White House, reporters from the wire services and the metropolitan newspapers gathered around us. I had been accustomed to newswriters on the New York City papers, but this was on an entirely different scale.

I held an informal press conference on the spot. Almost immediately I was asked what department of government I intended probing first. I tried to duck that one, not having made any plans.

"Look, gentlemen, you know that I've just come to Washington. I haven't even an office to hang my hat in yet . . ."

McGrath broke in with a vigorous flourish of his cigar. "I would be the first to welcome an investigation."

"In that case," I finished, "we might as well start with the Department of Justice."

One reporter broke in to ask me (this was the period during which Taft and Eisenhower were being mentioned prominently for the Presidential nomination) whether I was a Taft Republican or an Eisenhower Republican. Not wishing to become involved in that political dispute, I answered, "I am an Abraham Lincoln Republican."

With the first interview behind us, Howard McGrath took me to lunch at the 1925 F Street Club. Before long we were on a first-name basis. I was assured that my job would not be a taxing one; that it should not disrupt my private and professional life too much. "You can clean the whole thing up in several months," I was assured.

It was late in the afternoon by the time we reached the Department of Justice. The Attorney General administered to me the oath of office and handed me a formal letter of appointment dated February 1, 1952, as follows:

MY DEAR MR. MORRIS:

You are hereby appointed Special Assistant to the Attorney General, with headquarters at the seat of

Government in Washington, D.C., to perform the following functions:

1. Conduct investigations leading to the detection of, and appropriate action with respect to, any officers or employees of the Federal Government, and other persons, who may be guilty of improper or illegal conduct relating to the performance of official business of the Federal Government.

2. Conduct investigations, undertake studies, and make periodic recommendations to the President and the Attorney General for the correction and prevention of improper or illegal acts relating to the transaction of official business of the Federal Government.

3. Recommend to the Attorney General the initiation of prosecutions and other legal actions which may be warranted on the basis of facts ascertained in the course of such investigations or studies.

4. Report to appropriate authorities any facts ascertained in the course of such investigations or studies which indicate that removal or other disciplinary action would be warranted with respect to any officer or employee of the Federal Government.

Very truly yours,
J. HOWARD MCGRATH
Attorney General

After a further conference it was decided that I would commence my duties the following Monday, February 4th. Before I left McGrath sent out a press release of my appointment, as follows:

Mr. Newbold Morris is a distinguished lawyer with a reputation for courage, firmness and fairness in dealing with problems that affect the integrity of

public service. He served as President of the City
Council of the City of New York during the administration of the late Mayor Fiorello LaGuardia and
shares with the memory of Mayor LaGuardia the
respect with which his administrations are univer-
sally held. His many other public services and the
causes to which he has devoted his life are a matter
of public record.

In asking Mr. Morris to accept this assignment, I
have assured him that he will have my complete,
enthusiastic and unlimited cooperation, and that all
of the facilities of the various agencies of the Government which I administer or which can be made
available through the office of the President will be
at his disposal. No one is more anxious than I, as Attorney General, to have the charge of misconduct in
public office thoroughly and impartially sifted, for
I realize that the strength of our system of Government depends upon the faith that all men must have
in it.

Whatever staff and financial assistance Mr. Morris
will determine he needs in the performance of his
duty has been assured to him.

I recognize the undertaking to which Mr. Morris
has committed himself is a difficult one. I earnestly
ask the American people to place their trust in the
rectitude of his efforts no less than my own in en-
deavoring to find the full and complete answer to
the question that has been raised as to the extent of
venality in the Federal service.

Only by determining this in a truly objective
manner, unmoved by personal or political consid-
erations can we hope to retain for the faithful public
servants of our Government the honor and respect
they so richly deserve.

Mr. Morris owes no allegiance whatsoever by rea-

son of prior association or otherwise to myself or to
the present Administration. I have asked him to
undertake this task solely as a service to his country.

I remember feeling at the time that this was somewhat exaggerated and, perhaps, a too expansive estimate,
and what a contrast it proved to the curt letter of dismissal which was served upon me two months and two
days later!

I was fingerprinted, given an identification card,
handed a key to a private elevator for Very Important
People, and I was launched on the job. It was a bewildering atmosphere in which I found myself. As the days
went by, I recalled the proverb about people being
killed with an excess of kindness, and I began to wonder
whether this would possibly apply to me.

At the end of my first working day, McGrath invited
me to meet the chiefs of his department divisions. They
were all there, with the exception of J. Edgar Hoover,
head of the Federal Bureau of Investigation, who was
recuperating from an attack of grippe in Florida. I was
to meet and talk with him later.

Howard asked me if there were any remarks I would
like to make. I thanked him for the opportunity and
did speak a few words. I discussed political pressures,
and how difficult it was to administer a government
operation efficiently with constant interference from
politicians. I pointed out how appointments given out
of political consideration impair the morale of those
who have won their places by competitive civil service
examinations. I also touched on another fact I had discovered during my few days in Washington. I had been
disturbed to discover that some federal district attorneys

and a number of assistants in the Department of Justice were engaging in the private practice of law "on the side." I stated my conviction that you could not have efficient public service with loyalty divided between private clients and public duties.

Toward the end of my first week in Washington, Matthew Connolly, the President's secretary, informed me that an appointment had been arranged with Mr. Truman for the following Monday in Blair House. I arrived for my appointment at eight, and was conducted into the study that the President used for his evening work while the White House was being renovated. Mrs. Truman and their daughter Margaret were out, and so he was alone. The first thing that impressed me was the utter loneliness of a President.

Mr. Truman greeted me cordially. I started off by telling him how much I had enjoyed meeting his daughter at a recent luncheon in New York.

The President seemed pleased. "Margaret is a good girl; and that's because her mother is a wonderful person. In general I've found that children are no better or worse than their mothers."

I took a seat next to the President's desk, which was piled high with papers—reports from Korea, from the State Department, from the Department of Defense— all to be read before he retired for the evening.

The President commenced to shuffle through his papers, saying that he had a document dealing with the business that had brought me to Washington, and he wanted to turn it over to me. As he continued to leaf through his papers, without success, I suggested that he abandon the hunt. I explained that the time we had together could be more fully exploited if he permitted me to talk freely about my work. If, later on, he found the report, he could send it to me.

The President swiveled his chair around, looking steadily at me through his steel-rimmed glasses. I couldn't help admiring the physical fitness and mental alertness of one I had really known only through the newspapers. He bade me proceed. Since McGrath had moved me into headquarters in the Justice Department to carry out my assignment, many people had deduced that my investigation would turn into a whitewash. Pointing out to the President that the public could hardly have confidence in a bona fide investigation if I was operating in one of the departments which was to come under my scrutiny, I asked to be given independent office quarters. "I don't know where twenty thousand square feet of space can be found, but if I were President of the United States, I guess I could arrange for it."

He agreed and promised that by the following Monday I would have an office of my own.

I pointed out that there was no appropriation for my work and for the payment of a staff. He asked me how much I would need, and I said at least half a million dollars. He replied that he would make available $750,000 which would come out of the President's emergency fund, over which he had complete control, so that it would not be necessary to go to Congress, at least for the present.

I told him that it was impossible to proceed without the proper tools and that the most important of these was the power of subpoena. Again he agreed and promised to have a bill introduced, and to send a message to both houses of Congress.

Then, I asked for an executive order directing the heads of all departments, bureaus and agencies in the Federal Government to comply with my requests for personnel or papers, documents and records. I emphasized that I wanted him to use the phrase "prompt compliance," because that would show the country that he and I meant business. This he agreed to do.

I then told Mr. Truman that what the Federal Government needed was not just a one-shot investigation like mine; that an investigative agency should be established as part of the Executive branch working three hundred sixty-five days a year, looking into complaints and into sensitive spots in the Government where there might be opportunities for graft. I told him that I was astonished to find that in Washington not even the Attorney General and the Director of the Federal Bureau of Investigation had the power of subpoena. I told him about the Department of Investigation we have in New York City which is at the disposal of the mayor; that citizens of New York sending complaints to City Hall at least knew that the machinery was in existence for following up their charges.

"Mr. President, you must have hundreds of letters coming in to the White House every day complaining of one thing or another, some of them even alleging acts of misconduct by officers and employees. What happens to them?"

The President replied that all complaints were sent to the head of the department to which they related;

that it was up to the department head to decide whether to investigate within his department.

The President received my idea of a Department of Investigation with genuine enthusiasm and asked me to prepare a memorandum on it for him.

Finally I pointed out, "Mr. President, it's obviously impossible for me to investigate two and a half million government employees. But I believe it is feasible to look into the performance of about ten thousand employees at the top. The conduct of these administrators sets an example which is usually followed in the ranks.

"Of course, Mr. President, when I say top levels, I mean exactly that. *I intend to examine the affairs of employees right here in the White House.*"

The President assured me that no one in a responsible position should be exempted from inquiry. But he asked me how I proposed to investigate the conduct of ten thousand people.

There was only one way I knew of proceeding, I told him. I would begin by circulating a questionnaire. Such a questionnaire would elicit information concerning the net worth of the employee, including cash in banks and elsewhere, real estate, jewelry and furs. Liabilities would have to be listed, showing notes and mortgages payable as well as a list of unpaid debts. All bank and brokerage accounts would have to be listed, also the names of nominees, trustees, escrow agents and fictitious names. Another important question would be whether any substantial sums of money had been won or lost in gambling in any one year. The answers to the questionnaire would be kept confidential, as in the case of income tax returns.

I discussed with the President the standard of living check that could be based on the questionnaire. Of course, the vast majority of public officials were honest. However, if a federal official reported an annual salary of $12,000 and an independent income of $2,500 from investments, and it turned out that he had a mansion in Washington, a house in Florida, belonged to an expensive country club, owned three automobiles and had bought his wife a crested mink coat, it becomes apparent that there were hidden assets somewhere.

The President not only acquiesced in all my points, but he approved enthusiastically. At the end of the meeting he grasped my hand warmly as he said good night, and he asked me to report to him once a week. He told me that Charlie Murphy, his legal counsel, would forward the various documents I needed and that Donald Dawson, his administrative assistant, would be in touch with me about office space and clerical help.

As I walked back to the Carlton Hotel I felt that with the support of the President of the United States, I ought to be able to do the job.

Three days later at a press conference, the President issued a statement on our meeting:

> I have had a good conference with Mr. Newbold Morris about his plans for carrying out his job as Special Assistant to the Attorney General.
>
> I am directing all departments and agencies of the Government to cooperate fully with Mr. Morris in the performance of his duties, and to give him any information and assistance he may require, and to give the *highest priority* to any requests made by him. Adequate funds will be provided for the ac-

tivities of Mr. Morris and his staff, and they will be given separate office space outside the Department of Justice.

I intend to see to it that Mr. Morris has access to all information he needs that is in the possession of the Executive branch, and the authority to examine and require testimony from all officers and employees of the Executive branch. However, in many cases where Government employees have been subject to outside influence, the most essential evidence is not in Government hands. Mr. Morris cannot conduct a thoroughgoing and effective investigation of cases such as these unless he has the power to subpoena witnesses and documents from outside the Government. The Executive branch cannot confer such power on Mr. Morris. It must be provided by statute. Accordingly, I am going to ask the Congress to give Mr. Morris the subpoena powers necessary to the proper performance of his duties.

The Attorney General wholeheartedly concurs in these recommendations and in the arrangements we are making to enable Mr. Morris to do an independent, thorough and efficient job.

Mr. Morris will have my full support, and I intend to follow the progress of his work very closely. I hope that he will also have the full support of the Congress and the public.

At a meeting of the House Judiciary Committee, I had a friendly reception—particularly from the chairman, Representative Chelf from Kentucky, and from the ranking minority member, Congressman Emanuel Celler of New York, and Representative Keating of New York. Congressman Celler was most helpful in introducing me to the individual members of the committee. They inquired about the necessity of the wide grant of powers of subpoena and the power to administer oaths. I tried to make it very clear that at no time did I ask for the power to grant immunity from prosecution and that as far as I was concerned the bill could be amended in order to eliminate that section from the joint resolution.

The President was as good as his word—in fact, the swiftness with which things happened exceeded my expectations. The following day I conferred with Donald Dawson at the Executive Offices. He introduced me to Carl Blaisdell, who was one of the experts of organization at the Pentagon. I was told that twenty thousand square feet of space would be available to me at the old *Washington Post* building and that Mr. Blaisdell was in charge of equipping it. When I took my first look at the place, I became slightly dizzy with agoraphobia. Compared to this setup, my Wall Street office was a chicken coop. Before me stood row after row of desks, each with a telephone—more than two hundred in all. The walls were banked from floor to ceiling with thousands of cabinet files. I realized that it would be quite a job to fill this space with qualified personnel. My first assistant upon my arrival in Washington had been a loan from the Justice Department, an attractive secretary. I had dictated several letters to her, and then, happening to glance over her shoulder, I discovered that she was taking down my dictation in longhand. She knew nothing about stenography.

It is no easy matter to go about investigating a government. In fact, the sheer weight of getting started was so overwhelming that there were moments when I felt like slinking back to New York and burying my nose in routine law work.

As the President had promised, the joint resolution which would confer the power of subpoena on me and members of my staff designated by me was introduced in Congress on February 14th. This bill contained one grant of power which I never asked for and which caused a great deal of apprehension on Capitol Hill. It was the power to compel testimony by granting immunity "in appropriate cases."

> I recommend that the Congress enact temporary legislation to give Mr. Newbold Morris, Special Assistant to the Attorney General, the power to compel the attendance and testimony of witnesses and the production of documentary evidence, and the authority to administer oaths. Such legislation is necessary to enable Mr. Morris to make a thorough and effective investigation of illegal or improper conduct in the transaction of Government business.
>
> The facilities of the Executive branch of the Government are being made available to assist Mr. Morris in performing his functions and responsibilities. He is authorized to obtain from the Executive branch such information and assistance, including papers, records and documents, as he needs to carry out his task. Officers or employees of the Executive branch assigned to Mr. Morris' staff will work under his direction and control for the period of their assignment.
>
> This authority from the Executive branch, however, is not enough. Much of the necessary evidence will have to come from the records and testimony of persons who are not connected with the Federal

Government. To do his job thoroughly, therefore, Mr. Morris must be able to obtain testimony and evidence from persons and organizations outside the Government. Without such testimony and evidence, Mr. Morris will be unable to make a fully effective and conclusive investigation. It is therefore essential that he be given the power of subpoena, the power to compel testimony by granting immunity in appropriate cases and the power to administer oaths.

Attached is a draft of a joint resolution to accomplish this purpose. I earnestly recommend its speedy enactment by the Congress.

The powers the proposed joint resolution would confer are to be exercised by Mr. Morris, as the Special Assistant to the Attorney General designated for this important task, and a limited number of his personal assistants. In no event, would the authority extend beyond December 31, 1952.

In short, the legislation requested is for a limited, specific purpose, but a very necessary one.

I know that every citizen wants Mr. Morris to clean up any wrong-doing there may be in the Government, and to recommend measures to safeguard against any future misconduct. He has my complete support in his important task. I urgently request the Congress to give him its support by enacting this necessary legislation.

Someone in the Justice Department had slipped that request for power to grant immunity into the draft of the President's message, without my sponsorship. In retrospect it looks as though this extreme request had been deliberately sneaked in to irritate the Congress needlessly and to drive it into turning down the granting of *any* powers. And that is exactly what happened.

I feel that I was tripped up from behind before I even reached the scrimmage line.

In the meantime I managed to recruit some high-caliber assistants among the people who knew me best and who had faith in me from personal experience. I was very fortunate in persuading an old friend and colleague in the city government, Morton Baum, to come to Washington and fill the post as Deputy Special Assistant. He had an organizing genius, and was well known as a tax specialist. He went to work immediately on one of the most difficult preliminary phases of the operation—the determining of which positions and titles would be subject to scrutiny.

I was also fortunate in persuading Samuel Becker to come to work as Chief Counsel. Sam was originally from Wisconsin and had been in charge of public utility investigations for Governor Philip La Follette. I persuaded Albert Pleydell, an outstanding authority on government purchasing, to come to Washington. He was slated to direct what was intended to be one of the most important areas of the investigation—the procurement methods of the Federal Government.

Louis Weintraub, who had been a trusted advisor of Mayor LaGuardia, acted on a consultant basis for me and he helped chart the course of my investigation with representatives from the Office of the Budget Director.

I commenced hiring a few young lawyers; I obtained George Cutler, a Boston attorney, Alice Kupferman, a keen woman lawyer, and James J. Lyons, the son of my old colleague the Borough President of the Bronx, who had just come out of the Navy with the rank of Lieutenant Commander.

There is an interesting story concerning one appointment I managed to put through. Rudolph Halley, who had been counsel for the Kefauver Crime Committee, recommended a remarkable individual, George H. White. White had been a government narcotics agent for eighteen years. In 1948, he received the Treasury Department's top medal for his work in breaking up a coast-to-coast dope ring run by leading underworld figures. White collected much of the evidence linking Lucky Luciano to the international dope traffic, and he presented the Kefauver Crime Committee with a devastating record of Frank Costello's activities. During World War II, White served as a counter-intelligence agent in India and the Middle East.

A short, barrel-chested individual, White had been born with the crusading bug in his blood stream. When I made inquiries about him upon my arrival in Washington, I was surprised to learn that several months previously he had been transferred from Chicago, where he had been active in running down criminals, to Boston, Massachusetts, where he had been given the title of District Supervisor of the New England Bureau of Narcotics. Transferring him to Boston was like sending the vice squad out to raid a ladies' seminary. New England was relatively free of the narcotics traffic. Actually White had been exiled to "Siberia" for embarrassing certain influential parties.

But the politicians had not gotten White out of their hair. Since the Narcotics Bureau is under the jurisdiction of the Department of the Treasury, I requested Secretary Snyder to assign White to my staff for a period of several months as my chief investigator. I received a courteous note from the Under Secretary of the Treasury, Edward H. Foley, Jr., advising me that White was vitally necessary in his present post (in New England!) and suggesting another Treasury employee in his place. I decided to make an issue of the matter. The President had promised to give me a completely free hand in my investigation. I put in a phone call to Donald Dawson at the White House and strongly urged the transfer of White. The call was placed on a Friday. On Monday morning, when I arrived at my office, I found White waiting for me.

After we discussed investigative techniques, I said to him, "Look, White, I'm afraid that if you come up with something that will hurt this government, you may be in for further reprisals."

He shrugged. *"If I do my job properly, whoever has it in for me will not be around any more."*

In the course of business, White turned over to me leads that were of interest. One file called my attention to the disquieting report that the special assistant to a high-ranking government official had been the former vice-president of a corporation that had been financed by underworld money, according to the sworn testimony of its president before the Kefauver Crime Committee. Frank Costello, Meyer Lansky and Joe Adonis had admitted under oath that they owned substantial shares of stock in this corporation.

Another report White called to my attention was that the special assistant of another government official had been the public relations counsel for a Latin-American gambling syndicate. Over a period of years, numerous complaints had been brought to the Justice Department by citizens who claimed they had been swindled by the syndicate in crooked gambling deals. But the Justice Department could not be persuaded to launch an investigation.

A third report I received from White had to do with a United States district attorney who was collecting fees from distilleries throughout his state in return for giving them immunity from federal prosecution for income tax evasion.

A fourth matter White brought to my attention was the friendship that allegedy existed between Thomas Luchese (a notorious hoodlum) and an assistant in a district attorney's office. Luchese, better known as "Three Finger Brown," was a colleague of Luciano, Costello and numerous other hoods. White's report described how Luchese had taken an automobile trip with the D.A.'s assistant to Florida and how both men had vacationed together at a Miami hotel. White also pointed out that the D.A.'s assistant lived, while at home, in a $400-a-month suite, a remarkable circumstance in view of his modest salary.

While my associates gained headway on their several assignments, I was rummaging around for investigative tools. I have already mentioned that, despite President Truman's request, Congress had refused to grant me power of subpoena; and I would have to get around this obstacle with other techniques. I consulted a series of attorneys who were experts in criminal investigations. Among those I called were Virgil Peterson of the Chicago Crime Commission; Warren Olney of California, now Chief of the Criminal Division of the Department of Justice; William H. Jackson, who had recently resigned as Deputy Director of Central Intelligence Agency; Fowler Hamilton, former Assistant Attorney General; and Francis M. Shea, formerly an associate counsel for the prosecution of major Axis war criminals. I had been particularly impressed with the way the grand jury in Kings County, under the handling of the Brooklyn District Attorney Miles McDonald, had probed into racketeering and had helped to accumulate evidence that finally damned the O'Dwyer administration. The attorneys I consulted confirmed my own ideas about the procedure to be followed. This was to convene grand juries, similar to the Kings County jury, in sensitive spots around the nation; to swear in prominent members of the bar in each locality as special deputies of the Justice Department to bring evidence and compel the appearance of witnesses before the grand jury. I talked over my plan with McGrath and he consented to it.

We set the date for consulting a federal district court judge for the convening of a special grand jury on April 3rd. In the meantime I was preparing my investigation along a second front. I had assigned Willard Carmel, until recently one of the top men in the New York City Department of Investigation, to prepare my questionnaire. Over a long week end, Carmel and I hammered out draft after draft, with the assistance of friends who had experience in investigation and eliciting pertinent information. We completed the final draft in two copies. One copy was retained by Carmel. I returned to Washington with the other copy in my brief case.

On the following Thursday I had a conference with President Truman. He was about to leave for a visit to

Key West. I came to the conference a bit apprehensive. The previous Sunday evening I had appeared on the television show, "Meet the Press." One reporter had asked me how I felt about President Truman's appointment of former Mayor O'Dwyer as Ambassador to Mexico. Despite the fact that his city administration had been riddled with scandals, I tried to dodge the question by pointing out that O'Dwyer had beaten me for mayor in two campaigns and that I was not an exactly unbiased party. But the reporter persisted: Would *I* have appointed O'Dwyer Ambassador to Mexico? I replied in the negative.

Then I was asked to express my opinion of President Truman's military aide General Harry Vaughan. I replied that I knew nothing about Vaughan except what I had read in the newspapers. I was asked if I would have appointed Vaughan my military aide if I were President. Again I answered in the negative.

The Monday morning newspapers carried headlines to the effect that O'Dwyer and Vaughan were "targets" of my investigations. Of course, I had not said that. Nevertheless, I felt that this business might have annoyed the President. I was surprised to find him as chipper as ever. It was he who brought up the subject. He declared that headlines were often misleading, and, that although he had not seen the television program, his staff had reported to him that I had said nothing in bad taste.

I introduced the topic of my questionnaire. I told him that eleven versions of the questionnaire had been hammered out, and that each time I went over it I had eliminated questions which might seem too burdensome or objectionable in any way. I pointed out that the answers would be classified as confidential, and that I was going to take very special pains for the security of these questionnaires when they came back. I asked him if he would like to look at the final draft before it went to the printer. He held up his hand. *He said that he didn't want to see a copy until he himself received one to be filled out!* I gasped a little at that. I told him that I had never considered investigating the President of the United States.

Mr. Truman insisted that he wanted to answer the questionnaire. He said he had nothing to hide himself and that he knew about his wife's and daughter's interests and that he felt certain that he could fill out the questionnaire in a very short time. He suggested that after sending him one, I mail a copy to each member of the Senate and House with a polite letter explaining that I realized the Executive branch had no power to investigate the Legislative branch, but if the members would voluntarily fill out the questionnaire and send it back to me, it would be kept completely confidential. Of course, the President added, it would be interesting to prepare, on the basis of the questionnaire, a report, without identifying personalities, showing the amount of time pre-empted by outside interests, the time devoted to public duties, and other information that some day might be of interest to students of government.

Buoyed by the President's encouragement, I left the White House, unaware that this was the last time I would see Harry Truman while he was President.

When the questionnaires were printed, I decided to deliver them personally to the heads of the agencies. On

March 18th, with the help of two porters, I carried about six hundred forms of the questionnaires to the Justice Department. To avoid publicity I entered by the back door. McGrath was on vacation at Sea Island, Georgia, but I gave the questionnaires to Philip Perlman, the Solicitor General, who examined a copy with an assistant. Perlman pointed to one question that asked for the amount of fees charged by government lawyers to clients in relation to the time spent with them. "Why do you want to know this?" Perlman asked.

"Suppose," I answered, "you have a client and have received from him five thousand dollars for three hours' work. With this information I can go to the client and say, 'Are you in the habit of paying a lawyer sixteen hundred and sixty-six dollars an hour?' He may reply, 'True, that lawyer *did* spend only three hours with me, but he put in a call to the RFC and I got a five million dollar loan.' "

Nine days later when McGrath had returned from his vacation, the questionnaires had still not been distributed to the top people in his department. I tried to make an appointment to see McGrath, and, failing that, I tried to reach him by telephone, first once a day, then two or three times a day. When I still couldn't reach him, I began calling his office every two and three hours to find out why the questionnaires had not been distributed.

While this cat-and-mouse game was going on, I read in the newspapers that McGrath had been called as a witness before the House Judiciary Subcommittee and that he had been asked by Congressman Kenneth Keating, "Have you filled out this [Morris] questionnaire?"

McGrath answered, "No."

"You are, of course, planning to fill one out?"

"I'm not sure, Mr. Congressman, whether I am or not."

Upon reading this, I picked up the telephone and put in a long-distance call to Key West. I told Charlie Murphy that it looked as if the Attorney General was going to dig in his heels, and that resentment was beginning to accumulate against me. He replied that the President had already instructed Leslie Biffle, Secretary of the Senate, to arrange a lunch at the Senate Office Building for me with the Vice President and leading members of the majority to try to thaw out the climate of opinion.

After repeatedly calling the office of the Attorney General, I finally received a telephone call from a mutual friend. Howard McGrath would be willing to meet me for lunch. When we met on Tuesday, March 25th, I did not bring up the subject of the questionnaires and I was as tactful as possible. I told him I would like to get going in his department so that the investigation would be completed there as soon as possible, and he appeared to welcome getting it over with. I asked him if the chief counsel on my staff, Samuel Becker, could call at his office on Wednesday, March 26th. I told him that Colonel Becker would arrange with a number of accountants and attorneys to go over his records. He appeared to be completely agreeable to this. As we parted, he promised that the questionnaires would go out immediately.

Becker called on the Attorney General and spoke to him for three-quarters of an hour. At first McGrath seemed his old friendly self. But when Becker came to the nub of his visit he ran into trouble. He informed McGrath that, in addition to having the questionnaires distributed, we were prepared to begin a routine examination of the Department. We wanted to examine correspondence, diaries, appointment books, records of telephone calls.

Why had Morris singled out the Department of Justice for this investigation, McGrath wanted to know.

Becker reminded the Attorney General that it was McGrath himself who had suggested at the press conference preceding my appointment that the Department be the first to be investigated. Becker added that we had no reason to doubt that the affairs of the Department were properly handled, but that if any irregularities turned up, it was in the interest of the Department to make the facts known promptly, so that any rumors or charges could be set at rest.

McGrath retorted angrily that he would not consent to an examination of the Department's files, and he added that in no case would he permit the examination of his own records.

Faced with this impasse, Becker returned to his office and wrote me a memorandum: *This problem must be resolved promptly. Unless this question is answered satisfactorily before the end of next week, I see nothing further for us to do.*

To this I added, "Amen."

Now, at last, I saw the handwriting on the wall. If the Justice Department was unwilling to open its records to me, what Department would? Indeed, Secretary of the

Treasury Snyder had already shown even less enthusiasm for my investigation than McGrath (if that is possible!). For weeks, the reporters, among them my old friends, had been telling me that "nobody"—and they emphasized the word "nobody"—wanted me in Washington.

With regard to McGrath, in particular, I suppose a psychoanalyst would tell me that at no time did McGrath want an investigation; that when he found I really meant business he prepared his defenses, but he waited until the last moment in the hope that lightning might strike. In Washington the traffic is even more bewildering than in New York, and it was perfectly possible that I might be run over by a streetcar.

I heard later that the Attorney General had been privately dismissed from his office some months before, but that he had pleaded for one more chance. In appointing me he was carrying out his promise to set up some kind of machinery for a cleanup. I often wonder whether Howard McGrath has ever picked up a copy of a book containing the writings of Harry S. Truman and entitled *Mr. President*. In that book there is a paragraph whose directness appeals to me:

> I think that every public official who gets more than $10,000 a year ought to show exactly what his outside income is, if any. That should include District Attorneys, Senators and Congressmen—everyone in the federal service. I don't see any reason why that shouldn't be done. If a fellow is honest, he doesn't care.
>
> One of the most important steps to be taken in dealing with the whole problem of corruption in public life is to put key Government officials under

Civil Service. There is going to be a howl from the
patronage boys all the way down the street. But I
will fight for this vital and urgent change.

Actually, my experience in Washington was not unprecedented. When Senator Kefauver, who was at the
Yale Law School when I entered, had first organized his
Senate committee, most Democrats from the Justice
Department down had been bitterly opposed to him.
Spokesmen in the Criminal Division of the Justice Department had declared that a nationwide crime syndicate was a myth. Then, when the committee was finally
organized, the Justice Department backed an amendment to a pending tax bill that, if passed, would have
blocked the Bureau of Internal Revenue from bringing action against mobster tax dodgers who offered to
cough up taxes once they had discovered that the Government was after them. This coddling of hoodlums by
the Government had been going on for a long time
before Kefauver hit the trail.

They didn't want me any more than Kefauver—
certainly not the Department of Justice whose district
attorneys in certain localities were tied in with political
bosses and the underworld. I was not welcomed by the
Department of the Treasury, whose internal revenue
collectors were dropping out of office like flies under
grand jury indictments from Boston to San Francisco.
I was certainly not befriended by the Reconstruction
Finance Corporation, which was under investigation at
the time by a Senate committee. I was not greeted with
enthusiasm by the Federal Housing Administration,
some of whose officials were in virtual partnership with
unethical builders to swindle rent payers, home owners

and the general taxpayer out of a quarter of a billion dollars. Surely I was not endorsed by certain military officers in the War Production Authority who, while serving their country in uniform, had been privately retained on the payrolls of contractors to whom they handed padded contracts which were parlayed into fortunes.

From the day of Colonel Becker's unproductive session with Attorney General McGrath, events moved rapidly toward a climax. For example, after returning from one week end in New York, I discovered that my payroll had been held up. Assistant Attorney General Andretta telephoned me that orders had been received from "upstairs" that no pay check could be issued to members of my staff until a field security check on each individual had been conducted by the F.B.I. This was a body blow, because it would take several months before the security checks could be completed. The crisis was upon us.

One event particularly underlined the tension. The President returned from Key West in time to greet Queen Juliana of the Netherlands, who was on a visit to the United States. Awaiting her arrival at the airport were Mr. Truman and members of his cabinet. I read in the evening papers that the President, the Presidential Secretary, Joseph Short, and the Attorney General had been seen standing apart from the group, engaged in a heated discussion, apparently over my questionnaire. It seemed to observers that the Attorney General was being given a piece of somebody's mind.

I worked and waited, and appeared on television to mobilize public opinion behind me.

Arthur Krock, chief of the Washington bureau of the *New York Times,* arranged a dinner for me at the Metropolitan Club to meet a group of newspaper writers, editors and network commentators on April 1. Among those invited were the late Bert Andrews of the New York *Herald-Tribune,* James Reston of the *New York Times,* Frank Kent of the Baltimore *Sun,* Roscoe Drummond, then of the *Christian Science Monitor,* Bill Hillman of the Mutual Broadcasting System, Eric Sevareid of the Columbia Broadcasting System. It was the consensus of opinion among the newsmen that my problem would come to a head within a matter of hours. They agreed unanimously that the President had to take a stand; the only question was, would he support his long-time friend (who was in public defiance of his executive order), or would he back up the position of a man he hardly knew and who had played no part whatever in his own climb to ascendancy.

In view of everything he had done and said, logic would seem to demand support of my work. However, even as we talked, I had a feeling that the political system was too strong even for a President to buck. No one at that dinner foresaw what actually would happen before the curtain was lowered—that two bodies would be left lying on the stage as in the finale of a Shakespearean drama.

On Thursday morning, April 3rd, two days after the news dinner, I commenced dictating a memorandum to the President. He had asked me to remind him of my suggestions for establishing an investigation agency in the Executive Department which would receive complaints from the public and carry on investigations as a routine business. I had been deeply impressed by a remark J. Edgar Hoover had made to me during my first week in Washington. He had told me that the FBI was too overloaded with ordinary security investigations and with the job of protecting the nation against Communist espionage agents to be able to handle adequately the specialized problem of corruption in government. I felt that my proposed "watchdog" agency would be the answer. This agency—a newly constituted arm of the Executive to be headed by a commissioner and deputies with broad powers of subpoena, and responsible directly to the President—would function not only to receive complaints and to detect wrongdoing in public office, but even, more important, to act as a deterrent to it. No one has ever provided me with a solid argument as to why a President of the United States should not have this machinery.

At 12:45, while I was putting the finishing touches on my Presidential memorandum, the telephone rang. Ruth Montgomery of the New York *Daily News* was on the wire. *She informed me that the Attorney General had just announced my dismissal as his Special Assistant!*

I hung up, and almost immediately, a member of my staff came in to confirm the news. He had taken it off the ticker tape. Ten minutes later, a messenger from the Department of Justice arrived at the office and insisted on handing me personally a note from the Attorney General.

SIR:
   Please be informed that your appointment as a
Special Assistant to the Attorney General is hereby

terminated and your services as an employee of the Department of Justice shall cease at the close of business today.

You are hereby requested to deliver all files, records and documents in your offices to the Federal Bureau of Investigation.

Very Truly Yours,

J. HOWARD MCGRATH
Attorney General

As I read this curt message I couldn't help remembering the expansive statement the Attorney General had made to the press on my appointment only two months previously, describing me as "a distinguished lawyer with a reputation for courage, firmness and a fairness in dealing with the . . . public service."

Within several minutes, newspaper reporters and photographers arrived in droves at my office. They sent in a request for an immediate interview, but I decided to wait before making any statement. I heard that the President was to have a special press conference at 4:00 P.M.

As the afternoon wore on, I completed the memorandum for the President which I wanted to have ready for him in case he sent for me. I wanted to give him every opportunity for taking such action as he saw fit. However, I had no inkling of the sensation that was to develop. *At his conference, the President announced the resignation of J. Howard McGrath as Attorney General.* What had taken place between the President and McGrath I have not discovered. But, at any rate, McGrath was out along with me. There was a certain logic to this development. When a President is unable to decide which of two subordinates merits his support, he cuts the Gordian knot by abandoning them both.

One fact generally overlooked by the press and public at this time was this: *The day of my dismissal was the date on which Attorney General McGrath and I had agreed to call on a United States District Court judge for the purpose of convening a grand jury in Washington, D.C., to begin the probe into the criminal phases of corruption.* At six o'clock I agreed to meet with representatives of the press, as Department of Justice employees started removing all files and papers from the office. For the reporters, I reviewed all the events leading up to the present debacle.

Before I left my office, I reached Joe Short on the telephone and told him that I would wait until the following day before departing from Washington in the event the President indicated a desire to see me. I made no request for an interview, preferring to leave the matter entirely with the President.

On Friday morning, April 4th, I called together all members of the staff and thanked them for their loyalty. After saying good-by to each and every one, I prepared to leave on an afternoon train for New York. Gathered at the station were reporters and photographers, but I was just too exhausted to make any comments. Arriving at Pennsylvania Station, I found a number of my old friends reporting for the metropolitan newspapers on hand to greet me. We gathered in the stationmaster's office for a quiet smoke. The reporters seemed to be fascinated by the questionnaire. I gave a copy to Bill

Henderson of the Hearst Press, as he appeared particularly anxious to have one.

When I reached my apartment, I learned that Colonel Becker had been phoning from Washington. When I reached him he asked me whether the President had gotten in touch with me. A call had come in from the White House both at my office and at the Carlton Hotel, after I had departed on the train. Whether it was a message from the President himself, I do not know. But I decided that if Harry Truman really wanted to get in touch with me his secretaries would have no trouble finding me.

I had two curtain calls in Washington. I had been invited as a guest speaker at the National Press Club on Wednesday, April 9th. I protested that now that my mission was over they would not want to hear from me. Evidently tickets had been sold and I was urged to keep my appointment. I am glad I did, for I found a most sympathetic audience and I had an opportunity to leave an impression that there was still unfinished business in Washington.

The following day, in response to an invitation of Chairman Chelf of the Special Subcommittee of the House Judiciary Committee set up to investigate the Department of Justice, the questioning commenced in an effort to find out if I had any "leads" for the committee to follow. Counsel for the committee was Stephen A. Mitchell, at present Chairman of the Democratic National Committee. The members of the committee wanted to go all through my proposed method of investigation. I felt that they were wasting their time, because my employment with the Federal Government was over and there seemed no purpose in reviewing my plans which had been frustrated. However, as a sight-seer, I relaxed and answered questions as well as I could.

Just before picking up my belongings at a hotel and leaving Washington, I sat for a time on a park bench facing the White House, watching the fountains playing in the late afternoon sun. I decided that the rights, privileges and immunities of private life were much too precious to relinquish for another excursion into public service. I reflected on how much fun it would be to read in the newspapers about something happening to someone who wasn't me.

So this was the end of the venture. McGrath retired to his Rhode Island law office in favor of Federal Judge James F. McGranery who succeeded him as Attorney General. I returned to my Wall Street firm, a little wiser from having learned at first hand that Washington's Number One industry is the political shell game.

I had come to Washington wondering like millions of other Americans who was really running the Government. I had discovered that the Government was being run by a collection of self-seeking politicians (often in defiance of the President himself), whose will was being felt either by direct order or by implication in a thousand political echelons from Maine to California. I had found that cabinet members and other highly placed officials were openly disregarding Presidential directives when they didn't agree with them. Shortly after my dismissal, in addressing the National Press Club, I said, "Someday we are going to have politicians in public office who, instead of saying 'To the victor belongs the spoils' will declare, 'To the victors come the responsibility for honest government.' "

Since the birth of our nation, the "Big Fix" has been a curse of our party politics. The *Crédit Mobilier* scandal under Grant, the Teapot Dome tragedy under Harding, the five-percenters and bribed tax collectors under Truman, are the recurring outbreaks of a chronic illness.

Indeed, a "brain truster" in the Eisenhower campaign called and asked me to turn over to him any data I had compiled on corruption in Washington together with my recommendations for dealing with it. He at least must have recognized that no matter how honest the President and his immediate associates might be, the potentialities for corruption are inherent in the very nature of our political system.

Furthermore, Washington has a large quota of former government officials who are doing business with friends in key places in the Government (many of them in the bureaus from which they themselves have recently departed). The capital is always teeming with influence peddlers, ex-Congressmen turned lobbyists, and other folk whose zeal for protecting the taxpayer's money is not exactly overwhelming. Instead of being able to extend the coverage of Civil Service, President Eisenhower has been under continual pressure to lift several hundred top policy positions out of Civil Service and make them available to the party faithful.

Eisenhower, like Truman, has had trouble with family black sheep. His party has been forced, for instance, to accept the resignation of one chairman of the National Committee who, when he was a public relations counsel, had allegedly accepted a fee in trying to sell a privately owned hospital to the state, when it appeared that the state already possessed title to the building.

Yes, although Truman and company have left public life, the trouble lingers on.

Incidentally, while all my life I have been disgusted with the pattern of corruption, I have never adopted a "holier-than-thou" attitude toward individuals. When I arrived home after my frustrating experience in Washington, my friends asked me how I felt personally toward President Truman. I replied by telling them a story.

A leading industrialist completed a tour of service with the Federal Government and upon his return was given a welcome-home dinner by his "silk stocking" Republican friends. When the guests were seated at the table, the hostess turned to him and asked, "Ernest, tell us what you think of Harry Truman."

He shook his head. "No. I can't possibly tell you. It would shock you."

The conversation turned to other topics. When the ladies had retired to the living room and the men gathered over their cigars and coffee, the host reopened the subject. "Now, Ernest, the ladies have left. We aren't easily shocked. Tell us, what is your opinion of the President?"

But Ernest shook his head and remained silent.

Shortly after midnight when all had departed with the exception of the guest of honor, the host sidled up to him and whispered as he helped him on with his hat and coat, "Ernest, we're alone now; my wife is out of earshot. What do you think of Harry Truman?"

"All right, I'll tell you then. *I like him.*"

CHAPTER 2 "An Indian Named Charlie"

WITHIN a few hours after my appointment as Special Assistant Attorney General, political attacks began to be leveled at me. It was a source of bewilderment to find that most of them came from Republicans. Senator Mundt from South Dakota, Senator Nixon from California, Representative Potter from Michigan, none of whom knew me or probably had ever heard of me before, gave out statements to the newpapers implying in one way or another that I was not a person of integrity. Doubts were raised as to my sincerity of purpose in accepting an appointment in the Truman Administration. I suppose it would have been naïve to expect help and support from my fellow Republicans, who would have termed whatever the President had tried to do by way of cleaning up corruption a "whitewash." But I did not expect any politician to question my loyalty to the United States. While I was spending my last Sunday at home before commencing my task in Washington, reporters reached me by telephone to ask for a comment on Congressman Potter's statement charging me with having been a member of subversive organizations dedicated to the overthrow of our institutions!

The late Senator McCarran of Nevada joined in the attacks along these lines. He did not know me and I knew little of him. All I knew of Nevada was its scenic beauty, its easy divorce laws, its gambling and its sheep industry. To my amusement, some time later, I discovered that a committee, organized to aid the campaigns of internationally minded candidates for Congress, made this isolationist Senator from Nevada one of its prime targets. I was a member of this committee. Modest funds were sent to that state to help finance the campaign of his opponent. So, from Senator McCarran's point of view I guess that indeed made the committee "subversive."

I shrugged off these statements. They dried up after a few days. A friendly Republican Senator explained to me that the cloakroom strategy was to throw a cloud over me and try to keep me under it. If there was to be any investigating of the Administration, it must be done by committees of Congress. The Executive branch would be prevented from cleaning house, particularly in an election year, and, of course, an examination of department records might show constant interference and pressure by some congressmen, particularly in the Reconstruction Finance Corporation and Federal Housing Administration.

About two weeks later, another cloud appeared on the horizon. At the time, it seemed "no bigger than a man's hand"—if it could be developed into a cloud at all.

Back in 1947, Chinese Petroleum Corporation, an agency of the Chinese Nationalist government, sought to obtain the use of tankers to carry petroleum products from the Persian Gulf to refineries on the mainland and at Formosa. The communists had not begun to move across China, and, as a fighting ally in the Second World

War, China was one of those devastated countries which was included in plans for United States economic aid. Many countries whose shipping had been destroyed by the Germans and Japanese were acquiring surplus vessels from our country.

Representatives of a private concern, China Trading and Industrial Development Corporation, financed by Chinese capital, consulted one of my partners, Houston H. Wasson, with regard to certain provisions of the Shipping Act. This company hoped to acquire tankers to charter to Chinese Petroleum, but on a visit to Washington, I discovered that no further vessels of this type were available for foreign allocation. It was decided to organize a corporation in the United States which could qualify as a "citizen" within the meaning of the Act and to submit an application for surplus tankers in the event that any of these ships might become available.

Before China Trading took any action I had a conference with Admiral Smith, Chairman of the Maritime Commission, and also with officers of the State Department, to make sure that the use of tankers for the purpose of aiding in the rehabilitation of China was in accordance with government policy. In December 1947 I called at the Maritime Commission again and left two applications for tankers. One was submitted on behalf of China Trading and the other on behalf of the United Tanker Corporation which had been organized in Delaware with a president, vice-president and directors, all of whom were United States citizens. The certificate of incorporation required that the voting should be controlled by United States citizens. Officers and directors were not "dummies" in any sense, but were respected in shipping circles because of their backgrounds and experience.

It later appeared that tankers could be purchased from owners who were willing to dispose of them at premium prices. Three American flag vessels were bought by one corporation, United Tanker, whose stockholders included a number of eminent citizens, such as the late Edward Stettinius, at one time Secretary of State, Admiral William F. Halsey, General Julius C. Holmes and others of standing in the community. The stock in this corporation was subsequently sold to United.

After all these arrangements had been consummated, the young Chinese engineers who had brought China Trading's finances into the picture told me that they were interested in establishing a foundation and that they wanted to turn over to it all their rights to profits from their investment in United and its affiliated companies. They were all graduates of American schools of engineering and had seen what American education could do for young Chinese. They had an idealistic conception of training more and more of their fellow Chinese in the professions, so that they could lead the way for China in the years to come to better living conditions, educational facilities, sanitation and hospitals. They had turned to me because of my interest and experience in philanthropy in New York, in the hope that I could build a board of trustees of the foundation to carry on the work. I was very happy to be able to persuade Dr. Edward H. Hume, of a family with a long missionary tradition, to join the board. Dr. Hume's son Ted had been killed on a mission for the church, shot out of the

air over Sweden during the war. Others whom I per-
suaded to serve with me were Dr. Magnus Gregerson,
Head of the Department of Physiology at the Columbia
College of Physicians and Surgeons, and Arthur M.
Tode, well-known in shipping circles.

The Foundation in its brief history has made many
grants out of operating profits earned by United Tanker
Corporation. Fellowships have been granted to Chinese
students stranded in America as a result of the Communist seizure of their country; scholarships have been
granted to American students specializing in Chinese
art, history, economics; grants have been made for in-
service training courses for high school teachers and also
for the listing of Chinese professionals and intellectuals
in this country, available for specialized service.

I speculated on how any politician could make anything out of this setup. But I had underestimated the
capacity of certain individuals for doing just this.

For almost four years after their acquisition, these
petroleum carriers operated in unfavorable as well as
favorable charter markets.

The United Tanker group managed to meet payments
on ship mortgages held not only by banks but by the
United States Government itself. These American flag
vessels checked in with the consular offices if they were
operating abroad, or with the United States Coast Guard
if they were operating in domestic waters. They were in
constant touch with United States authorities.

The language in Section 9 of the Shipping Act must
have bothered someone in the Maritime Administration.
Another law provides for the forfeiture of a United
States flag vessel owned by a citizen which is transferred

to a person who is "a subject or citizen of any foreign prince or state."

In December, 1951, a tanker operated by a company, wholly owned by our foundation, was seized and a test case commenced. Its importance transcended United Tanker, for the troublesome sections of the Shipping Act and of the Registry Statutes affected many vessels whose acquisition had been wholly or partially financed by foreign capital.

This litigation, if pursued to the end, would have resulted in an interpretation of the citizenship requirements of the Shipping Act. Other questions to be resolved and raised by the Government would include the following:

> Is a charitable foundation, whose officers, trustees and members are United States citizens, but which, in carrying out its purposes, has aided some non-citizens in obtaining an education, disqualified as a citizen?
>
> If a vessel is purchased from a government agency relying upon legal advice of counsel for the agency as well as the advice of the purchaser's attorney, should the purchaser lose both the purchase price and the vessel?
>
> If the Commission delivers a bill of sale for an American flag vessel to a purchaser, must it also formally approve its own act?

The United States Supreme Court granted our client's application for a writ of certiorari and would have heard this case except for the fact that the litigation has been settled even as I write this chapter. This settlement is agreeable to both the Government and our client, the controversy is at an end; but the Senate hearings and the line of questioning will remain in my memory as long as I live.

On March 4th, 1952, my partner, Houston Wasson, who had handled all the legal details with regard to the organization of United Tanker and its subsidiary companies, appeared before the Senate Committee. He told the story fully and patiently. One matter about which he was asked was three or four shipments of petroleum to Communist China after the Nationalist Government had retreated to Formosa. He explained that our firm was legal counsel and was not engaged in oil transportation; that the agents operating the ships made charters in a world market, and in this case they took the precaution of asking the State Department what American policy was with regard to trade with Communist China. This was before the Korean War, and it was American policy to keep the lanes of trade open wherever possible all over the world.

Of course, I have always regarded legislative investigations as important because their primary and ostensible purpose is to obtain facts which will ultimately lead to corrective legislation. In this particular instance, it seemed ridiculous to me that surplus government property should be disposed of at an arbitrary price fixed by law. The best method for disposing of surplus government-owned vessels is to take advantage of a favorable market and advertise for public bidding. Then the Government takes advantage of a good market and of competition.

After hearing the questions directed at Mr. Wasson and the method of questioning by some of the members of the Senate subcommittee I realized they were not interested in remedial legislation or in my views with regard to the disposal of government property. Indeed, even at this writing, no member of the Senate has suggested any amendments to the Shipping Act which would provide for the sale of surplus ships at public auction.

When counsel for the committee called and courteously invited me on behalf of the committee to appear, I told them I would be glad to testify and that it would be unnecessary to subpoena me.

Accordingly, on the morning of March 11th I arrived at the Senate Office Building, alone, and made my way to the subcommittee room. Senator Hoey, as Chairman, introduced me to a few of the committee members, and during the time reserved for photographers I had a few brief moments to study the faces of some of these Senators. I had a good long look at Senator Joseph McCarthy of Wisconsin.

After being duly sworn as a witness and after a few primary questions I was somewhat baffled by the following exchange:

SENATOR MUNDT. Mr. Morris, who made the appointment for you? Was the appointment [with the Chairman of the Maritime Commission in 1947] made by the White House?

MR. MORRIS. What? Excuse me?

SENATOR MUNDT. Was that appointment made by the White House?

MR. MORRIS. The White House? No sir. I think Admiral Smith called, or his office.

SENATOR MUNDT. Did anybody from the White House go with you to the office of Admiral Smith?

MR. MORRIS. Goodness sakes, I wish they had. I didn't know anybody in the White House.

SENATOR MUNDT. Your answer is that they did not? Who introduced you to Admiral Smith?

MR. MORRIS. It was just the way I introduced myself to you. I came up and shook hands with you. You never saw me, although we had been corresponding quite a bit.

SENATOR MUNDT. Your testimony is that you went into Admiral Smith's office alone?

MR. MORRIS. Absolutely alone, and cold.

SENATOR MUNDT. And nobody introduced you to him?

MR. MORRIS. And I never knew him before.

SENATOR MUNDT. Nobody preceded that with a phone call?

MR. MORRIS. I think I probably called his secretary and asked for an appointment.

SENATOR MUNDT. But nobody else?

MR. MORRIS. Absolutely nobody. I don't know anybody in Washington yet.

SENATOR MUNDT. You and I got acquainted this morning, so you are getting acquainted slowly.

MR. MORRIS. Now I know one Senator. So I am one up.

SENATOR MCCARTHY. Do I understand your testimony to be that no one from the White House helped you make your original contact with the Maritime Commission?

MR. MORRIS. Senator, as many times as I am asked that question, I will say "No." I swore to tell the truth, and that is the truth.

SENATOR MUNDT. Mr. Morris, do you know a man in Washington, or did you know a man in Washington, at that time, in the White House, by the name of Turner?

MR. MORRIS. Turner?

SENATOR MUNDT. Turner.

MR. MORRIS. I never heard of anybody by the name of Turner working in the White House.

The only Turners I could think of were Gene Turner, Amateur Skating Champion of the United States in 1939, and Professor Turner at the law school who taught the law of Negotiable Instruments. Certainly I never heard of any Turner at the White House.

It appeared that this mysterious character Turner was no longer employed at the White House, but someone located him in a remote part of the country, and he stated that he had never met me at any time. I suppose the purpose of the questioning was to insinuate that I had sought "influence," or perhaps it was an effort to throw me off balance. In any event, it will always remain a mystery to me.

Other questions revolved around my "profits" from the operation of tankers. I explained that I had no stock participation in the venture and that all the profits went to a foundation engaged in philanthropic work and that none of the trustees of the foundation received any compensation for their work. But the Senators did not want to have any misapprehensions straightened out. In fact, some of my own friends got the impression that the ships were my property, that I had made more than $3,000,000 in selling them, whereas it was the Halsey-Stettinius-Casey group which made a profit selling a number of ships, including three to our clients. It was our clients who contributed to that profit by paying an amount to that group which resulted in a profit to them of $450,000.

Out of approximately two hundred charters of ships, three or four of them involved the carrying of petroleum

products to China after that country had become occupied by the communists. I explained that I did not
operate ships; that I did not know of these voyages, because in the late summer and fall of 1949 when the
charters were made, I was too busy running for mayor
of New York.

They evidently did not have enough of me that day
and asked me to come back for a return engagement on
March 12th. I have been buffeted about quite a bit in
New York City politics, but the only really sordid experience in my life was when I appeared before the committee on this second day.

In this book, I do not intend to characterize the
technique of the Junior Senator from the State of Wisconsin. His methods are known to newspaper readers
and particularly to television viewers all the way from
Maine to California. A "select committee" of the Senate
and his own "peers" characterized his conduct as "con-
tumacious," and as this book goes to press, the United
States Senate has censured and condemned his behavior.
I will merely quote a few excerpts from the record:

SENATOR McCARTHY. Now, Mr. Morris, I want to ask you
    several questions, and so that you will not, in view of
    your attitude yesterday, think that you are being trapped,
    I want to tell you the purpose of these questions before
    I ask them, so that there will be no doubt in your mind.
MR. MORRIS. Senator, I am sorry. I didn't think I was being
    trapped.
SENATOR McCARTHY. Let me finish my question.
    Can we have an understanding that you will not inter-
    rupt until I get through?
    Mr. Morris, in view of the fact that you are the presi-

dent of China International Foundation, in view of the fact that the China Foundation held all the stock in United Tankers, in view of your testimony yesterday that whoever controlled the common stock was responsible for the actions of the corporation, in view of Louis Johnson's letter in which he points out that the activities of your corporation are a threat to national security, in view of the ECA memorandum pointing out that while ECA was trying to build a fence around the Communists you were supplying the oil and lighting the fires that burned it down, in view of the money which your corporation made carrying material to Red China which contributed to the Chinese war effort and helped sign the death warrant of American boys, I would like to know this. I would like to ask you some questions.

I would like to know whether you were the active controlling president responsible for shipment of war materials?

.   .   .   .

SENATOR MCCARTHY. Do you understand the purpose of the question?

I want to find out, Mr. Morris, whether you were the dummy head of this corporation, had no control over its activities, whether it was being run by these Chinese, who, according to ECA, were loyal to the Communist cause. Or were you the head of the corporation? It would appear that either you were the greatest dope and dupe of all times, or you are directly responsible for making a vast amount of money, which the Defense Establishment pointed out would be and has been soaked in American blood. I want to ask you some questions.

Did you, at any time, try to find out where your tankers were running? During the operation, did you try to keep track of where they were running?

MR. MORRIS. Well, you asked me about fifty questions. I will have to answer each one of them.

The last question almost took the wind out of me! Even Tammany had an unwritten code of fair play. The skillful Senator from Wisconsin adopted so many major premises which were false and raised so many implications which had no foundation in fact that it was impossible to answer the question with any degree of intelligence. In the first place, until this hearing, I had never heard of any letter from Secretary of Defense Louis Johnson, and, in any event, the Secretary had not pointed out any activities of United Tanker that were a threat to national security. Of course, the Senator erred when he said that United Tanker Corporation was my corporation. Furthermore, ECA did not point out that while ECA "was trying to build a fence around the Communists you were supplying the oil and lighting the fires that burned it down." At the time the shipments were made, no one knew that a war would commence between North and South Korea and nobody foresaw that after the war broke out Communist China would aid the North Koreans. In other words, the Senator who can pick up a set of facts which occurred in one stage of history and make them fit into entirely different historical circumstances knew perfectly well that I was not the sort of person who would order the transportation of material to Red China in order to "sign the death warrant of American boys." This kind of searing attack I was unfamiliar with.

Senator McCarthy was charging that United Tanker was "run by these Chinese who according to ECA were loyal to the Communist cause." As a matter of fact, the

Chinese to whom he referred did not run the corporation nor were they communists. *The corporation was run by American citizens of fine reputation and well known in shipping circles, while the Chinese he referred to were hardly communists. The families of several of them have been executed or imprisoned by the communists and their property confiscated.*

The Senator returned to the witness as follows:

SENATOR McCARTHY. What part did you take as president in selecting the officers?

MR. MORRIS. Well, I voted the stock which was held by the foundation, and in turn elected a board of directors in whom I had confidence. They, in turn, elected officers in whom I had confidence. They, in turn, selected Sieling and Jarvis, a well-known and world-renowned shipping agency, as brokers, in whom I had confidence. And I discharged my responsibility.

SENATOR McCARTHY. Then, in view of that control that you had, had you known that the tankers were hauling oil to Red China, would you have put a stop to it?

MR. MORRIS. I would have made sure that whatever those vessels were doing, they were carrying cargoes to any part of the world in accordance with the policy of the United States and in accordance with the law. And that is my duty, and that is where it ends and where it begins.

SENATOR McCARTHY. Well, some of the other tanker firms felt their duty extended a bit further. You said you followed the policy of the United States. In view of the fact that the Secretary of Defense said these activities were endangering the national security, keeping in mind that other firms refused this business with Red China, my question now is: Had you known of the operation of these tankers hauling oil, war material, to Red China, would you have put a stop to that operation?

MR. MORRIS. Now, you have got three questions there. Wait a minute, Senator. Had I known of the Secretary of Defense's letter?

SENATOR MCCARTHY. Yes.

MR. MORRIS. Well, if it was written at the time those charters were made, of course I would have been against those cargoes being carried. I think you will find that letter— I have forgotten the date—was after these runs were made.

MR. FLANAGAN. The record will show that the first letter by the Secretary of Defense was in October 1949.

MR. MORRIS. Well, put yourself in the position of those operating the ships, who are anxious to be sure that they are carrying out their operations in accordance with United States policy. You would normally turn to the State Department. They make foreign policy.

SENATOR MCCARTHY. I would not normally turn to the State Department.

MR. MORRIS. Well, you wouldn't. You wouldn't turn to any Department. You just sound off.

Looking back on it now, perhaps I should have quietly and with dignity risen from my witness chair, addressed the late Chairman Hoey, McCarthy's predecessor as Chairman of the Senate Subcommittee, and told him that since I had come as a guest I expected to be treated with courtesy and that I would like to leave and await a subpoena should the committee desire any further testimony from me, but I did not. I "talked back" to the Senator who had made the hearings particularly disagreeable. Later, Arthur Krock, head of the Washington bureau of the *New York Times,* advised me that that was a mistake. I asked him what else I could have said when McCarthy accused me of helping to "sign the death warrant of American boys" in Korea. He gave me the right answer very simply: "I didn't and I wouldn't." How simple it sounds now and how far away that Washington nightmare seems.

I used to wonder what motivated Senator McCarthy in his attack upon me. While I was working on the material for this book, I picked up a daily newspaper and read the answer. During the hearings before his committee in which the Department of the Army was accused of all kinds of disloyalty and after the Senator had been particularly savage with a high-ranking Army department official, he stated that in his early life he had been tutored by "an Indian named Charlie." Charlie taught him to hit hard and hit first. I don't remember now whether he told him to hit low, but anyway, Charlie has been responsible for a great deal of turmoil, false accusations, mental anguish and outraged feelings.

CHAPTER 3 Dutch Schultz and the Hard-drinking "Drys"

Peopl continually ask me how I ever got into politics. Why should anyone accustomed to comfort and security want to enter the most demanding and cruel occupation in American life?

My political "handicaps" were humorously enumerated during a dinner given me by friends shortly after I had been elected to my first city-wide office under La-Guardia. At the point when everybody's fancy was bubbling on the tide of sparkling spirits, Joe McGoldrick, the city Comptroller, rose to direct a few remarks in my direction.

"Our hero tonight is part of a great political tradition. I propose to show you how he has surmounted the handicap of birth and education. Born of rich but honest parents, he comes from the immigrant group which, however numerous in the eighteenth century, is today the least politically potent. The Greeks, the Poles, the Czechoslovaks, even the Turks and Armenians muster more effectives on election day. No such solid phalanx stood ready to march behind our young standard-bearer into power. Alas, those early immigrants are almost as extinct as the Indians whom they once exterminated. Such handfuls of them as remain are mostly found on reservations in Newport, Bar Harbor, Southampton . . .

while a few cling to their pueblos on Park Avenue.
"Did time permit, I could expatiate on the handicaps
of our hero's birth, but I must hurry on to the hardships
of his upbringing. His . . . parents denied him a chance
to sell newspapers. Imagine a future politician robbed of
the opportunity to point to his youthful career as a newsboy! Not only had the coming of the electric lights prevented him from learning his three R's by firelight, but
his unrelenting parents did not even let him go to night
school. I ask you how was a young man to succeed in
politics in our great city without a chance to go to night
school and learn the American language as it is spoken!
"Instead, an unkind fate bundled him off to Groton
and Yale. A lesser man would have abandoned hope in
face of such adverse fortune. . . . But it is such trials
which try man and prove his mettle. Undaunted, un-
swerving, unflinching, this fearless young man followed
Fate into the lists, and today we find him President of
the City Council—a Daniel in a den of lions!"

I was born in a high brownstone house on East Seventy-
second Street, Manhattan. My earliest memories were
similar to those described by Clarence Day in his "Life
With Father" sketches.
My father was an attorney, but he was actually more
interested in education than in his own profession. He
was one of the first trustees of Teachers College and took
a keen interest in its affairs. Even after he received his
LL.B. degree from Columbia, he read Greek and Latin
for pleasure. He was an enthusiastic family historian. The
hero of the family seems to have been Captain Richard
Morris of the Cromwellian Cavalry. It was Richard who

decided to find a home in the new world and who fled
from England with the restoration of the Stuarts. The
Morris family had already revolted against tyranny,
burning Chepstowe Castle that belonged to Charles I.
Upon coming to the throne, William and Mary made
amends for the lands that had been confiscated, giving
the Morrises a vast tract of property in the southeast
Bronx.

Lewis Morris (a typically rebellious forebear) was a
prosperous New York landowner and lawyer when the
Revolutionary War broke out. Like the later Civil War,
the American Revolution in many cases set families
against one another. Lewis had a brother who was a
general in the British army. He wrote warning Lewis
not to dare sign that "radical manifesto," the Declaration of Independence. He painted a frightening picture
of what would happen to Lewis if he took up arms
against King George. Lewis read his brother's letter
pleading with him to "think of the consequences," and
growled—so tradition has it—"Damn the consequences,
give me the pen!"

My mother's grandfather was Ambrose Kingsland, a
mayor of New York in the eighteen fifties. He was the
mayor who first planned a wide-open space in the center
of Manhattan, which was later developed as Central Park.
He also advocated the construction of a "steam elevated
railroad" to get people downtown faster than they could
travel in a horsecar. Mayor Kingsland had his fights with
Tammany politicians, and it was reported that one alderman, in an angry argument with His Honor, leaped
over the mayor's desk and grabbed him by his whiskers.

The most famous of my forebears was Gouverneur

Morris, Lewis's half brother, the Federalist who is credited with having written the final draft of the Constitution and who spent two years as George Washington's minister to France. Gouverneur lost a leg when he was twenty-eight, as a result of being thrown from his carriage by a stampeding horse. Yet he continued to hunt and fish. He even shot the St. Lawrence rapids in a canoe. Morris served as our minister to France during the French Revolution and he remained on the job during the height of the Terror to protect the rights of Americans and to offer asylum to French citizens threatened with the guillotine. He was a close friend of Washington's and is said to have contributed the greatest number of speeches to the marathon debate that hammered our Constitution into shape.

In my boyhood I was supposed to be insulated from the harsher facts of life. My father gave me an allowance of twenty-five cents a week, and he would have been terribly shocked to learn that I squandered the money, taking elevated rides through the city slums, gazing with fascination at the colorful immigrant peddlers and their pushcarts, stopping off to peer into barrels stuffed with herrings whose odor tore at the nostrils. That nickel carfare actually took me across an ocean into a world stranger than any dime novel. And occasionally people from this world strayed to my doorstep. Sometimes a hobo from the Bowery would appear at our kitchen door, asking the cook for a cup of coffee. And while he gulped it down, I'd sit with him and try to wangle from him stories of the saloon. I discovered that there were people who didn't like the rich. Even our cook would sometimes mutter darkly against us, as she stood at her coal stove perspiring from sunrise until evening. I listened to her in awe as if she were one of the sisters in *Macbeth,* uttering a curse over the witches' cauldron.

When I was nine, I was taken by my parents on a trip to Europe. We spent a couple of months in Germany, France and Austria, drifted down through the Dolomites and stayed an entire spring in Italy and the Riviera. We booked passage home, but illness in the family prevented us from boarding ship at the last moment. If one of the children hadn't come down with German measles, this book might never have been written. The ship was the S.S. *Titanic.*

When I entered my teens, the greatest influence in my life was Groton School in Massachusetts. The reigning deity there was the Reverend Endicott Peabody, who doubled as the headmaster and as the coach of the crew. I made the crew. I was growing very fast and in those years was a little stooped. When I bent over my oar to row, I hunched my shoulders and failed to get the proper leverage. The Reverend Mr. Peabody was in the habit of sitting me down on the float. "Morris, you've got to pull your shoulders back!" To illustrate, he put a bony knee into the small of my back. I have never slouched since.

At Groton, I tried unsuccessfully to make the football team. I played in all the early games. During the climax of one game with Saint Paul's the snow began to fall, and the coach called me from the bench. I thought that my hour had come. But the coach only wanted me to give my uniform to a first-string end who had gotten too wet to hold onto the ball. I went to the showers.

From Groton I went to Yale. The last Morris to have

gone there before me had been Lewis Morris, the father of the signer of the Declaration of Independence. At Yale my passion was rowing. I was on a very celebrated freshman crew. Grantland Rice prophesied the day before the Harvard race that our freshman crew was sure to win—unless it sank. And it did! Since I had a habit of jumping my slide, just before the race I nailed my trunks down to the seat. Midway over the course, when we were leading Harvard by three lengths, a surfaced submarine from the New London naval base overtook the shells. We were suddenly caught up by two tremendous rollers. The heavier members of the crew were in the waist of the boat; and as it lay suspended in mid-air, the frail craft buckled. Nailed to my seat, I had to decide in an instant whether to sink with my pants on, or swim without them before fifteen thousand pairs of eyes. I swam.

The rest of my college career was pedestrian. I never could make the varsity crew, and I still have recurring dreams about it. In the middle of a deep slumber, I suddenly receive a telegram from the Yale coach on the eve of the Harvard contest, pleading with me to get my shorts out of mothballs and take the next train to New Haven. It seems that there has been an epidemic of influenza among the student body, and Old Eli is desperately in need of a few stout souls from other years to row for her.

I suppose that even if I had not come from a comfortable brownstone house, the age in which I lived would have spoiled me. It was the era of the twenties. Jimmy Walker sat in New York City Hall. People believed there would be no more wars, except for the intertribal bloodletting of the local bootleggers. Folding money was as plentiful as the ticker tape that deluged Lindbergh on his return up Broadway. Life was just one huge Ziegfeld Follies, and practically everybody seemed able to afford two front seat tickets for the spectacle. This was the era of Peaches Browning; of the courtroom trial in Dayton to outlaw evolution; of women who left their millinery shops to enter the "red eye" trade and who drove smart tourist cars loaded with moonshine across state borders, taking along their children as "cover ups."

Soon after I graduated from the Yale Law School, my father died suddenly. I was an executor of his will, and I entered the old family firm of Morris & McVeigh that specialized among other things in decedent estates. I felt somewhat removed from the stream of life. There is material compensation in taking care of the dead, but I itched to have something to do with the quick as well.

Fortunately I had a means of working off some pent-up energy. My father had been a member of the New York Republican County Committee from the 15th Assembly District, and at his death I was elected in his place. This was my entrance into politics, although I scarcely suspected the implications. I received a letter from Keyes Winter, the leader of the Assembly District, notifying me of my election. Winter had been a close friend of Booth Tarkington's. Together as kids they had fished from the banks of the Wabash. Indeed, Tarkington had used Winter as the model for his Penrod.

The 15th Assembly District was the last Republican stronghold in New York City. The Democrats referred to it as the "silk stocking" or the "surtax" district. And they circulated ogrish stories about it. They told how a campaign girl who was hired by our party to check upon a list of registered voters picked up the phone and asked for a "Mr. Duveen." A sepulchral voice answered, "There is no Mr. Duveen here." "Well, is there a Mrs. Duveen?" "There is no Mrs. Duveen," boomed the voice. "This is the residence of *Lord* Duveen!" The girl hung up in a tremble. This was one of the more cheerful tales whispered by the Democrats about this dragon-haunted neighborhood.

Informing me of my election to the County Committee, Winter used phrases of such enthusiasm as to convey more than a hint that I would play a major role in direction of Republican policy for years to come. I was therefore a bit deflated upon attending my first meeting of this committee to discover that there were four thousand other Republicans present, all aspiring to local thrones. What was more, my hero Winter, when he got up to vote on an issue, wasn't even asked to make a speech. He just delivered 253 votes from the 15th Assembly District, one of which was me.

My introduction to politics on a national scale came in 1924 when I attended the Republican National Convention as a sergeant-at-arms. I was given a badge and told to stand outside the convention hall to examine delegates' credentials. I almost despaired of getting into the hall at all when William Jennings Bryan, covering the convention for the Hearst papers, came up to me and asked if I could sing. He needed tenors for a chorus of newspapermen to keep the delegates entertained before the convention was called to order. I was glad to oblige and put my sergeant-at-arms badge into my pocket

for the time being. When the song fest was over, I joined
the New York Delegation and found our ambassador to
Mexico, James R. Sheffield, Dr. Butler and Ogden Mills.
They asked me to lunch with them after the morning
session. Senator Albert Beveridge joined us and I felt
that I had at last "arrived"!

In 1928 I again attended the Republican Convention
—the one that nominated Herbert Hoover. This one
provided me with some real excitement. The Democrats
planned to make an issue of prohibition during the
campaign. The Republicans, who had originally put
through prohibition and had supported it through
thick and thin, were divided amongst themselves as to
whether to continue to nuzzle their noses in the sand or
face up to the overwhelming sentiment of the people
and come out squarely for repeal.

I heard that the Republican Resolution Committee
was to meet in a certain hotel suite to thresh out the
party stand. I was eager to get into the room to witness
the political fireworks. But when I arrived at the door,
a national committeeman spotted my sergeant-at-arms
badge in my lapel and he decided he had better use for
me. "Young man, stand outside and make sure no one
comes in except members of the committee."

My heart sank. There were five hundred assistant
sergeants-at-arms, but I seemed to be the one who always
had to stand at the door. No sooner had I taken up my
post than a bellhop appeared carrying a bucket of ice. I
tried to keep him out, but he told me curtly that an order
had come for him. He knocked and was let in. Within
several minutes a second bellhop arrived, carrying ice,
and then a third. Each was admitted into the room. I

was bursting with curiosity. When a fourth bellboy appeared, I asked him if I could borrow his jacket and deliver the ice myself. A dollar tip persuaded him to cooperate. I put on the jacket, knocked and entered. The lawmakers in the smoke-filled room, who had put across prohibition, were in a convivial mood on the stuff Carrie Nation had whetted her hatchet on. They did not notice me standing in the corner.

I witnessed an extraordinary incident. Mrs. Charles Sabin, a tall, beautiful woman who for years had led the fight among Republicans for repeal, was standing in the center of the room, flushed with anger. She pounded the table and I heard her say, "Let's stop being hypocrites and put a repeal plank into our platform."

One committee member, who was not mellow enough yet to have forgotten the dry vote, growled, "Aw, Pauline, I wish you women would leave politics to us. There are certain things you just don't understand."

Another member said, "Come, Pauline, have a cocktail."

The drink was poured. Mrs. Sabin lifted her glass as if to toast the GOP. But, at the very last second, she flung it to the floor, turned on her heel and strode from the room. The prosperity issue won out over repeal and Herbert Hoover was elected by a landslide. But the campaign of Mrs. Sabin and Al Smith against hypocrisy finally prevailed.

I was not prepared at this time to become seriously involved in political campaigning. As I have previously mentioned, I had just commenced to practice law, and I didn't like to take so much time away from my work. Once you become active in politics people start telephoning you, and for a young lawyer to be receiving a lot of extracurricular phone calls makes a bad impression on the firm.

Nonetheless, in 1930, I assisted my election district captain in the state campaign. One evening he confided to me that he was in serious financial straits. He asked me for seventy dollars. I loaned the money and never saw him again. He disappeared from his jobs and from his usual haunts. I was promoted to be district captain in his place. My territory consisted of two city blocks, and I felt immensely important.

Gradually I learned the tricks of ward politics. All through the year and particularly during registration, I visited my voters and learned something of their needs. The Democratic captain in my district came from a family that had been in the undertaking business for three generations. On election day, I volunteered to watch over the corpses while the family went out to vote. Of course they voted the straight Democratic ticket. But I enjoyed their friendship. At no time did they ask for my business!

Two of my associates during the early political days were Joseph Clark Baldwin III and Clendenin Ryan, a grandson of Thomas Fortune Ryan. The three of us decided to open a restaurant in Yorkville in the heart of a Democratic district. What was even more audacious, we designed our restaurant in French décor and had Joe Baldwin's Gallic wife prepare Parisian recipes—this in a neighborhood that for generations had been saturated with the odors of wienerschnitzel and sauerbrauten. We even invited Democrats to bend a foot over our brass rail. Some jaundiced folk misconstrued our policy of fraternization. They accused us of hatching a fusion plot to take over the political machinery of the district! Actually, our motive was to raise money for neighborhood welfare work. And if, in the process, a few hungry Democrats became converted to our "socially conscious" brand of Republicanism, we weren't prepared to repudiate them.

The date for the opening was set for the middle of June, and we invited not only newspaper and magazine reporters, but people well known in high society. Baldwin's function was to lend "taste" to the venture, developed from long experience in France; Clen Ryan was our financier; I was the attorney who prepared the lease.

I arrived about four in the afternoon of the opening and found the place in utter confusion. Prohibition beer was warming up in the hot afternoon and sixty-five pullets were lying on the tables, waiting to be casseroled. The petunias and begonias had not yet been planted in the topsoil just outside the kitchen. I telephoned Consolidated Edison, and before long the stove and refrigeration equipment were connected and the chef was at work. Then Joe Baldwin appeared and we planted the flowers. By seven o'clock the guests began to arrive. By eight o'clock everyone was seated. But suddenly the rain came down in buckets, driving our patrons to cover. The flowers we had planted so hastily were washed into the kitchen.

The next day Clen Ryan departed on a fishing trip to Alaska and Joe Baldwin sailed for France to occupy an eighteen-room château he had rented for the summer. I was left holding the bag. I arrived at the restaurant for dinner that night. The waiters stood briskly alert for business. But no one showed up. I dined in royal loneliness. Gradually, however, in the following weeks business picked up and the restaurant became popular after a fashion, even though the main view from the tables consisted of rows of neighborhood laundry hung out on the lines. Our music was supplied by a fellow who had come to me begging for a meal with a safety pin holding the lapels of his coat together. Noticing an upright piano that had been left on the premises by the previous occupant, he sat down to play. He performed so beautifully that I asked him to come every evening and play Strauss and Schubert for his meals.

Unfortunately, we had failed to provide for suitable eating space when the autumn winds came and it was too cold to eat out of doors. By October we had to close the restaurant. I'm sure this made many politicians happy.

In the meantime I had become increasingly involved in politics. During a three weeks' vacation I took from my law office in 1931, I was elected Assistant Treasurer of the New York County Committee for my district. Shortly afterward, Frederick Warburg, the Treasurer, resigned, and all the books were turned over to me.

In the summer of 1932, I received one of the biggest shocks of my political life. One afternoon in August, a Packard limousine with shades drawn pulled up at the district clubhouse. Out stepped four men, their hats thrust down over their faces. They stood by the door while a fifth man, a short, blubberly fellow, got out. Then they closed in around him, and the five went upstairs to see the district leader.

I had observed the arrival of these men from the opposite curb and was curious about the nature of their visit. Late that afternoon, after they had left, I called on Keyes Winter. "Who were those men who came to see you?"

"Arthur Flegenheimer and his bodyguards."

I was astounded. Arthur Flegenheimer was better known to me and to millions of newspaper readers as "Dutch Schultz," the beer baron—one of the nation's overlords of crime, a man who wielded almost as much power over the underworld in the East as his opposite number Al Capone in the Middle West.

Winter informed me that Schultz had called on him because he was in trouble with the Government due to his failure to pay income taxes. Schultz had made a proposition to Winter. He declared that if Odgen Mills, who was at that time Secretary of the Treasury in Hoover's cabinet, would "lay off" investigating him for income tax evasion, he would guarantee to deliver the 17th Assembly District to the Republican candidate for the New York State Senate in the coming election.

"What did you answer Schultz?" I asked Keyes Winter.

"I kicked him out of my office," Winter replied.

I rolled up my sleeves and really pitched into the campaign from then on, aghast—God bless my youthful innocence!—at this incident of a gangster attempting to negotiate a deal with a political party.

On election day, Walter Mack, later the president of Pepsi-Cola, who was the Republican candidate for the State Senate, lost the 17th Assembly District, which was in the middle of the Senatorial District, by 13,000 votes —enough to give Tammany a victory. Dutch Schultz had worked his revenge thoroughly. It was afterward discovered that one voting machine after another had rung up thousands of votes for Mack's opponent *two hours before the polls opened!*

The scandal that followed Walter Mack's defeat led to a series of convictions, and several of Dutch Schultz's henchmen served time in Sing Sing for vote frauds. Schultz himself, who during the course of an enterprising career had placed a Tammany boss on his payroll at a thousand a week, left this world dramatically one evening in October 1935. While he was seated in a Newark saloon going over his accounts, three mobsters entered and riddled him with bullets. He died like a frightened child, screaming out "Mama, Mama!" and taking the names of his killers to the grave with him. His career was ended at thirty-eight.

In the spring of 1933, my political fortunes took an upward turn. I was elected president of my district political club. By this time New York City politics had reached one of the dramatic crises in its history. The moral laxity of the Jimmy Walker administration had brought on the Seabury Investigation. And when Governor Franklin Roosevelt summoned the easygoing mayor to Albany and threatened to oust him from office, Jimmy Walker resigned and exiled himself to Europe. An interim mayor, John P. O'Brien, was selected by the Democrats to finish out the year that remained of Walker's term. But everywhere reform was in the air.

Just after I had been elected president of my club, Adolf Berle, a professor at Columbia, whom I had first met through my father and who had married a childhood friend of mine, invited my wife and me to dinner at his home. There were only two other guests present, a stocky, florid little Italian and his wife.

"Newbold," said my host, "I want you to meet Major Fiorello LaGuardia."

It is perhaps not an exaggeration to observe that this evening was the turning point in my life.

CHAPTER 4　The "Forty Thieves"

WHEN I first met LaGuardia, on the eve of the 1933 mayoralty election, he was fifty-one. He had already lived not one, but several colorful lives. Through his veins flowed the blood of rebels and dissenters. His grandfather fought with Garibaldi's Red Shirts to liberate Italy from the domination of foreign troops in the middle of the nineteenth century. This ancestor married a descendant of a Jewish refugee who had fled from the Spanish Inquisition. LaGuardia's father was a musician. During the Spanish-American War, he served as bandmaster with the American infantry. Fiorello was born in New York City. But the family moved West, and the boy grew up in Prescott, Arizona, which in those days was an Army frontier post swarming with Indians.

Throughout his life LaGuardia remained very sensitive about his immigrant ancestry. When he was only ten, an organ-grinder visited Prescott. Fiorello's friends were delighted. "A dago with a monkey! Hey, Fiorello, you're a dago too. Where's your monkey?"

The child was bitterly hurt. And his embarrassment increased when his father appeared and began chatting with the organ-grinder in Italian. It was his first chance in years to use his native tongue and he was overjoyed at the meeting. "Perhaps he considered an organ-grinder a fellow musician," LaGuardia recollected ruefully.

During the war with Spain, LaGuardia's father became seriously ill from the "embalmed" beef served by the scandal-ridden Quartermaster's Corps. He was discharged from military service and he died several years later, shortly after the family had moved to Trieste to live with his wife's relatives.

Beginning at nineteen Fiorello held a series of un-usual jobs. He entered the United States Consulate at Budapest as a clerk and within two years was appointed the acting consul at Fiume, then under control of the Austro-Hungarian Empire. His flamboyant temper perfectly matched the surroundings. He punched a Hungarian officer in the nose at a masquerade ball and narrowly escaped paying with his life. He became in-volved in a dispute with Maria Josefa, the Imperial Highness of Austria-Hungary, and he had to go into hiding until the storm blew over. Aware that thousands of immigrants were being rejected at Ellis Island and sent back to Europe because they couldn't pass their physical examinations, he insisted that the Fiume au-thorities give the immigrants examinations at the port of embarkation (the cost to be borne by the steamship companies). It took twenty years before the immigrant regulations in most ports were altered to provide this simple justice. But LaGuardia lived to see his views generally adopted.

At twenty-three LaGuardia returned to the United States and took a job as interpreter on Ellis Island during the day while he attended the New York University Law School nights. At thirty-three he hung out his shingle as an attorney.

This little man—he stood only five feet two—disclosed a genius for sponsoring unpopular causes. He served as a sort of one-man legal aid committee for the underprivileged. He took the cases of foreigners in his neighborhood, battling in the courts frequently without a fee, and he became an accomplished linguist in French, German, Croatian and various Slavic dialects. "I even speak a little English," he confessed. His temper flared whenever and wherever he saw a goat exploited by the wolves. Once he became embroiled with the chairman of the New York Prizefighting Commission—a Tammany wheel horse—who decreed that all boxers appearing in New York arenas must spend a minimum of twenty dollars to buy red and blue fighting trunks (which were worth a couple of dollars) from a firm with Tammany connections. This low-blow ruling stung the pugs to fury. Delegations descended on LaGuardia's office demanding a fight in the courts. LaGuardia accepted the challenge and he succeeded in having the order rescinded.

After two years of working for practically nothing on behalf of the city's clothing workers, LaGuardia entered politics—and as usual he joined the underdogs, the Republicans who were a minority in the Tammany-controlled Fourteenth District. He received the nomination to run for Congress in a curious manner. One evening as he was sitting in the district clubhouse while the local Republicans were filing petitions for nominations, the district leader suddenly muttered, "We haven't got a candidate for Congress, boys. Who wants to run?"

Immediately LaGuardia was on his feet. "I do."

"O.K. What's your first name?"

"Fiorello."

"Hell, let's get somebody whose name we can spell!"

LaGuardia had to argue vigorously to receive the nomination. He lost the election to the Tammany incumbent, Mike Farley, a saloonkeeper. But he made such a strong showing that the Republicans appointed him Deputy Attorney General of the State of New York.

LaGuardia recalled to me that he had a clash with Jimmy Walker while he was Deputy Attorney General. The Albany legislature had recently passed a Weight and Measures Law, according to which manufacturers were required to state the true weight on all food and containers. LaGuardia was assigned to try a case against a leading meat packer for misstating the weight of ham. Jimmy Walker appeared in court for the defense. As soon as the trial got under way, he rose and declared that he had been the author of the Weights and Measures Law and that it had not been designed to apply to ham in "wrappers," but only to containers of glass, wood, or tin.

The Judge, a Tammany appointee, dismissed the case. His Honor and Jimmy invited LaGuardia to have a drink with them. LaGuardia exploded. "Look, Jimmy, you know damn well that a lot of little storekeepers have been fined for selling hams in wrappers short-weight. How can you, the *author* of the law, appear in court to defend a *violation* of it?"

"Fiorello," Jimmy answered, "why do you suppose we introduce bills? We pass many of them just to kill them. You're not going to remain a deputy attorney all your life. Make the right connections, and you will be able to pick up a lot of cash defending the cases you are now prosecuting."

The Judge nodded his head wisely in agreement.

In 1916, LaGuardia campaigned with a four-piece band and beat Mike Farley for Congress. He voted for war with Germany in 1917 and enlisted to fight. Turned down for infantry officers' training because of his size, he took private flying lessons and maneuvered his way into the pioneer air corps. Returning from action on the Italian front, he re-entered politics. He ran for the presidency of the New York City board of aldermen to serve out the unexpired term of Al Smith who had been elected governor of the state. And he was the first Republican to win the office in twenty years.

But LaGuardia's most congenial stamping ground was the Congress. He returned to the House of Representatives in 1921. Here he continued to espouse unpopular causes that ultimately became respectable. During the era of stock market speculation, he exposed the swindles of stock market manipulators who bribed financial writers to circulate false tips. He fought against prohibition. He demonstrated to the House how legal near-beer could be mixed with a legal malt tonic to make an alcoholic beverage, and he defied the prohibition agents to throw him in jail for imbibing it. He fought for the eight-hour work day for labor, and he was a sponsor of the Norris-LaGuardia bill that prohibited the use of federal injunctions in labor disputes.

This stocky little politician was not a dewy-eyed idealist, as his enemies found out time and again. "A man who extends the hand of friendship to LaGuardia,"

remarked one observer, "is in danger of losing a couple
of fingers." His political enemies called his tactics "black-
guardia" and one of them, goaded into fury, threatened
to "hit that goddam little wop over the head!"

LaGuardia became known in Washington as that
relatively rare animal—an insurgent politician. He was
as likely to attack the Republicans as the Democrats.
Once when a critic charged him with being disloyal to
his party, he retorted, "What party?" During his seven
terms in Congress he ran, among other things, as a Republican, a Progressive, a La Follette Independent, a
Fusionist and a Farmer-Laborite. He continually bucked
both major party machines and drew his support from
the unattached groups of voters. "I am interested not
in party labels but in issues." He based his politics upon
the recognition that there were millions of Americans
who had absolutely nothing to do with the palace ma-
neuverings of the major parties. He reached beyond
labels and campaigned on behalf of the independent
groups. "I'd rather be right than regular."

The Republican leadership, of course, was exasperated
by his tactics, but members of Congress who had served
with him told me there was universal respect for his
industry and shrewdness. He not only read, but studied
the background of every bill. He knew more about
legislation pending in committees than any other
member of the House.

While Republican leaders in New York City had a
natural suspicion of an unpredictable officeholder, by
1929 LaGuardia had made a sufficient name for himself
so that he was the obvious candidate to run against
Jimmy Walker in the municipal campaign. And, of

course, it is always easy for a Republican in New York City to obtain a nomination on the municipal ticket because the chances are so overwhelmingly against him.

But the party left LaGuardia pretty much to his own devices as to how to conduct the campaign. The Republican machine was not greatly interested in freeing the city government of Tammany control. LaGuardia told me an amusing story about one of his evening engagements to speak. His manager, Paul Windels, a well-known Republican of Brooklyn, who later served as Corporation Counsel of the City of New York, told him he had a most important speech to make that night.

"Where am I going?" asked the candidate.

"To the National Republican Club, and, Fiorello, you have to get your suit pressed and be sure to be shaved and have your hair combed, because this is the most important evening of the campaign."

At 8:30 that evening LaGuardia and Windels climbed into the limousine hired for the evening and were followed by the press in another car.

As they entered the National Republican Club on Fortieth Street, they discovered that the lights were out. A porter turned one on in the hall. They asked him where the meeting was to be held, and he answered that he didn't know, but would the two of them like to fill out an application for membership in the club? They switched on the other lights, and, followed by the representatives of the press, found the stairs to the meeting hall. Since LaGuardia had given out a release of his speech, he was compelled to go through with it. He delivered a fighting address in an auditorium that was empty except for the reporters. As he talked, he noticed a green-shaded light over a billiard table in a room across the hall. Two members were enjoying their evening game, and all through his speech the billiard balls clicked ceaselessly. The players did not deign to look up once.

LaGuardia was beaten for the mayoralty by Jimmy Walker in 1929. New Yorkers were still basking in a dream of prosperity. Three years later, LaGuardia was swept out of Congress by the Democratic tidal wave that put Roosevelt into the White House. To add vinegar to LaGuardia's wounds, he had been defeated for the first time in seventeen years in his own district, by a Tammany candidate.

Thoroughly disgusted, LaGuardia announced his retirement from politics. "I'm going to get a little place in the country," he told friends, "and settle down to raise chickens." He rented a cottage in Westport, Connecticut, and moved there with his family. Less than a year later, by one of the most unexpected turns of fortune in American political history, LaGuardia became mayor of New York.

The event that boosted LaGuardia to the top of the political heap was the Seabury Investigation. But this investigation might never have taken place, and certainly would never have assumed the significance it had in people's minds, if the economic and moral climate of America had not undergone a profound change since 1929.

In late October of 1929, the bottom dropped out of the stock market and out of the hearts of a hundred and forty million Americans. Bankers, storekeepers, taxicab drivers, and stenographers lost their savings. Families that had been wealthy went on relief. Daily, the obituary columns were swelled with notices of suicides. All of us over forty recall the standard joke of radio comedians in those days—that when a man applied for a hotel room, it was a tossup whether he wanted it for sleeping or jumping.

We remember, too, how the international Apple Shippers' Association, loaded with an oversupply, sold apples on credit to unemployed men, and how the street corners blossomed out with these salesmen selling apples for a nickel each.

By 1932, there were twelve million unemployed. A million migrants were wandering over the nation looking for odd jobs. Two hundred thousand children, torn adrift from busted-up homes, were on the bum from town to town. Everywhere people tried desperately to keep up their self-respect. Wives whose husbands had only recently been high-priced executives now operated beauty parlors on their front porches, took in clothes for pressing, sold baked pies and preserves in the kitchen. Families moved from expensive city homes into country shacks to raise their own food. Lawyers pretended to their friends that they were taking the 8:30 train daily into an office full of clients. But when they emerged from Penn Station, they pounded the streets for jobs that were not to be had.

The depression left scars within people that will not be healed in a lifetime. All of us who lived through that experience are even today influenced in our attitude toward security—at least subconsciously—by the panic that then uprooted us. In the early 1930's, folk were in a bitter mood. They began to examine certain basic assumptions of their economic structure, and to ask how some of those among them had previously acquired their wealth. They discovered that certain leading citizens of the community had made their money by political horn-swoggling that set into sharp focus the relationship of City Hall with thieving pressure groups.

One of the most celebrated victims of this reprisal by a short-tempered public was the administration of Jimmy Walker in New York in 1931. Before 1929, the people howled with laughter when a guest of honor said to Jimmy during a civic reception, "You don't have to give me the key to the city, Mr. Mayor. The town is wide open!" After 1929, New Yorkers felt these jokes were far too dear for their pocketbooks.

Shortly after the 1929 election, Al Vitale, Walker's campaign manager and city magistrate, was guest of honor at a lavish banquet. During the middle of festivities, gunmen broke into the dining room and relieved the guests of their wallets, unburdening one of them, a city detective, of his revolver. Vitale made phone calls to highly placed politicians and the revolver was returned by the triggermen to relieve the detective of any further embarrassment. Police Commissioner Whalen, upon investigating the incident, discovered that a number of the guests who had been present at the dinner had criminal records and that Magistrate Vitale had borrowed ten thousand dollars from Arnold Rothstein, the recently murdered gambler. A preliminary investigation of the magistrate's courts had already shocked the city.

Now, the New York Bar Association and William J. Schieffelin of the Citizens' Union demanded a thoroughgoing investigation of the Walker administration. The legislature in Albany authorized a joint committee of the Senate and the Assembly headed by Senator Hofstadter to carry out the inquiry. The investigation was directed by its counsel, Samuel Seabury. Before it was over, the people were shown in detail just how the city had been taken over lock, stock and barrel by a Tin Pan Alley song writer and his Tammany pugs. Every branch of the government was found to be suffering from the itching palm. It was discovered that Crain, the New York district attorney, was associating with racketeers and manipulating bogus stocks that robbed the city of more than fifty million dollars a year. Sheriff Farley of New York County was removed from office for permitting organized gambling in his clubhouse. It was revealed that the city piers had been leased to steamship companies for kickback fees of fifty thousand dollars and up. The mayor himself was discovered to have stock in a bus corporation seeking a franchise from the city and in other questionable firms receiving city privileges. Large sums of money were deposited for his benefit in bank accounts and safe deposit boxes held jointly with several people who were known to be fattening on graft. His own brother, a doctor, was found to be splitting fees with physicians assigned to city compensation cases.

One wealthy businessman who had put the mayor in the way of some juicy profits testified blandly, "This, of course, I figured was for my friend Jimmie Walker, rather than for the mayor of New York—but he happened to be the mayor!"

The people had previously received a vivid picture

of how corruption hits the average man and woman on the street, when the city magistrate's courts were exposed in all their rottenness. It was discovered that city magistrates, members of the vice squad, attorneys and bondsmen had for years been cleaning respectable women out of their savings and throwing them into prisons.

Women of every class took the witness stand and told a story whose pattern varied very little. A stool pigeon for the vice squad would ring the doorbell. When he was let in by the woman of the home, he would take off his outer coat, and in the course of questioning her, suddenly remove his suit coat and put some money down on the table. Immediately, the door would open, a member of the vice squad would enter and accuse the woman of running a house of prostitution. The stool pigeon would testify that he had come up for an immoral purpose and point to the money he had taken out to pay the woman. The woman would be bundled off to the magistrate's court. But before she was brought before the judge, she would usually be taken to a lawyer's office (one of the gang), cowed into assigning over her bankbook and surrendering any cash she had in her pocket to pay him for "defending" her in court. The judge was frequently in on the deal. In most instances, the woman, after being relieved of her savings, would be thrown into prison to serve a term as a prostitute!

One businesswoman told the Seabury Committee that she was at home waiting for her husband when the doorbell rang, a stool pigeon forced his way into her apartment, pushed her into the bedroom, and slammed the door. The vice squad officer immediately followed into the house and charged her with prostitution. She told

him that it was a mistake. She showed him her marriage
certificate and business card. The officer arrested her
and brought her to a police station. She was given an
attorney who, before he was through with her, took
five hundred dollars in cash and over a thousand dollars'
worth of jewelry. Although her husband, together with
the superintendent of the apartment and two friends,
swore to her good character, the woman was found guilty.
She was locked up in prison and forced to undergo the
venereal tests prescribed by law for convicted streetwalkers. The woman spent five and a half months in
jail and was then released on probation.

Another woman told the committee that her fiancé
had just left her home after discussing plans for their
marriage when the bell rang, and a voice called out
"Telegram." She slid the chain bolt into the slot and
cautiously opened the door. As she reached through the
opening for the telegram, her hand was seized and
pressed against the chain until her fingers bled. A policeman forced open the door. The woman became hysterical,
and a maid came to her help, only to be ordered away
by the cop. A second officer entered the room, the charge
of prostitution was made, and she was booked at the
station house. She was hustled over to a bondsman and
ordered to give $50 for a bond. (The legal rate was $15.)
At her trial the cop testified that he had found the
woman in bed with a man who alleged that he had
paid her $5 for the visit.

In spite of the testimony of her maid, her fiancé, and
her former employer, the defendant was found guilty
and sent to prison where she suffered brutality from a
woman doctor who made the required physical tests.

She was sentenced to six months' probation. Her fiancé, whose belief in her remained unshaken, married her. Their honeymoon was interrupted by a required visit to the probation officer.

As the Seabury Investigation continued to unfold the dirty Tammany washing, and Governor Franklin Roosevelt threatened to take action to remove him, Jimmy resigned as mayor and sailed to Europe. Tammany Hall elected one of its own surrogates, John P. O'Brien, to serve out the remainder of Walker's term. When Judge O'Brien, upon his election, was asked whom he would appoint to be his police commissioner, he blurted out, "I don't know. I haven't heard yet."

This was the political situation when I met Fiorello LaGuardia at Adolf Berle's home in the spring of 1933. It turned out to be an historic year. That spring, President Roosevelt's New Deal had been born in Washington; a few months previously Adolf Hitler had seized power in the Reich; the Japs, who had already invaded Manchuria, marched into Jehol in defiance of the League of Nations; Sally Rand, who had been broke in 1932, stumbled upon a gold mine as she danced with whirling fans at the Chicago Century of Progress. In Washington, before a Senate committee investigating banking operations, a midget suddenly plopped into the lap of stately J. P. Morgan; Max Baer knocked Max Schmeling cold in Yankee Stadium; just about everybody from Bar Harbor to San Diego seemed to be tucked up with a copy of *Anthony Adverse,* the new best seller—and in New York, the political parties were preparing for a new mayoralty election.

That night as I spoke to LaGuardia in Berle's home,

the conviction grew upon me that this peppery reformer, who was certainly available for the office of
mayor, had an excellent chance of obtaining it this year.
Long before the Seabury Investigation, he had been
making charges against the Walker administration; in
fact he had been the only man in public life to have
doggedly pursued the issue. He had laid the groundwork
for Samuel Seabury, and everything he claimed had
turned out to be true.

Before we parted that evening, I said to LaGuardia,
"Major, would you be willing to address my district
Republican club? I have got to get a speaker for the next
meeting."

He told me that he would like to think it over. The
next morning he phoned me and accepted.

I sent out notices to the membership, and you would
have thought that an earthquake threatened to uproot
the silk-stocking Republican Club. I received letters
from leading members advising me that my sainted
father would turn over in his grave if he knew that I
had invited "that filthy radical" into the sanctum of the
Republican party. The newspapers played up the controversy. I stood by my guns and LaGuardia appeared
for his speech.

The clubhouse was packed. People stood ten deep
along the aisles, the men resplendent in their boiled
shirts, the women in their low-cut gowns and jewelry.
The press had effectively beaten the drums. The controversy drew Republicans from all over the city to see
the "fireworks."

LaGuardia arrived about ten minutes late. After we
had disposed with the routine business of the meeting,

he strode down the center aisle and mounted the platform. People expected him to launch into a typically flamboyant speech, spiced with histrionic gestures. But he began to speak in so low a voice that the audience had to strain its ears. "I apologize for being late. Marie, my wife, sent my suit out to be pressed, and it didn't come back until a few minutes ago. I couldn't leave the house until it was returned." The audience howled.

He continued slyly, "I'm very proud to be here tonight. But I don't know whether you ladies and gentlemen have decided to admit me to the social register, or whether you just wanted to go slumming with me."

From that moment he had the audience in the palm of his hand. He launched into an exposé of Tammany politics, similar to his campaign charges of 1929. When he had finished, Bill Hoppin, one of the most conservative members of the club, arose and offered a resolution thanking the former Congressman for his speech.

LaGuardia's conquest of my audience marked a turning point in his political fortunes. The newspapers covered his talk generously, and the Major emerged almost at once as a leading candidate for the mayoralty nomination.

To provide against the possibility that the Republican organization might stand pat with a machine candidate, a group of civic leaders, men of different parties and various views on national issues, but united in their desire to see a bossless government in New York, met at the City Club on August 4th, under the chairmanship of Charles C. Burlingham, a former president of the New York Bar Association. Samuel Seabury was present to boost LaGuardia's candidacy, and after six hours of vigorous discussion, the Major was named as the standard-bearer of the new Fusion party.

Major General John F. O'Ryan, who had been put forward by old-line Republicans, withdrew his candidacy in the interests of harmony, and the way was open for Republican endorsement of LaGuardia.

Tammany Hall nominated its wheel horse John O'Brien, but Ed Flynn, the Bronx Boss, convinced that the public could no longer be fooled by the O'Brien type of candidate, put forward his own man, "Holy Joe" McKee, as a "reform" candidate. This running of a Tammany insurgent on the "Recovery Ticket" was a shrewd maneuver by Flynn who, feeling O'Brien would be beaten badly, sought to save jobs and patronage for the Bronx County organization.

While President Roosevelt did not publicly come out for Flynn's "New Deal" candidate, James Farley endorsed him. However, Adolf Berle, who was looked upon as a Roosevelt spokesman by liberals, came out flatly for LaGuardia and took much of the sting from the Farley pronouncement.

The Fusion party interjected a new element into New York politics. Thousands of young men from every walk of life joined its ranks; and as election day grew near, they insured that Tammany would not terrorize the polls. Flying squads under Clen Ryan called "Fusioneers" were formed and detailed to strategic points throughout the city. Scouts in speedy autos were assigned to reconnoiter and telephone back to Fusion headquarters whenever trouble broke out; these calls were then relayed to the combat squads. College heavyweight boxers were enrolled to escort independent voters through the ranks of

Tammany hoods who stood near the machines. On election day, Fusioneers got up unusually early to make the rounds of the flophouses. They routed out all the inhabitants who were registered to vote and escorted them to the polls, giving them coffee and doughnuts on the way. This was the first time so many bums had ever voted anti-Tammany—and cold sober!

LaGuardia won out in a close race in the three-way struggle. He received eight hundred thousand votes out of a total of two million cast. Yet despite the narrowness of his victory, the defeat turned out to be one of the most costly ever suffered by a political machine.

In one area of town alone, the Fusioneers were unable to cope with Tammany, and as a result the Democrats salvaged two key offices. They elected the president of Manhattan Borough and a district attorney of New York County by a plurality of twenty thousand votes, many of which were fraudulent. During the voting, groups of Manhattan hoods, wearing gray snapbrim hats, invaded one polling booth after another in the area south of Fourteenth Street. They told the cops to "scram," and the coppers took a walk. Men and women waiting in line to vote were shoved out into the street. At each poll, several mobsters took over the registration book and signed for those who had not yet voted, while others rang up votes on the machine. When Republican captains entered the polls and tried to interfere, they were rounded up by the police for disorderly conduct and taken away in paddy wagons.

It was the incompetency of the Tammany district attorney who was elected by these methods in 1933 that launched the political career of Thomas E. Dewey. The

Dewey racket investigations were initiated as a direct result of the Tammany district attorney's failure to convict racketeers who had monopolized large areas of the city's economy.

On election night, shortly after LaGuardia's victory had been conceded, word reached the mayor-elect that Tammany workers at the polls were tampering with the vote for comptroller. Although technically he didn't as yet have the authority to do so, LaGuardia acted boldly. He ordered the police to send patrol wagons out to the suspected voting polls to load up with the ballots and bring them back to police headquarters for the counting of the votes. Whether there had in fact been illegal tampering has never been proved. But in any event the Fusion candidate for comptroller was elected to the office.

My association with LaGuardia during the campaign made an everlasting impression on me. I accompanied him during his speech-making tours into sections of the city I was hardly aware existed. We toured the East Side and the slum areas of Brooklyn and Harlem. LaGuardia had raised himself by his bootstraps; a descendant of immigrants himself, he felt close to these people. The crowds that gathered to hear him speak responded with an enthusiasm that had to be seen to be believed. One evening, LaGuardia spoke before a gathering of garment workers who packed the Manhattan Center. At every reference to low-rental housing, slum clearance, social security, the audience applauded vigorously. I had been brought up in a circle that regarded such proposals as spawned by long-haired Bolsheviks. But as I looked upon the faces of these citizens, I felt that there could be nothing alien or treacherous about these ideas. The fact is that the hammer blows of the depression had forced our society into a state of fluidity that permitted the immigrant to play an increasingly important role in American affairs, and that offered this little Italian-Jewish American who so perfectly expressed these aspirations a unique opportunity to lead him.

The press found something humorous in LaGuardia's association with me, passing sly digs about the friendship of the "Little Flower" with the "Mayflower." The fact is that LaGuardia came into my life at a most politically impressionable stage and gave it a driving energy that it might otherwise have not possessed.

LaGuardia won more than an election in 1933. He ultimately broke the hold of a political machine over the resources of the mightiest city in the world. And yet he was restrained in his victory. That election night, after both the Tammany candidate and the Eddie Flynn insurgent wing of the Democrats conceded their defeat, LaGuardia stood on tiptoe straining to speak into a microphone that was strung slightly above him. "We licked both wings of Tammany," he told his party workers, "but I have only the votes of a plurality. I am determined to give this city the kind of administration that will provide me with a thumping majority four years from now!"

Apart from the independents he had wooed and hoped to keep loyal, the mayor-elect had no illusions about his support. He knew he faced a battle to survive. He could never forget how when he won his first seat in Congress —he was the first Republican ever to be elected south of Fourteenth Street—the local Republican organization, instead of receiving him with jubilation, was plunged into deep gloom. The members of his district club barely nodded to him. That night of victory, he actually heard one Republican on the telephone in a rear office saying to the Democratic leader of the district from whom he had been getting political favors for years, "Honest, Joe, we didn't double-cross you; we didn't do anything to help this guy. We just can't control him." The life of an insurgent is no bed of roses. LaGuardia knew that he would ride or tumble on the tides of reform.

For his inaugural, LaGuardia repeated the oath of the young men of Athens, given in the heydey of Pericles. "We will never bring disgrace to this, our city, by any act of dishonesty or cowardice. . . . We will battle for our ideals and sacred things. . . . We will transmit this city far greater and more beautiful than it was handed over to us."

The New York mayoralty is generally regarded to be the nation's most exacting elective office after the United States Presidency. The mayor today handles a budget second in size only to the federal one. He has been granted an immense authority to do good or evil. For one thing he is the chief law enforcement officer. The police commissioner is appointed by him and serves at his pleasure. The judges of the lower courts are appointed by him and the county judges and district attorneys are paid from his budget. His chief limitation is financial, since the state controls the major sources of taxation. But the mayor, as chief magistrate, has almost unlimited power to control or condone crime in the city.

Even during the last century, before the five boroughs

were incorporated into the present city, New York mayors were powerful political figures. And an exceedingly motley crew held the trust. There were picturesque mayors and some whose distinction was not so much their color as their smell. One classic stooge was A. Oakey Hall who was mayor during the 1880's and who was arrested for helping Boss Tweed empty the public purse. Hall was so completely under the thumb of Tweed that he wouldn't put on a suit until the Boss approved its cut. He started life as Abraham Oakey Hall, changed his name to Abraham O. Hall, and called himself A. Oakey Hall when he entered society. Politically he belonged at various times to the Whigs, the Know-Nothings and the Republicans. He was only consistent in his grafting.

An even greater rascal than Hall was Fernando Wood, the Civil War mayor who had previously run a grogshop where he clipped sailors of their purses. This politician was virtuoso enough to have taught Boss Tweed tricks of the political trade.

But there have been some respectable mayors too. During the presidency of Jefferson, Edward Livingston served in City Hall. He was considered to have the keenest legal mind of his time. Another cut above the average was Philip Hone, who kept a diary that turned out to be a treasure trove for historians, replete as it was with glimpses of Webster, Clay, Washington Irving and other well-known contemporaries.

Then there was John Purroy Mitchel who was elected mayor at thirty-four during World War I. Mitchel came of fighters. One of his uncles had been killed while defending Fort Sumter; another had died in Pickett's charge across the fields of Gettysburg. Young Mitchel had been a boxer in college and he could punch hard with both hands. He was undoubtedly the roughest character Tammany faced before LaGuardia. Like the Major he had been swept in on a wave of reform. But the machine retired him from office after a single term. When he entered City Hall, Mitchel's hair was completely brown. Before he retired, it had turned gray. That's what fighting for reform does to a man in one term. One can surmise the strain under which LaGuardia labored for three terms.

Shortly after LaGuardia took office, he asked me to come and work in his administration. I was thirty-one years old, and only just starting to make a place for myself in a law office. It was quite a decision to make, but the restlessness of the times gave me a spirit of restlessness.

I thought carefully about the kind of job I would want to do in the LaGuardia administration. I knew that a great many of the city's problems would have to be solved in Albany. The city had very limited financial power. I told LaGuardia I would like to go into the city law department as assistant corporation counsel (which would keep me in touch with my vocation) and join the legislative division in Albany.

I arrived in Albany on New Year's night, 1934, with Reuben Lazarus, who was then, and still is, considered the outstanding financial authority on municipal government.

That first winter in Albany was a very busy one. The Assembly met at eleven in the morning, and the Senate met in the late afternoon or the evening. Sometimes the two houses would be in session concurrently, which made it difficult to cover both. I spent my time under Lazarus' direction preparing bills and amendments to bills that would give the LaGuardia administration power to effect economies in the courts and in education, areas over which the city ordinarily has no control. We had to institute economies because the tax delinquencies were very high. The city budget, the last prepared by the O'Brien administration, was thirty-one million dollars out of balance. The bankers had the city's revenues pledged first to the payment of indebtedness. To balance the budget it was necessary to effect a two per cent salary cut among all city employees. But it seemed unfair that the employees in the city-controlled departments—the police, fire, sanitation, hospitals—should have to accept the two per cent cut while those in the state-controlled Department of Education, the courts and the Board of Elections could get away without having to carry their share. Of course, it was a very unpopular thing to cut salaries. However, the employees of other cities, during these days of the depression, either didn't get their pay checks at all or received scrip. Several cities were issuing a scrip money enabling their employees to buy bread and other necessities. But we felt that it was more in keeping with the dignity of the City of New York to restore its credit and to pay in United States currency.

One bill before us this session had to do with consolidating the five Park Departments. In place of the five previous Borough Commissioners of Parks, Robert Moses emerged as the city's single Park Commissioner.

The thing that amazed me most during my stay in

Albany was the spectacle of a handful of upstate rural legislators, some of whom represented a constituency that would have been lost in Times Square at midday, telling the people of New York City how to run their government. As a matter of fact, the American city is a bastard development utterly unprovided for by the founding fathers. The Constitution was framed on the assumption that the rural community would remain the basic political unit in America. The early Americans sought to discourage the political growth of cities. They were only too aware of the reign of terror established by the Parisian street mobs during the French Revolution. However, due to waves of immigration and shifts in our native population because of industrialization, a century and a half after the Constitution was framed the American city has become the frontier of democracy. Two out of every three Americans live in cities, and it is here that the most vexing social problems of our times arise.

It is apparent that the social problems of New York and other American cities can never be solved until the state legislatures, established when farmers were the politically dominant element, are fairly reapportioned. Only then will we have truly representative government, and only then will the legislature give broad home rule power to cities.

In August of 1934, when I had been in Albany for eight months, Joe Baldwin, a Republican member of the city Board of Aldermen, resigned his seat to become a candidate for the state Senate, and I was asked by Kenneth Simpson, district leader, to fill the vacancy. I turned the offer over in my mind for several days, and accepted. I said to myself, I've seen what can be done or rather what can't be done in Albany. Let me see what can be done in New York.

The chief obstacle to reform in New York City was the Board of Aldermen—the city legislature established in 1830. During various periods of its activities, it became known as the "Boodle Board," and the "Forty Thieves." In the past, even when Tammany Hall lost a mayoralty election to the reformers, it had enough strength in the district organizations to give it a majority on the Board of Aldermen.

When I joined the Board it consisted of sixty-two Democrats and three Republicans. But life was not unpleasant. The Tammany politicians were gentlemen of wit. Most of them had been given their seats as a reward for a lifetime of party service, and, although Murray Stand, majority leader, was an industrious fellow, the others did not break their backs with work. The sessions rarely lasted over half an hour, and even less when Babe Ruth put on a show at the Yankee Stadium.

I had no sooner taken my seat on the Board than I got into a cat-and-dog fight over introducing six bills to reorganize or abolish some county offices, consolidate others, and put all positions under Civil Service. My bills would have abolished the five county sheriffs and set up a single city sheriff, selected by Civil Service, cutting out about three-quarters of the aggregate budgets of the five. This had been the Citizens' Union program for years.

The sheriff was a favorite political pawn of Tammany. He was nothing but a glorified process server. And under the sheriff, hordes of Tammany henchmen had been given jobs as deputy sheriffs. Upon investigation I discovered that one such deputy served only three court papers during an entire year.

The Board suceeded in blocking my bills, and as long as it remained in existence, the sheriffs stayed in office. However, in 1940, when I was president of the Council, a civic uprising resulted in having the proposal placed on the ballot by petition. And the voters, many of whom until then had never even known about the sheriff racket, abolished or consolidated the county offices out of existence by a wide majority.

I uncovered one fantastic situation while I was on the Board of Aldermen. I found that volunteer firemen who had been injured in the course of duty and the widows of volunteer firemen had, since the early nineteen hundreds, been the beneficiaries of revenues from an ancient tax which was still in the legislative books. At the turn of the century, this tax had been a very much needed source of revenue to take care of injured men or dependents of those who died fighting fires. Although the city had a regular fire department with a paid force for almost half a century, I discovered that there were seven volunteer companies organized in Queens and Staten Island who were still receiving income from the old tax. Their chief activity, however, was parading on the Fourth of July. (Occasionally they put out brush fires.) I discovered that the old Benevolent Association of the Volunteer Firemen of the Old City of New York was still in existence. And 45 per cent of the taxes collected was still being sent to a home for retired firemen at Hudson, New York, that hadn't been functioning for years! Yet the administrators of the home kept up offices and received the money.

I introduced a bill to correct the situation. It provided for keeping the tax, but using the revenues totaling $500,000 a year to defray the expenses of the regular fire department pension fund, which was running at a deficit of two million dollars a year. I expected no opposition to my bill. After all, how many volunteer firemen were left? I was amazed to receive telephone calls, letters, telegrams, numbering 1,800 in all. The Volunteer Firemen's Associations of the cities of Troy, New York, and of Binghamton asked me how I could do such a dreadful thing. Sitting next to me on the Board was Eddie Buhler, an alderman, who said: "Newbold, this is a terrible mistake. Do you know that you are cutting *me* out of a pension when I am old? I'm not making a fortune, and if I die, you are taking bread away from my family."

"Eddie," I replied, "I didn't realize that while I am sleeping in comfort on Park Avenue, you are out fighting fires!"

"No. I'm not fighting fires. I'm the chief of a volunteer company."

"Where is it?"

He named a section of Queens. He explained to me that every year a number of popular young men in the community were elected to the volunteer fire company. (They didn't fight fires; they just collected from the fund.)

One old company of New York had nine trustees— the only survivors of the original organization. They exercised sole discretion over the disbursement of a pension fund that had accumulated reserves of $400,000. Every year they met and awarded themselves an annual allowance of $3,600 each and pensions to ninety-one widows of deceased volunteers. One year they declared themselves a bonus of $1,800.

My bill to remedy this didn't pass the Board of Aldermen. Years later, I believe it was Assemblyman Herbert Brownell, now United States Attorney General, who corrected this situation with legislation in Albany.

During my term as alderman, I got into one stormy row with LaGuardia. A bill to dispense with public letting in the purchase of fire equipment by the city was sent in by the mayor just before the summer recess. I knew nothing about the matter. And I was determined not to vote on any legislation, whether it came from La-Guardia or anyone else, without preliminary study. I rose and objected to the Board's considering it that day. Unfortunately, this happened to be the final session of of year. The Board adjourned and departed for the ball game.

LaGuardia was furious. As a result of my action, the American La France Company, an organization LaGuardia looked upon with disfavor, might have gotten the contract instead of the company he desired to obtain it. I knew nothing about the American La France Company, or the politics involved. But LaGuardia wrote me a little note. *I would just like to know if by any chance you are a stockholder, a director, or attorney for the American La France Company.*

I went down to the mayor's room and without inquiring whether I could enter, walked right in and confronted him.

I held out the handwritten note. "Did you write that?" He answered, "Yes, what have you got to say about it?" "A lot of people have accused me of a lot of things.

But nobody ever questioned my personal integrity. If
you mean that, it's the end of any relationship between
you and me."

He took his glasses off, looked at me, and said, "Gee,
I'm sorry," and he put his hand out.

"Well, you'd better tear that up and put it in the
basket!" He did, and although we had disagreements,
we never had a quarrel again in our subsequent years
together.

By and large I enjoyed my personal relations with the
Tammany members of the Board. One day I stole a march
on Majority Leader Murray Stand and proposed a resolution to give all city employees a holiday with pay on
Saint Patrick's Day. It was adopted unanimously! Henceforth, my fellow members, many of whom were Hiber-
nians, accepted me as a "regular guy." To this day I have
a soft spot in my heart for these representatives of an
old New York.

After the Board was replaced by the City Council, I
hankered after their fellowship. I invited the boys to a
reunion at Bill's Gay Nineties, on East Fifty-fourth
Street. During the meal I suggested that we form the
Association of Past Members of the Board of Aldermen,
and nominated for president Peter J. McGuinness, the
then Assistant Commissioner of Borough Works in
Brooklyn. Headquarters for this association were set up
in the Yale Club; and thereafter, on each Saint Patrick's
Day, I was host to my friends before we joined the parade.
Old Pete McGuinness was a symbol of a New York that
is no more—New York of the corner saloon, Peacock
Alley, the Tenderloin, and Betcha-Million Gates. Like
the political bosses described by Lincoln Steffens, Pete

McGuinness and his cronies were more sinned against than sinning. They were the victims of a political system inherited from the past. I have in my files a quaint letter Pete McGuinness sent to me at the time when, as president of the City Council, I was fighting the Tammany forces tooth and nail. The letter is eloquent of Pete's affectionate nature.

DEAR PAL NEWBOLD,

I was just speaking of you to Judge McGrate and Judge Lockwood, and we were discussing what a fine fellow you are.

I consider you my very dearest pal, and I have been advised of the way you accept some of my friends who have had occasion to request a meeting with you.

Newbold, old pal, no words I can speak can express my proper feelings and thoughts about you, and while the sun is shining on the Great Irish, the sun will shine on us two, while we are enjoying that splendid luncheon at the Yale Club, and basking in our wonderful friendship.

Your pal

PETE

In 1936, due to the untimely death of Bernard Deutsch, elected with LaGuardia, there was a vacancy in the office of President of the Board of Aldermen, and Kenneth Simpson, the county chairman, asked me if I would like to run for the seat. I accepted. Simpson, who was the original spirit behind my nomination to this city-wide post, was the most powerful Republican in city politics. For an organization politician, he was an unusual person. He loved classical music, and collected Picasso and

Bracque paintings with the same shrewdness that he collected delegates for political conventions. His bristling red mustache was a tip-off to his colorful personality. Once while we were on a vacation together off the Cap d'Antibes, he took time out from a discussion of political strategy to chat with me about the meaning of a Prokofiev symphony.

Nineteen hundred thirty-six was a presidential election and state election year. Roosevelt and the New Deal were riding the high tide of popularity, and Simpson admitted to me when he suggested I accept a place on the Landon ticket that there was practically no chance for me to be elected, but that if I ran well in the five boroughs, it would lead to future opportunities. The Republican organization put most of its energy into the campaigns for Alf Landon and Frank Knox on the national ticket, and for Bill Bleakley running for governor. I was left pretty much to my own resources.

Curiously enough, LaGuardia had been cool at first to my nomination. Even now he had lingering suspicions about me because I lived on Park Avenue and because I had blocked some of his bills on the Board of Aldermen. But before the campaign got under way, members of LaGuardia's official family drifted into my camp. I was elated to receive a telegram from Paul Windels, La-Guardia's brilliant corporation counsel, notifying me of his support. Mary K. Simkovich, dean of Settlement House Directors, Marie Winter, wife of my former district leader, Mrs. Ogden Mills and Mrs. Ruth Pratt, a member of Congress from my district, and her lovely daughter Virginia Thayer, headed up a woman's committee to support me. Dick Lawrence, President of the

New York City Y.M.C.A. and of the State Chamber of Commerce, and Samuel Seabury and the Citizens' Union rallied to my support, and LaGuardia eventually followed suit. Even the New Deal newspapers supported me.

For my city-wide campaigning I purchased an open secondhand Packard out of my own funds for $700, and sold it to an undertaker a year later for $900. Just how large I loomed in the political picture was demonstrated to me when I put in an appearance at my first Republican rally in Brooklyn. According to the schedule, I was to arrive a few minutes after Judge Bleakley, the candidate for governor. Preceded by a motorcycle escort, I drove up to the Erasmus High School. A brass band was drawn up in front of the steps. As he heard the wail of motorcycle sirens, I saw the bandmaster raise his baton. The trumpeters and drummers were poised for the fanfare. I stepped from my auto and the maestro looked over his shoulder at me. "Hold it, boys. It's a false alarm!" By some accident I had arrived ahead of Bill Bleakley.

Local issues were completely obliterated by the great national struggle. This was to be the first major political test of the New Deal.

One must recall the atmosphere of the times. In the four years since Roosevelt had entered the White House, a radical experiment in government had changed the lives of the American people. The New Deal attempted to build prosperity from the bottom up, rather than from the top down. Roosevelt, as he put it, "planned the national conservation not only of physical forces, but of human beings." In implementing his government welfare program, he had taken the country off the gold standard, raised agricultural prices by subsidizing farmers for underproducing. He put the government into industry by building federal power dams in the Tennessee Valley. He sent thousands of jobless young men off to CCC camps, set up a social security system of unemployment insurance and old-age assistance. He put four and a half million jobless to work on federal relief programs. Through NRA and, later, the Wagner Act, his Administration granted labor its magna carta, prescribing maximum work hours, minimum wages, and the right of collective bargaining.

The economic headquarters of the nation had been moved from Wall Street to Washington. For the first time in our history, no important decision could be taken by the financiers without approval of the White House. Everybody felt the impact of the "new look." H. L. Mencken, whose *American Mercury* had been the bible of the intellectuals in the nineteen twenties, lost his place in the sun as his followers turned from the sport of intellectual debunking to the social economics of Keynes. Masses of people, convinced that the economic system was doomed to remain chronically ill, expressed themselves in a series of Utopian movements. Huey Long raised the standard of a "Share the Wealth" program which at its height attracted over four million people. Dr. Francis Townsend of Long Beach, California, unveiled a plan for revolving old-age pensions. Upton Sinclair, running for governor of California, came forward with an EPIC (End Poverty in California) plan, according to which the unemployed would be put to work producing goods for one another and bartering them.

Not only was President Roosevelt's program harassed by these fratricidal flank attacks on his left, but Al Smith, the leader of the right wing elements, broke with him and took a walk at the Democratic National Convention. And within Roosevelt's own command post, as it were, labor leaders were engaged in a bitter struggle over the issue of craft versus industrial unionism—a struggle that led to the A.F. of L.'s casting John L. Lewis and the unrepentant C.I.O. organization out the front door in 1936. The rash of sit-down strikes that followed as the C.I.O. flexed its organizational muscles plagued the Administration still further.

The international situation was disturbing. In 1936, Hitler had seized the Rhineland, Mussolini's armies were converging upon Addis Ababa after a sudden invasion of Ethiopia. While Americans were whistling to the tunes of Ginger Rogers-Fred Astaire motion-picture musicals, and buzzing over the sensational new fiction heroine Scarlett O'Hara, civil war had broken out in Spain, and, by election time, Franco had reached the outskirts of Madrid. But there was one event that provided an emotional escape this year. King Edward announced from London that he was abdicating the throne for "the woman I love."

In the meantime, the Republicans, disturbed by Roosevelt's program for coping with the depression, disagreeing with his deficit spending, his inflationary manipulation of the currency, his putting the government into industry on a large scale, contested his re-election in a campaign that turned out to be one of the bitterest in our history. Alf Landon, the Kansas governor, was a kindly, liberal man. But he simply didn't have the

personality to match Roosevelt's. The President won the
election, carrying every state but Maine and Vermont.
The *Literary Digest,* which had predicted a Landon
victory, sank into oblivion.

However, despite the Roosevelt landslide, I managed
to run 150,000 votes ahead of Landon and the rest of the
ticket in New York City. This showing assured my
nomination for the Number Two spot on the LaGuardia
ticket the following year when the mayor ran for re-election. This ticket was overwhelmingly elected, and as
president of the newly created City Council (the Board
of Aldermen had been abolished with the adoption of
a new city charter), I entered into an intimate association with LaGuardia for eight years.

Next to the re-election of LaGuardia, the year 1937
was important for another reason. On the New York
County ticket, supported by the Republican, American
Labor, and Maurice Davidson's Progressive parties,
Thomas E. Dewey was elected district attorney. A young
attorney who had stepped into the shoes of the United
States Attorney for the Southern District of New York,
Dewey was persuaded to run for this first elective office
by Kenneth Simpson, Sidney Hillman, and David
Dubinsky. Launched into politics by this curious assort-
ment of bedfellows, Dewey's career was meteoric. After
nine months as district attorney of New York County,
he was to run for governor against Herbert Lehman, and
in 1940, after only two years in elective public office, he
was to become a leading candidate for the Republican
nomination for President. In my opinion, Dewey is the
most resourceful politician on the national scene today.
The only two politicans who have equaled—and perhaps

surpassed—him in this regard, Roosevelt and LaGuardia, are both dead.

Mrs. Alice Longworth delivered an unkind quip when Dewey was a candidate for his second Presidential nomination in 1948, *"You can't make a soufflé rise twice."* But I predict that Tom will return to public life and rise a third time on the national scene.

CHAPTER 5 The "Little Flower" and the "Mayflower"

I WAS to know the mayor in his later years as well as any other political associate of his, but the man became a legend long before I undertook to write about him. He was, in fact, a legend while he lived. The people of New York called him the "Little Flower" and "The Hat." Whenever the aggressive little figure under the big-brimmed Stetson trudged across the newsreel screens of the nation, audiences were engulfed with laughter. The high-pitched voice declaiming in righteous wrath was well worth the price of a ticket to any movie house. But, as mayor, he had a certain majesty that added cubits to his stature.

The fact is, LaGuardia was a new kind of mayor for New York, a new kind of administrator in American politics. True, the immigrant strain had long before been injected into the blood stream of American politics. But LaGuardia's ancestors came from the Mediterranean. He had been exposed as a young man to the countries of central Europe. He was perhaps the first to bring to the problems of American city government the temperament, not of the businessman, but of the Old World *artiste*. He saw government not merely as an exchange house for political and economic transactions, but as a living, exfoliating organism that could develop into something ugly or beautiful, depending upon the environment in which it fed and the *aesthetics* of the people who guided it. The great American reformers of the past, John Purroy Mitchel of New York, Tom Johnson of Cleveland, for example, had been businessmen who conceived of their job in business terms—the trimming of expenses, the elimination of waste and inefficiency, the guaranteeing of honesty in political transactions. They would have been astonished at the conception that good government is also an *aesthetic* problem; that to the dimensions of honesty and efficiency, must be added the judgment of *beauty*.

Shortly after his inauguration, LaGuardia expressed this feeling he had inherited from the Old World. "I am in the position of an artist or a sculptor. I can see New York as it should be and as it can be if we all work together. But now I am like the man who has a conception that he wishes to carve or paint, who has the model before him, but hasn't as yet been given a chisel or a brush." (This was his way of requesting money and state-delegated powers to carry out his program.)

Yes, LaGuardia was a funny man. He was an unsparing, opinionated man. And he was a man of political genius. Taking over the helm of the largest city in the world, in the throes of the depression, LaGuardia restored it to financial health. The stock market crash and the panic that followed had hit New York harder than any other city in the country. The luxury business which supplied a living to so many of its inhabitants was practically wiped out. On January 1, 1934, when LaGuardia entered City Hall, the people of New York had reached the bottom of the toboggan chute after three years of downskidding. Bank failures had depleted personal savings. No adequate system of public relief had been set up. The city's credit was eliminated.

One out of every three jobholders was out of work and the state relief funds available for the unemployed were woefully inadequate. One-fifth of the students in the city schools were suffering from malnutrition and were unable to attend classes regularly. Physicians, chemists, teachers were put on relief jobs that brought in fourteen dollars a week for a husband and wife with two children. Experts from the relief agencies advised recipients how to budget their earnings "realistically" —ten dollars a month for rent; five dollars a week for food; twenty-five cents a week for electricity and gas; forty-five cents a week for household expenses. When it was pointed out that heated apartments for ten dollars a month were unavailable in New York even during these times of depression, and that the Edison Company charged a minimum of one dollar just to turn on the electricity, the authorities shrugged and bemoaned the lack of funds. Street begging had become so prevalent that the Brooklyn-Manhattan Transit Corporation placed ads in its trains and subway stations forbidding its patrons to give handouts. "It is a mistaken kindness to hand money to street beggars," declared one city magistrate as he passed sentence on a vagrant. And an editorial writer in a contemporary magazine inquired, "What would this . . . judge who enjoys an appointment for ten years at an annual salary of $12,000 have us give the man who is less fortunate than he—a revolver?" All types of private charity had been tried and found inadequate to cope with the crisis. "There is hardly an American," wrote one observer, "who would allow another man to starve on his doorstep if there was a loaf of bread in the house, but we are reaching a point where we are willing to let thousands die of starvation provided only that they crawl off out of our sight to do it."

Before 1929 LaGuardia had remarked to friends, "It's damned depressing to be a reformer in the richest country in the world." But now reform was not only popular. It was inevitable. The mayor's social philosophy predated the New Deal. His roots were those of progressive Republicanism typified by Theodore Roosevelt, George Norris and the La Follettes. Their compassion for the public welfare had none of the taint of foreign ideology, none of the dogmatic intellectualism of Marx or Bakunin. The progressivism of the La Follettes was as American as the homespun optimism of the Middle West they came from. It was simple and devastating. "We are opposed," declared La Follette the elder, "to any form of class dictatorship either of the plutocracy or of the proletariat."

Since LaGuardia had spent his formative years in the Middle West, physically at least, his roots were close to those of Harold Ickes, who, as Secretary of the Interior under Roosevelt, presided over the Public Works Administration. Despite a difference in party label LaGuardia had no hesitancy about accepting federal relief money. He believed that mass unemployment was a concern of all the people of the country. And he did not consider relief charity. He had to match the federal expenditures by raising additional millions on his own. Furthermore, at a time when too many other communities were flagrantly sponging on federal relief and getting little or no results with the money, LaGuardia put thousands of men to work on a job program that transformed the physical aspect of the city.

Under his regime New York blossomed into a community of beauty. Old parks were restored; new ones were built. Plans for arterial highways that had gathered dust in the files for years were put into operation. In addition to his works program, the mayor put an end to the land condemnation racket that had been bleeding the city treasury for the profit of landowners, lawyers and politicians. He established in each borough a small claims court where the man in the street could get speedy justice without having to resort to lawyers. He helped to push through the reorganization of county governments, wiping out old sinecures and putting the remainder on a civil service basis. LaGuardia appointed Lewis Valentine, a career policeman, as his police commissioner, and New York mobsters had a very bad time of things. Frank Costello and Dandy Phil Kastel were driven from town. The tinhorn gamblers were compelled to transfer their operations west of the Hudson.

The mayor refused to flinch from facts. When he entered office the credit of the city was at low tide. The city was able to borrow from the banks only at exorbitant rates. As a member of Congress, LaGuardia had continually resisted a sales tax. But as mayor he advocated a sales tax under a power delegated by the state to give the city a necessary source of revenue. Emergency relief taxes including the sales tax were needed to augment the real-estate levies to cope with unemployment. The sales tax LaGuardia initiated was the best conceived one in the country. And it has since been used as a model in many places.

The mayor displayed the passion of the *bon vivant,* exhibiting the idiosyncracies of some of his Bohemian forebears. He rushed to fires in a fireman's helmet; he stood before symphony orchestras and conducted them with the *bravura* of a professional. He read the Sunday comics over the radio to the children of New York during a strike of newspapers. He was so popular a broadcaster that whenever he spoke, there was a marked falling off of water consumption. Taps were turned off throughout the city. People sat glued to their radio sets.

Historically LaGuardia was a phenomenon. He was the only New York mayor ever to serve three consecutive terms. Even more significant, he was the only reform mayor to be re-elected to office. This had profound consequences. As Eddie Flynn, the Democratic boss of the Bronx, has pointed out, Tammany had always operated on the assumption that reform movements would expend themselves in a single term. The Tammany machine had been capable in the past of withstanding four years of a reform administration because of its carry-over appointees. However, before the twelve years of LaGuardia's administration were over, there was not a single official outside of the state and county courts and the Board of Elections who owed his position to Tammany. Starved from a prolonged lack of patronage, the machine had come apart at the joints. Its headquarters on Seventeenth Street, erected during the lush days, had to be sold out by the bank that held the mortgage, and David Dubinsky's International Ladies' Garment Workers Union moved into it. In only one area was Tammany able to maintain a fingerhold. It lived on the judges it had nominated and elected to the bench. And even here it experienced a depression. There has always been a lively *sub rosa* commerce in the judgeships. At one time, Tammany was able to sell a nomination to an ambitious lawyer for $100,000. But when LaGuardia obtained the power to cut judicial salaries, Tammany had to scale down its price. There is a bullish and bearish cycle even in the graft market.

The present system of electing judges has resulted in a sorry mess. Sometimes, political district leaders have even been named secretaries to judges. Patronage running into millions of dollars a year in special guardianships for infants or mental incompetents, receiverships, refereeships are parceled out to attorneys who have served the machine. When the public has finally been treated to a thorough exposé of this sordid business, the notion that justice is blind will go the way of all delusions. Actually justice, when dispensed by machine-picked judges, has at least one eye cocked open to do its master's bidding.

When LaGuardia entered City Hall, his personal savings were at a low point. He didn't even own an automobile. Yet one of the first things he did was to cut the mayor's salary from $40,000 a year (the Walker level) to $22,500. Until he was given an official home (during his second administration), he lived in a small six-room apartment on upper Fifth Avenue.

He became mayor of the world's largest city with practically no administrative experience. Through twelve years of an active, turbulent administration, he undertook not only to lay down policy, but to carry out the details of it. He not only directed the government, he acted it out as a one-man show, taking the leading roles and the parts of the supernumeraries as well.

There never was a more autocratic democrat. Like old Frederick the Great, he swooped down suddenly, unexpectedly, on various parts of his domain, meting out awards and penalties with equal promptness. Every appearance was dutifully reported in the press; each was meant to dramatize a point, to function as a tableau in a morality play. Only weeks after his inauguration, the mayor, calling attention to the fact that under the law he was entitled to sit as a judge, suddenly appeared in the West 100th Street Police Station and presided as magistrate, sentencing a slot-machine operator to jail. A week later, he sat on the bench in Brooklyn, sentencing a second gambler—and then, to make sure that the point was not missed by the public, the mayor personally presided over the smashing of "one-armed bandits" throughout the city and posed with a sledgehammer for a photographer before they were dumped into the East River.

One afternoon he directed a police inspection of a hundred movie houses throughout Manhattan, Bronx, and Brooklyn to discover whether the owners were complying with a new city regulation requiring them to set aside a section of the theatre for children—under the supervision of a matron.

He pounced down upon the Harlem prison and released two young boys, held as material witnesses in a murder case, turning them over to the Children's Society.

In between times he found the energy to ride to

murders, automobile accidents, railroad wrecks (in the sidecar of a police motorcycle when the mayor's limousine was laid up for repairs).

LaGuardia was one of the hardest-working men I ever knew. His recreation was pretty much limited to listening to music, or attending a baseball game with the children. Once he asked what my plans were for a warm July afternoon. I replied that I had a date to play golf. Somewhat wryly he observed, "I thought you did that *last* week."

His commissioners and assistants rarely succeeded in getting a vacation. His indefatigability set the pace. Once when one of them managed to get away, and LaGuardia heard he had just arrived in the Canadian woods for a few days' fishing, His Honor concocted an emergency and summoned the commissioner back to New York before he could land a single trout.

The mayor was a man utterly without physical fear. I never knew when even a social evening spent with him would turn into a physical crisis. One hot summer night, I accompanied the mayor to Radio City Music Hall, primarily to take advantage of the air-conditioning system. As we entered, the feature picture had just ended. An organist was playing under a spotlight. "Newbold," LaGuardia whispered to me, "that's how our city must be run. Like that organist, you must keep both hands on the keyboard and both feet on the pedals—*and never let go!*"

The new show had just gone on when a police officer came in to tell us there was a fire outside. LaGuardia leaped from his seat and rushed out of the theatre. I followed. Smoke was pouring from a restaurant on Fifty-first Street. Without breaking his stride, before the fire-fighting equipment arrived, LaGuardia disappeared inside the building. After a while firemen entered and I heard one of them mutter on coming out, "Will somebody get the mayor out of there." Minutes passed. The last fireman emerged from the entrance, and still the mayor hadn't appeared. Smoke continued to billow from the doors and windows. I became genuinely alarmed. Finally, after what seemed an interminable time, LaGuardia emerged from the entrance. His clothes were covered with soot. His face was barely recognizable. "I gave the refrigeration system a personal going over," the mayor explained to me. "I wanted to find out whether the building code had been violated." He hadn't trusted the eyesight of the fire battalion chief, a dozen trained fire fighters and experts from the Bureau of Combustibles!

Rarely did LaGuardia miss the chance to dramatize his ideas. Due to the fact, perhaps, that he was of Italian descent, and because so many pushcart peddlers in the lower East Side were Italians, he was especially sensitive to the problems of these peddlers and the spectacle they created. He decided to abolish the pushcarts and establish enclosed public markets. He was opposed by taxpayers' lobbies. The plan was held to be too expensive. Besides, many sentimental people argued that the peddler with the rusty scales hanging from the side of his cart (which were in many cases giving short weight to housewives) was one of the quaint sights of New York City. They hated to see him go.

I shall never forget how, during a similar campaign to clean up the streets of organ-grinders (most of whom

were simply licensed beggars), a woman came up to La-
Guardia at a social function and begged him not to
deprive her of her favorite organ-grinder.

"Where do you live?" he asked her.

"On Park Avenue."

LaGuardia successfully pushed through his plan to
eliminate the organ-grinders and the peddlers, despite
the pleas of the penthouse slummers. I accompanied
him to the dedication of the first public market, and I
shall always remember the event. The peddlers were
attired in neat white coats. Each stood by his indoor
stand, his wares in orderly array. LaGuardia launched
into his address, and, suddenly, in the middle of it,
stooped and picked up an apple from one of the stands.
"There will be no more of this," he said, as he pretended
to spit on the apple, polishing it up on his coat sleeve and
putting it back on the stand. This was his way of dem-
onstrating that the new public markets were in the interest of public health. Pointing to his listeners in their
crisp white coats, he concluded, "I found you pushcart
peddlers . . . I have made you *merchants!*"

LaGuardia surrounded himself from the outset with
a cabinet of men who were as politically unconventional
as himself. Hitherto, the political district leaders had
been appointed to the jobs of city commissioners with
their control over millions of dollars. LaGuardia broke
the rule. He appointed for his fire commissioner Patrick
Walsh, a man who was actually a fireman. For his police
commissioner he selected Lewis Valentine, a policeman
who had previously been broken in rank for conducting
raids against the gamblers in Tammany clubs. He
shocked old-school politicians by inviting nonresidents

of New York City to enter the government. His commissioner of health was Dr. John Rice, an expert who had made a brilliant record in New Haven, Connecticut. Austin H. McCormick, who directed the city prison system, had achieved an equally distinguished record as chief of the federal penitentiary in Chillicothe, Ohio. Political labels, color of the skin, made no difference. Paul Blanshard, a Norman Thomas socialist, was appointed the first Commissioner of Investigation. Four distinguished Negroes were brought into public office; Hubert Delany was appointed to the Tax Commission, later to the Court of Domestic Relations, the first of his people to be so honored. Myles Paige and Jane Bolin were put on the magistrate's court; Frank Crosswaith was appointed to the city Housing Authority.

In the 1936 election, a new charter for the city had been adopted by popular referendum. It became effective January 1, 1938, when I took office. Among other things, it provided for the abolition of the old Board of Aldermen and the establishment of a city council as the new legislative body. Under the old system of election by districts, Tammany had completely dominated the legislative body by gerrymandering the districts, so that it had overwhelming representation. The opposition vote was practically worthless. However, the new City Council was elected by a system of proportional representation. This completely freed candidates from the necessity of being nominated in machine-dominated primary elections. Furthermore, it provided for a truer representation of the city's diverse elements. On the last Board of Aldermen, Tammany had sixty-two out of a total of sixty-five seats. In the newly elected Council, there were thirteen Tammany Democrats out of twenty-six members. Two seats were held by Independent Democrats, three by Republicans, two by Fusionists, six by American Laborites. Thirteen members, in other words, were beyond the control of the Tammany machine.

However, the political diversity of the Council justified my claim that proportional representation gave to New York exactly what it purported to give. It provided representation in direct proportion to the various political entities and, just as important, provided for representation in direct proportion to the population of each borough. Out of sixty-five members of the old Board of Aldermen, elected from gerrymandered districts, twenty-four came from Manhattan and twenty-four from Brooklyn, yet Manhattan's population was only a little more than half of the population of Brooklyn.

This very diversity made my job as the first Council's presiding officer a challenging one. Since Tammany's control over the old Board had been complete, it had named to it mostly candidates who would serve as messengers or liaison between district leaders and government agencies. Every district leader maintained his power by doing "favors" for his constituents. A manufacturer of fire equipment might want to make contact with the fire commissioner. It was usually the alderman who effected this meeting.

One of them told me he received $500 for arranging such an introduction. When I raised my eyebrows at this frank disclosure, he stated that I shouldn't worry about it because the books of the company were set up in such a manner that a $500 fee would have to be paid to someone who would act as public relations "officer" and why should an alderman be discriminated against! Another favor might include requesting the commissioner of housing and building to defer action on a violation for failure of a landlord to install fire-retarding equipment. Innocuous favors would involve an effort to speed someone's mother-in-law through the red tape of immigration or find a location for a veteran to establish a newsstand.

In any case, I found each alderman always had in his pocket an agenda of favors that he had to complete by sundown on a given day, and throughout the day he would check off the items as he completed each mission for the district organization. However, to the new Council, where Tammany was in a real fight for its interests, it sent the more articulate, shrewd and aggressive members of the old Board of Aldermen. They knew just exactly when to summon up their vocal power in bitter tirades against the Republican, Labor, Independents blocs (known as the Fusion or Coalition Group), which turned the chamber into bedlam. And they often contrived to make it look as though it were all my fault!

Just before we took office on New Year's Day, 1938, I invited all twenty-six members to a dinner at the old City Club. I arranged the seating at the table in such a way that members of the Republican, Labor and Democratic parties and those independently elected were interspersed instead of sitting together in parliamentary blocs. I explained to them that I thought this was the way we ought to plan to sit in the Council chamber. I preferred to preside at the head of a table instead of being perched on a speaker's dais. I had a theory that without an aisle to divide the members of a legislative body, across which one is tempted to shout, we would discuss city problems objectively. "But of course," I concluded, "you have the votes to do what you like."

John Cashmore, who seemed very likely to become the Democratic leader of the Council, looked at me quietly and smiled. I had known him well as a member of the old Board of Aldermen. His silence was more eloquent than words.

At the very first session trouble broke out. The first order of business was the election of a vice-chairman and majority leader of the Council. According to the new charter, no member could be elected except by a majority vote of all the councilmen.

However, one member of the Council, Mike Quill, had gone to Ireland to get married, and his ship had been delayed en route to the United States. Therefore, only twenty-five members were present to vote on the vice-chairmanship. The thirteen Tammany Democrats promptly nominated John Cashmore. The anti-Tammany forces united and nominated Jim Burke, an Independent from Queens.

The roll was called, and Cashmore received thirteen votes to Burke's twelve. I then called the members' attention to the section in the new city charter which provided that no local law or resolution could be passed except by a majority vote of *all* the members, not merely those present. And reminding them that Quill was absent, I declared the office of vice-chairman to be still vacant. At this, John Cashmore jumped up and yelled, "Hitler here is depriving the people of a vice-chairman!"

I was mindful of the situation under the old Board

of Aldermen when an arbitary number of members
could constitute a quorum and pass important legislation; this even if a minority were present. I didn't
want to see these days return. So I repeated my ruling,
reading from the city charter: "No local law or resolution
can be adopted except by at least a majority affirmative
vote of *all* the councilmen."

Then another Tammany member, Kinsley of the
Bronx, stood up and delivered a peroration, claiming
democratic government was being strangled in our
legislative chamber.

Since we couldn't agree on a vice-chairman at this
session, I entertained a motion for the election of a city
clerk. This office was one of the last strongholds of Tammany patronage. LaGuardia had been mayor for four
years, and the Tammany pickings were sparse. My candidate for city clerk was Lawson Stone, the son of the
Chief Justice of the United States Supreme Court. He
had never been in politics. But if I had succeeded in
having him elected to this office, he would have helped
us put it under Civil Service, and this would have
broken the grip of Tammany.

When the matter came to a vote, the thirteen Tammany members named Michael J. Cruise. I insisted that
the office was vacant. Cruise shouted hoarsely that he
was the legally elected city clerk.

Pandemonium broke out in the chamber. The Democrats took the matter into the city courts and obtained
from Judge McGeehan an order requiring me to recognize Cashmore as vice-chairman and Cruise as city clerk.

I found myself in a quandary. If I continued to insist
that these offices were vacant, I would be held in con-

tempt of court and might have to preside over the City
Council from a prison cell. On the other hand, I felt
strongly about the principles involved. I took the position that I could not recognize the court injunction because the legislative branch of the city could not be
handcuffed by the courts.

To make matters even more complicated, Mike Quill
suddenly arrived in New York. He took his seat for the
second session of the Council. I now estimated that with
Quill present (he was expected to vote with the Independents), the vote for the offices would be split
thirteen to thirteen, and I, as president, would cast the
deciding vote. So I immediately ordered a new roll call.
It was a game of cat and mouse. With the voting now
stacked against them, the Cashmore group reasoned that
if one of them left the chamber to go to the men's room,
the balloting would remain thirteen to twelve; and since
I had previously ruled that twenty-five votes did not
represent a quorum, this would prevent my candidates
from being chosen. Just before the roll call, a Tammany
member left the chamber according to plan, and the
vote was thirteen to twelve (in favor of Burke) as expected. Without turning a hair, I held up the order from
the court. "Gentlemen, yesterday I ruled that a majority
of only those members present was insufficient, but since
the court has declared that for parliamentary purposes
it *is* sufficient, I must obey the order. I therefore declare
James Burke elected vice-chairman of the Council."

The case finally reached the Court of Appeals, and
McGeehan, Cashmore and company were upheld. During the interim New York City was treated to the
spectacle of two city clerks and two majority leaders

holding office, each claiming the exclusive right to the position. At first, whenever I left my chair to speak for a bill, I would put Burke in my place as vice-chairman. But Cashmore made such a fuss that eventually I remained glued to my seat. Sustained by the Tammany-dominated courts, Cashmore was finally declared the vice-chairman and majority leader.

These tumultuous City Council sessions were broadcast over the radio and earned continual headlines in the press. Spectators jammed the galleries. Behind the comic-opera byplay was the serious struggle on the part of Fusion to wrest control of the legislative body from the grip of the political machine. Our attempt, partially successful at the outset, resulted in long-range failure. Upon the return of Tammany to City Hall under the leadership of Mayor O'Dwyer, proportional representation was abolished, and the City Council returned to the old two-party district system. In the first City Council to be elected in this manner (in 1949), there was exactly one opposition member to the Tammany majority. He was Stanley Isaacs, a general without an army. Named the Republican minority leader, he had no one to second the resolutions he introduced.

As has already been more than hinted at, the City Council sessions were hardly pink tea parties. More than once I had to caution members that they were pounding their desks at their own peril. "Please, Gentlemen, the beams under this floor were put in one hundred and fifty years ago and they haven't been inspected since." Once I had to call the cops to keep order in the chamber.

The vulgarity and rowdiness of the Council were the raw material of democracy in action in a turbulent

city. The epithets Cashmore and his followers hurled
at me were frequently unprintable. "You lousy ape"
was one of the more gentle references. "I can tell what
you are by the length of your arms and the shape of
your head!" This was a reminder that I loomed several
inches taller than the rest of them. I was called a half-
wit, a crook, a bastard, a hammerhead, a jackass, a drunk,
a brat. And more than once I was challenged to take off
my coat and fight. One Bronx councilman, Louis Cohen,
spent considerable time under the care of a physician
for what was diagnosed as chronic high blood pressure.
His colleagues cautioned him against arguing with me!
I am happy to report that at this writing he is in good
health and we are friends.

Joseph Kinsley of the Bronx interspersed his attacks
on me with some delightful mimicry of Mayor LaGuardia and his commissioners. He was frequently called
upon to repeat his performance by popular request.

There never was a dull moment during our sessions
—and even in between times. One night after a debate,
one member barged into my office, grabbed me by the
neck and pushed me half across the room, kicking my
shins as he knocked over the furniture.

I saw no reason to conceal from the voters the high
jinks of their elected representatives; and I considered
it a healthy thing that the sessions of the City Council
were broadcast over the city radio station. In front of
each member's desk stood a microphone, and our de-
liberations reached a large audience in New York and
outlying areas. The press dubbed us "The Greatest Show
on Earth."

One of the liveliest sessions over which I presided

occurred when my old Board of Aldermen bills to reorganize the county offices were introduced by Genevieve
Earle, our lady member from Brooklyn. The county
sheriffs and the office of City Clerk were among the last
roosting places of the Tammany ward heelers.

The Council session began at 12:20 in the afternoon
and lasted continuously until 8:20 the following morning. The sheriffs, registers and their deputies attended
in a body and hissed from the galleries when the pro-
ponents of the bill spoke. At 11:00 P.M., the official
stenographer collapsed and had to be carried from the
room. President Jim Lyons of the Bronx humorously
proposed that the Board of Estimate sell to the public
six-inch double-faced phonograph records of the twenty-
hour session. Eddie Cantor wired City Hall from a hotel
in the Catskills where he was entertaining: *I am offering $200 for these records to be used on my Monday
night radio program. I reserve the right to take out what
I think is too funny!*

The bills were defeated, and it wasn't until the following year when the forces of good government obtained
fifty thousand signatures to a petition and placed them
on the ballot that the county offices were consolidated
by popular referendum. The people took the matter into
their own hands.

One thing that always amused me during these Council sessions was the reaction of the Tammany Democrats
to taxes for unemployment relief. Although the Cashmore group won the right through the courts to be
declared the majority, no Democrat would ever take
the responsibility for introducing tax measures, even
though they were part of the New Deal program. It

always remained for me to sponsor the bills; the Democrats would talk for hours against them. And then when
it came to a showdown, they would provide just enough
votes for the measures to squeak through. The Democrats would figure out who among them had the safest
districts; these would vote for the taxes. When it was
once suggested that Fred Schick of Staten Island be
called upon to support a bill, Cashmore declared, "Oh,
no, he's too nice a guy. I wouldn't let *him* vote for
taxes!"

Yet there were high comedians as well as low ones,
serious members as well as buffoons, introverts as well
as circus barkers who met to transact business in this
chamber. The fact that men of such varied backgrounds
with nothing in common except that each was sanctified
with power from the people could rub shoulders in
deliberation within a single room was a tribute to our
vitality as a nation.

Here, for instance, sat Joe Baldwin, a member of the
Racquet and Tennis Club, who lived in the "silk stocking" district, and only a few feet away from him sat
Charlie Keegan who had once earned his keep as a
newsboy. Here gathered Louis Hollander, the self-
educated head of a clothing union, and Bobbie Straus,
the heir of a great department store fortune who had
been trained in political science at European univer-
sities. Here also deliberated Mrs. Genevieve Earle, a
graduate of the New York School of Social Research,
and Johnny Nugent who had bucked his way into
affluence from a humble job in a shipyard. And, presiding over this group as majority leader, when for a
time the anti-Tammany forces gained the upper hand,

was Baruch Charney Vladeck, a frail Jewish immigrant who had fled from a Czarist prison. Poet, scholar and newspaperman, Vladeck had fought thirty years for slum clearance and better housing, and although he bitterly opposed the machine politics of the Tammany group with a devastating wit, each St. Patrick's Day he swung vigorously up Fifth Avenue with a sprig of shamrock in his lapel and a carnation that had been dyed a brilliant green. Where else could this happen but in America?

From what I have written it would seem that the job of presiding over this heterogeneous Council occupied most of my waking hours. Actually less than ten per cent of my time was spent in the chamber, for the Council worked through legislative committees and met as a body once a week. My more important service was as a city-wide member of the city's governing body, the Board of Estimate, over which LaGuardia desired me to preside, so that he could devote his own time to administration problems.

On the very first day I took office, LaGuardia came in and looked around the room he had occupied as president of the Board of Aldermen in 1919.

"Do you really want to work?" he asked.

"What do you mean?"

"Well, Newbold, it you want to make this job a sinecure there isn't much for you to do. You preside over the Council on Tuesdays, and you attend the Board of Estimate meetings on Thursdays, and study items on the calendar in between. That's about all. But if you want real work, I'll keep you busy."

I agreed, and we started a partnership that was tremendously satisfying to me and, I like to believe, helped him effectively to implement his social program in the years ahead.

One of the major problems confronting a large city is the maintenance of an efficiently run, low-priced transit system. When I took office in 1938, both the IRT and the BMT, the two main subway systems transporting millions of New Yorkers daily to and from their work, were privately owned and in very poor shape financially. LaGuardia delegated Joseph McGoldrick, the city comptroller, and me to represent the Board of Estimate in negotiations with the security holders for the purchase of the properties so that they could be placed under comprehensive city management.

After months of negotiations, we settled with the representatives of both companies for $340,000,000. The following story is a typical illustration of how LaGuardia operated when his ire was aroused. In order for the purchase to be consummated, we needed the consent of 90 per cent of the underlying security holders. In the BMT group, 87 per cent acquiesced. But the biggest and most stubborn holdout was the Prudential Life Insurance Company. LaGuardia asked John Stedman, its president, to come in for a conference which I attended. Stedman remained adamant, refusing to turn in his bonds. If they were turned in, bondholders would receive approximately 90 per cent of par; holdouts would get 100 per cent. Finally LaGuardia said, "All right, Mr. Stedman, you've seen your bonds climb from thirty-four where they were before the city began negotiating to take over the properties, all the way up to ninety, at which you can sell them today. I will give you until midnight tonight to make up your mind. If I don't hear from you tomorrow, I will announce to the press that unification is off. You may be able to explain to your fellow bondholders why their holdings have dropped to thirty-four again."

I considered LaGuardia's tactics to be much too drastic. I couldn't believe that the mayor was actually willing to call off negotiations after all the work we had put into them for six months, and especially when we were so close to achieving our objective. Whether LaGuardia was actually prepared to quit or was simply acting out a bluff, I've never found out. At any rate, Mr. Stedman went home convinced that LaGuardia meant what he said. Eleven o'clock that night he phoned in his acquiescence. Unification went through, and it was a good deal for the city, for revenues after operating costs left a net of $25,000,000 a year, at a five cent fare.

Like many showmen, LaGuardia had a large slice of ham mixed in with his genius. He couldn't resist bidding for the jackpot with a pair of deuces. In September 1938, while he was on the Pacific coast addressing an American Legion convention, fifteen thousand New York truck drivers, without any warning, went on strike. The strike had not been authorized by union leaders. As acting mayor I brought the outlaw strikers and the employers together. And it was agreed that perishables, food and medicinal supplies would be moved off the piers. Anna Rosenberg and Arthur S. Meyer of the State Mediation Board brought their experience into the picture to help accomplish this.

The union leaders came back from an American Federation of Labor convention and negotiations for a new contract commenced. LaGuardia returned to New

York and quickly mapped his strategy to breach an impasse. One morning when the stalemate had lasted for several days, I was astounded, upon getting out of the subway on my way to my office, to see a number of antiquated vehicles with the Department of Sanitation insignia on them, crowded into City Hall Park. As I climbed over the vehicles to get into City Hall, I tried to picture to myself Bob Moses's purpling countenance when he found out what treatment his park was getting.

The mayor arrived shortly, and the representatives of the union and industry entered his office to continue their negotiations. By four o'clock in the afternoon, after hours of prolonged mediation, LaGuardia showed signs of irritation. I looked out of the window and was perplexed to see standing alongside of every Department of Sanitation vehicle a uniformed Department driver. Suddenly the mayor whispered to me, "When I give the signal, tell them to get those trucks started."

A few minutes later he announced to the union and trucking representatives that if the contracts were not signed in fifteen minutes, he would order food, perishables and other commodities to be transported in New York Department of Sanitation vehicles. Then he said to me out of the corner of his mouth, "Get those trucks moving."

I whispered, "Where do you want those junk boxes to be moved? Some of those engines haven't been tuned up since the nineteen twenties!"

"Move anywhere," he snapped. "Just get them going!"

I stepped out into the hall and told Bill Powell, the deputy commissioner, to give the order. It took a little time for the engines to get started. Several of the vehicles were so obsolete they had to be cranked by hand. But finally they lurched into a roar, punctuated by frequent spluttering and backfiring. The mayor's face remained impassive as he blew a ring of cigar smoke into the air. An industry representative stepped forward and agreed to sign. The others followed, and the strike was over. Not one of these hardheaded executives had the presence of mind to realize that no shipper in his senses would have put a valuable cargo on any one of our Sanitation trucks!

One interesting duty I undertook during these years involved the setting up, at LaGuardia's suggestion, of a foreign trade zone on Staten Island. We had to get an enabling act from Congress to permit us to set up a free port. We obtained WPA funds to enclose and rehabilitate the great Hylan piers which had been built at a cost of thirty or forty million dollars in 1919, just following the first world war, and had never been used. Piles were rotting. Surrounding each pier was a great apron with railroad tracks for the B. & O. locomotives. We enclosed them with barbed wire. We had to pay for nine customs guards at various entrances, had to put in an "electric eye" system; when a ship passed through into the pier, a great gong went off and alerted the customs people. Even on the restricted scale on which we were forced to operate, we did an immense amount of business. In the first year we brought in almost a half million dollars in revenues to the city from property which would otherwise have been idle.

The first shipment dramatized the whole purpose of the free port. It was not customs' territory, and heavily dutiable commodities came in for transshipment free. We brought in steel drums from Czechoslovakia which were cheaper than our American manufactured steel drums. We poured United States produced oil into the steel drums, transported them to South America and Central America, brought new shipping into New York harbor and gave jobs to thousands of longshoremen who were out of work. We brought in nonquota sugar, awaiting the lifting of the quota. We brought in heavily dutiable Brazil nuts which were dried and shrunken in weight. Those that came into the United States were charged a duty on the shrunken weight. The remainder was transshipped to Europe and other points in the world.

One of the greatest thrills I received was when three freighters steamed in from Sumatra with the last Sumatra leaf tobacco, just before the Jap invaders arrived. The tobacco had been shipped out, and it was cured in the Staten Island free port, transshipped to Cuba and the rest of the world. Sumatran leaf is used on the outside of every cigar. We had pony skins from Siberia, and rugs from Italy. One of the lift-vans broke open when it came in with heavily dutiable stuff. The possessions of refugees from Nazi Germany were in them, and a grand piano rolled out.

Watch parts, some of which were manufactured in the United States, and others in Switzerland, were put together in a regular watch factory on Staten Island. Those watches that didn't come into the United States were shipped to other parts of the Western Hemisphere.

As I worked with LaGuardia over these years, I developed a technique of side-stepping his explosions of temperament that toppled even the strongest-rooted of his advisers. I decided not to get ulcers, and, of course, as an elected official I could not be fired. Not even Sullivan's Lord High Executioner caused greater consternation among his subjects at times than the little mayor who barked orders from his desk in City Hall, his legs dangling a few inches from the floor, his spectacles whirling like a huge bee around his fingers as he stung his secretaries into continual action with six buzzers. As the mayor loquaciously administered his program, on the walls around him the former mayors and colonial governors looked down from their gilded frames, sometimes, I fancied, in consternation, sometimes with amusement. Every now and then a chandelier tinkled above the mayor (whether jarred into dissonance by the pounding of the outside traffic or by LaGuardia's invective, I could never discover).

More than once as he was in the very act of sending a blundering commissioner to hell, I would see LaGuardia suddenly change into a mood of tenderness and a smile would annihilate his frown. I would follow his eye to a window and observe, pressed above the rail of an iron fence, the face of a kid who had sneaked across the driveway to get a glimpse of him through the window. Someone once declared that if children could vote, LaGuardia would have been elected President of the United States. No other politician has ever been so greatly worshiped by the small fry. To thousands of children the mayor was a magnificent, fun-loving imp straight from the Sunday comic strip. And to grownups as well he was an irrepressible imp—with a giant's heart.

Occasionally, after a long day at City Hall, I would

relax with the mayor and his family. LaGuardia had married Marie Fischer, who had been his assistant in Congress and during his presidency of the Board of Aldermen. They had adopted a girl and a boy, Jean and Eric. Each Fourth of July, the mayor told me, he would take the children into his study and read them the Declaration of Independence. I venture to assert that George Washington, who first read this document to his troops in 1776 in the park outside the mayor's City Hall office, hadn't put more enthusiasm into the performance.

Speaking of how LaGuardia loved children, I recall that the mayor once took a trip to Washington on a matter of the highest importance. He was loaded down with official papers he planned to study on the way. Accompanying him was a child who had been staying with his children as a house guest. On the plane, according to a fellow passenger, the mayor fussed and fretted over the boy, looked every few minutes to see whether he was strapped in properly, whether he was enjoying the flight. Neglected were the papers of state. This mayor with a reputation for toughness acted like an overanxious hen around her smallest chick.

Just as he went silly over a kid, he grew moist-eyed over Mozart and Wagner. Music certainly hit the spot with him. The old-time politician used to relax over the spittoons in political clubhouses. But LaGuardia established his recreational headquarters at Carnegie Hall. Each Good Friday afternoon, he left City Hall to listen to *Parsifal* at the Metropolitan. During the election of 1941, the turnout of voters was small; the regular Republicans were hostile. LaGuardia won by a very small margin. All during the voting, his political advisers paced up and down in their headquarters nervously, afraid for his political life. The mayor himself did not put in an appearance. Emissaries were sent to find him, to discuss a strategy for policing certain polling areas. They frantically searched all over town unsuccessfully until one of them on a hunch went to Carnegie Hall. There, with the lights turned low, the mayor sat listening to Arturo Toscanini putting his orchestra through a rehearsal of Beethoven's Seventh Symphony.

LaGuardia's official family had many laughs, and not all of them were at the mayor's expense. He had a habit of calling his commissioners together at regular intervals and awarding a large bronze bone in a leather case to the official who had pulled the biggest boner during the period preceding each meeting. On the eve of one Fourth of July his fire commissioner, John McElligott, made a radio speech warning parents to keep their kids under supervision so that they wouldn't injure themselves with firecrackers. "Let's make this a truly safe and sane Fourth of July." The morning after the Fourth, the mayor received a phone call from a city hospital. The fire commissioner was *hors de combat*. He had burned both his hands lighting firecrackers! When the commissioner returned to duty he received a bone with his name inscribed over the date of his achievement.

Like Teddy Roosevelt, LaGuardia had no use for red tape. "There is no *ersatz* for justice." During the depression when 300,000 New Yorkers were unemployed and a million men, women and children depended upon public assistance for survival, he wasted no time with elaborate paper work or technical formalities, but acted directly with his welfare commissioner, Bill Hodson, to alleviate distress wherever possible.

When LaGuardia commenced his second term, William Allen White and other liberal Republicans began booming him for national office. But when friends asked the mayor for his reaction, he shook his head negatively. "The fellow in City Hall who has his eye on another office is like the automobile driver with a pretty woman at his side. He can't keep his mind on his work."

Indeed, LaGuardia's refusal to give out jobs on a political basis precluded his advancement along orthodox lines. For years after his election few of the Republican district leaders dared to be seen in the corridors of City Hall, such was the mayor's obsession against even the physical proximity of the breed. However, he did seem to be able to look upon several of the Republican leaders whom he had known through the years as individuals. After hearing him muttering about "politicians," I was somewhat surprised to see the mayor walk up to one who had come into City Hall, shake hands with him and display just more than a formal cordiality. But it was impossible for even that particular leader to gain access into LaGuardia's office alone to plead for any political favor or patronage.

LaGuardia was fully conscious of the fact that this policy was politically suicidal. He once declared that the supreme quality for office was the ability to say "No," and he said it again and again, rubbing it in for good measure. But he knew that this would make it impossible for him to go on to higher office. Gradually, important Republicans who felt that patronage was the lifeblood of the organization realized that he meant what he said.

When he came up for renomination after his first term, he did not find much support from these party officials. In fact, it was in 1937 that he was opposed in the Republican primary elections by Senator Royal Copeland, a Tammany Democrat, entered in that primary contest by reactionary and bitter Republicans. In 1941, LaGuardia had an even narrower squeak in obtaining the Republican nomination. A Republican "regular," Judge Davies, was entered in the primaries against him.

In 1937 an interesting arrival in the fight for good government was the American Labor party. It is not generally remembered how the American Labor party came into being. But it was fathered by one of the master politicians of all time, Jim Farley. Jim was the man most responsible for the nomination of Franklin D. Roosevelt in 1932. It seemed to him that with the Democratic party weakened in New York by LaGuardia's election in 1933, there should be a more vital political arm of the New Deal in the greatest industrial center in America. So, in 1936, to aid Roosevelt's first bid for re-election, a coalition of trade unions joined in the formation of the American Labor party. But Jim failed to look a year ahead. It must have been a great source of chagrin to him to discover that in 1937 the American Labor party, having helped to install Roosevelt in the White House for another term, espoused a Fusion good-government movement and helped to return LaGuardia to City Hall, to elect Thomas E. Dewey as District Attorney, and to keep the Tammany tiger starving for another four years.

Yet LaGuardia looked further into the future than his own political fortunes. He had a vision of an American society beyond the power of the bosses to create or desecrate. For instance, to one journalist who interviewed him, he made reference to the multimillion-dollar Criminal Court and jail the city had recently constructed. "I hope that one day my son Eric will go strolling downtown with his grandchild. And Eric will point to this courthouse and say, 'My boy, your great-grandfather built this building when he was mayor of New York.' And the little boy will look up in wide-eyed astonishment and answer, 'Gosh, what in the world did he want to build *this* for, Grandpa? The old boy was certainly extravagant, wasn't he!' "

LaGuardia was without doubt unduly optimistic in believing that the need for jails would ever be eliminated from our society and that courthouses would become "white elephants" for the city. But you can't blame a fellow for trying.

For twelve years I continued my association with LaGuardia, as a blizzard of brown, pink, green memos —drafted in various colors to indicate the degree of priority—poured from the inner sanctum upon my desk and into the lower echelons carrying orders for the advancement of the administration's program. I was impressed with LaGuardia's ability to avoid the fate of most reformers who find it rough going once they have abandoned the role of attacker and have assumed the position of the defender of a record. When Seth Low, the New Yorker, for instance, was asked why he was defeated for a second term for mayor, he replied, "When I first ran, I attacked vice—and everybody is interested in vice. But when I ran again, I had to defend virtue. And who is interested in virtue?"

LaGuardia made virtue *exciting*—a not inconsiderable feat. Indeed, it was an accomplishment of the sheerest sorcery which, in its detailed unfolding, kept me perpetually amazed.

CHAPTER 6 "I Would Rather Be a Lamp-post in New York . . . !"

ONE of my most interesting obligations under La-Guardia was in the formalities of office. I represented the city on innumerable ceremonial occasions when evening dress was required. The mayor abhorred a tuxedo. I remember him smiling at me when I dropped by at his house in evening clothes one evening before going out to a function. "That tuxedo looks so well on you, *why don't you buy it?*" This was the kind of crack he was always making, for most of his friends would rent formal attire on the few occasions which demanded it.

A man in public life must have a clear head—and a strong stomach. In a single evening it was not out of the ordinary for me to put in appearances at a formal dinner at the Waldorf-Astoria held as a social occasion for an industrial convention, a meeting of Local 802 of the American Federation of Musicians at the Manhattan Center, a dinner of the Patrolmen's Benevolent Association, the opening of a Red Cross drive, and an annual "affair" of the American Legion of Kings County. I would enter one dining room, nibble at a platter of anchovies, make an address, shake a few hands and leave for the next function, to be greeted by a platter of ice cream and maraschino cherries, only to find at the third

144

function a lobster supplemented with Viennese pastry. Then to top off the evening, I would be handed a roast turkey wing.

This crazy-quilt-patch diet would continue, evening after evening, week after week, and during the sunlit days of the World's Fair before the outbreak of World War II, these engagements were multiplied. During one stretch I kept going from six until after midnight for sixty-five consecutive evenings. Finally, I was hit by an attack of ptomaine poisoning and fatigue, which led to the temporary loss of sight in one of my eyes.

Let me mention, with all due modesty, that not long after this I ran into Jimmy Walker, who once was as firmly linked to Manhattan's night life as is Santa Claus to Christmas. He looked at me in admiration when I told him of the sixty-five consecutive nights on the town. "Gosh," he admitted, "I never did better than twenty-six nights straight."

While Jimmy Walker epitomized all that was irresponsible in Tammany politics, and I had always fought the things he stood for, I, like just about everyone else in New York, loved the man personally. I have even sung duets with Jimmy in public.

While I was president of the Council, Jimmy would visit City Hall in a nostalgic mood. One June day, he dropped in and suggested that we go to a ball game. I pointed to a stack of memoranda on my desk relating to the next day's Board of Estimate session. "I can't leave this work, Jimmy. We have a calendar tomorrow with three hundred and sixty-three items to be voted on, and I expect to be here late this evening studying these reports."

"Forget it," he said. "In all the years I presided at Board of Estimate meetings, I never knew what was on the calendar until I came in a half hour late."

Yes, Jimmy was perfectly genuine. He never pretended to be what he wasn't. That was what I liked about him.

In Jimmy's heyday, the luster of Grand Street had passed; Greenpoint was the "garden spot of the world" only in the minds of Pete McGuinness and its own residents, but Broadway was the brightest spot on earth. Jimmy was what the people wanted, a symbol of the hour.

I have often wondered whether if New York had been in the midst of a depression and not riding a carefree boom when he took over as mayor he might not have developed entirely differently. He had a good, sensitive heart and he was immensely susceptible to his environment. Change the moral climate, and you might have changed the man.

I saw something of Jimmy during his final years. I will never forget the story he told me about his meeting with Mussolini. While Governor Roosevelt was investigating the charges against him in 1932, Jimmy took a trip abroad with his secretary, Charlie Hand. He arrived in Rome toward dusk and was met at the train by the night-club crowd of the city. After changing into evening dress, he made the rounds of the "hot spots." About four in the morning, Charlie Hand reminded him that he must be ready for his meeting with Mussolini which was scheduled for eleven that morning. "Look, Boss," he whispered, "you ought to visit something else in Rome besides these night dives so that you can have an intelligent chat with Il Duce."

He grabbed Jimmy's arm, took him out of the night club, and an Italian friend escorted them through the Colosseum, the Forum and the Arch of Titus in the light of the moon. Then Jimmy went to bed for a few hours' sleep. At nine a masseur called, and after a cold shower, an aspirin, and coffee, Jimmy got into his cutaway and top hat and was ready. Still half asleep and suffering from a splitting headache, all he could afterward remember was that upon arriving at the palace, he was escorted to a great double door which was opened by men in magnificent uniforms and guided into a chamber. At the end of a long marble floorway was a desk. Behind it was a pair of wide, staring eyes above a protruding chin. Il Duce rose and extended his hand, then as Jimmy took his seat, he leaned forward and said, "Tell me, Mr. Mayor, what are your impressions of Italy?"

Jimmy cleared his throat and then launched into his great effort. He extolled the running of Mussolini's trains on time, the draining of the marshes, the reclamation of land, the projects which sent labor battalions singing on their way to work. "But what struck me most, your Excellency, was when I stood in the Colosseum which was so beautiful in the moonlight and I thought of the early Christian martyrs sacrificing their lives in order that Rome might be the center of Christian civilization—and now how under you the Roman Empire is being so magnificently re-created!" Finally, the mayor, exhausted by his rhetoric, pulled out his handkerchief and mopped his brow. Il Duce leaned across his desk and murmured, "Tell me more, Jimmy, tell me more."

This was a great victory for the Blarney Stone. The captivated Duce clapped his hands; doors opened on every side; attendants entered, each carrying a chair; and behind them walked the members of Mussolini's cabinet, who were introduced to the mayor. Mussolini seated Jimmy in the position of honor in the center of his cabinet to the right of an empty chair reserved for himself and personally adjusted Jimmy's tie and handkerchief while photographers assembled to take pictures.

Jimmy Walker's tongue had certainly been blessed by the Irish leprechauns. I feel that if he had ever chosen to run for mayor again, despite the Seabury investigation, he would have been a hard man to beat.

Another politician with whose politics I sometimes disagreed, and for whom I never ceased to have affection, was Al Smith. I had met the governor long before I got into public life through his daughter Emily and her husband, John Warner. Al's son was elected to the City Council under proportional representation, and the ex-governor came down to City Hall to see him take his seat. One day I was called upon to represent the city at a funeral at St. Bartholomew's. The "Governor" had wanted to attend the service and he phoned and asked me to take him along with me. He said he felt old and tired. Mrs. Smith had passed away, and he was very lonely. As we knelt together, during the most solemn portion of the service I suddenly felt the "Governor's" elbow digging into my ribs. "You know, Newbold," he whispered, "I can never come to this church without thinking of the old days when it was the site of Ruppert's brewery and we young fellows dropped in for a free beer!"

Sometimes it was my lot to entertain royalty during their visits to New York. No matter what the occasion, the mayor was never at a loss for wit when he associated with these dignitaries from abroad. When Queen Wilhelmina of the Netherlands was escorted through City Hall, she was much taken with the portraits of Dutch colonial governors hanging from the walls.

"Are these your ancestors?" she asked LaGuardia.

"No, your Majesty. They're *your* ancestors."

The mayor and his wife entertained kings and queens with a characteristic simplicity. I was present at a dinner given to Queen Wilhelmina at which only a maid was present. Marie LaGuardia did her own planning of the meal. I think that LaGuardia's grandfather who helped liberate the Italian peasant from the rule of foreign emperors would have relished this scene.

As acting host for the city, I welcomed a number of people whose lives had been turned topsy-turvy by the Nazi armies. Two such people were Crown Princess Martha and Prince Olaf who were exiled from Nazi-occupied Norway; another was General Wadislas Sikorski, commander of the reorganized Polish forces who were being trained with the British armies to fight their way back to their homeland. I also greeted Eduard Beneš, the President of Czechoslovakia, whose bitter tragedy was to be deferred until after V-Day when the Communists snatched up his country.

I welcomed the young expatriate King Peter of Yugoslavia to City Hall, and when he asked to be taken to one of those games "for which the mayor is always throwing out the ball," I escorted him to see the Yankees play the St. Louis Browns. The king posed for pictures eating a hot dog. But after DiMaggio and company had walloped the Browns for five consecutive innings, the king, who spoke an excellent English, declared, "Let's go home. There's a limit to everything!"

Politics crept into my most carefully scheduled pleasure excursions, even those away from the city. In 1937 I planned a vacation in Mexico to rest from the campaign which resulted in my becoming president of the Council. I thought I was leaving Tammany Hall behind me for a few weeks at least. But I had no sooner boarded the train than I discovered that one of my fellow passengers was Eddie Flynn, the Democratic Boss of the Bronx, whose official position was Secretary of State of New York. Flynn had tried his best to defeat us Republicans in the recent election, and now he was going to Mexico for a vacation. It turned out that we had reservations at the same hotel, the *Reforma*. Upon arriving in Mexico City, we attended an Armistice Day reception held at the United States Embassy. Flynn stood in the reception line just behind me as we waited to greet Ambassador Josephus Daniels and to be introduced to President Cardenas's Secretary. This gentleman understood very little English. Nevertheless when he greeted me he managed to put together a sentence. "Señor Morris, the President has received notice of your arrival and invites you to an audience with him in the palace tomorrow."

Eddie Flynn was the next to be introduced. He was announced by his official title, Secretary of State of New York. President Cardenas's representative caught the word "secretary" and he jumped to the conclusion that Flynn was my amanuensis. That night Flynn took a barbiturate to get a complete rest. But the official day begins early in Mexico City. Next morning at 8:00 A.M. the telephone rang, rousing Flynn out of bed. President Cardenas's Secretary barked into his ear, "Señor Flynn, will you tell Señor Morris that his appointment with the President has been arranged for twelve noon?"

Flynn grew purple. "Why the devil don't *you* tell Morris? He's just down the hall!"

The official decided Flynn had misunderstood.

One hour later, at 9:00 A.M., there was a knock at Flynn's door. Eddie opened up, shivering in his pajamas. Three men stood stiffly before him, dressed in morning suits and top hats. "Señor Flynn," one of them declared. "We must *insist* upon awakening you. Will you *please* inform Señor Morris that his audience is scheduled for noon."

For several seconds Flynn stared at them through the mists of sleep.

"Have you guys gone crazy!"

"You *are* Señor Morris's secretary, are you not?"

Suddenly, the reason for the misunderstanding dawned upon this politician whose candidate was one day to beat me in my effort to be elected mayor of New York. He threw back his head with laughter. Until his death Eddie Flynn continued to laugh at the remembrance of this misadventure. He told the story whenever we turned up together at a gathering.

Sometimes, as acting host for the city, I ran into disputes that would have tested the patience of Job. In 1938 I was invited to throw out the first baseball to open the season for the New York Yankees. I looked forward to a relaxing afternoon. But when I arrived at the Stadium I found that the park attendants had

gone on strike and were picketing the entrances. Inside the park, thousands of fans, who had crossed the
picket lines refusing to be frustrated by this sudden
row between management and labor, were waiting im-
patiently for me to make my appearance and for the
flag-raising ceremonies to begin. Colonel Jake Ruppert,
the owner of the Yankees, paced back and forth like a
whippet straining at the leash. I called together Ed
Barrow of the Yankees and the attendants and then and
there on the sidewalk negotiated an armistice. Both sides
promised to send representatives to City Hall the following morning to iron out the dispute.

I felt pleased with myself for having patched up the
trouble, at least temporarily. But the conference had
delayed the game and I hadn't reckoned with my fans.
As I entered the park I was greeted with a chorus of
razzberries. Not for nothing has the Bronx Cheer become
a celebrated item in our lexicon. I had to walk the
gauntlet of booers all the way from the flagpole to home
plate. As I passed second base, one voice bellowed, "Who
do you think you are showing up so late, Jimmy
Walker?" I no longer recall the final score of the game.
Perhaps I didn't wait around long enough to find out.

Playing host for New York was a fabulous, fatiguing
experience. New York isn't a city, nor even, as Harold
Ickes called it, the forty-ninth state. It is a large, palpi-
tating hunk of the planet. "Bojangles" Robinson, the
great Negro jazz dancer, like millions of others, was under its spell, and he once said to me, "I'd rather be a
lamppost in New York than a mayor anywhere else in the
world!"

In my day as a city official, New York was a far cry

from the bustling little hamlet of eighty thousand souls
that Gouverneur Morris knew; whose streets at nightfall
swarmed with the traffic of cows driven home for milk-
ing; whose only night noises were the croaking of frogs,
the buzzing of mosquitoes from the marshes and the "all
clear" of the night watch. Under LaGuardia, New York
developed a richer cosmopolitan flavor than ever before. Thousands of refugees of the arts and sciences,
fleeing from Hitler's storm troopers, sought asylum along
the Hudson and poured their skills and agonies into
our yeasty spirit. New York contains more Jews than
Tel-Aviv, more Irish than Dublin, almost as many
Italians as live in Rome. When I addressed a war bond
rally on Times Square or escorted a visiting dignitary
up Broadway, I felt frequently as though we were ac-
knowledging the cheers of crowds swarming over Tra-
falgar Square, the Place de la Concorde, the Ringstrasse
rolled into one.

Here within a sliver of space between two rivers, men
and women have risen from extreme human degradation
to leadership in the arts, the professions, business, and
here numberless others have broken their hearts with
unfulfillment. Here an unknown girl may step on the
boards and become a prima donna within a single afternoon, and here policemen rush each year to twelve hundred apartments where the gas has been turned on to
end a private nightmare. The struggle between free
men and the goons of totalitarianism the world over
has been reflected in the tavern, tenement, alley brawls
of the New York slums where a welter of races rub shoulders. During the peak of Hitler's attacks on the Jews,
I visited a crippled Jewish editor of an anti-Nazi news-

paper in a Brooklyn hospital. He had been slugged into unconsciousness by four Nazi thugs who had broken into his office. They had carved out the emblem of the swastika with knives on his chest and back, rubbed paint into the wounds and ripped an American flag from the wall. This editor survived and continued his campaign against Nazism. It was little victories like this that led eventually to V-Day and the surrender of the Wehrmacht.

As a city official I met Americans from every section of the country who had developed into the finest flowering of the races represented in New York. During the war I received the battle flag of the aircraft carrier *Franklin,* which, after being struck by Japanese bombs, successfully undertook a twelve-thousand-mile trip home under its own steam. Her crew was made up of many of our racial strains, sailors whose ancestors had left their squabbles behind them in Europe. Eight hundred and thirty-two Americans were left beneath the waves. Two hundred and thirty others suffered wounds. The flag that I hoisted on the roof of City Hall was still black with the smoke from the fires that had raged all day and night on the flight deck and below, after the ship was hit.

On another occasion I received Colonel Devereux of French origin, who, with his marines of various ancestries, fought off successive waves of Japs storming Wake Island in the days following Pearl Harbor, losing three-quarters of their numbers before they surrendered. When I officially welcomed Colonel Devereux to our city, he made what was probably the shortest acceptance speech on record. "I don't know what I can say, but thank you."

This then was the New York I came to know so well when I played master of ceremonies for a brief interval. I cannot describe precisely why the Morrises, the Cohens, the O'Reillys, the Schmidts, the Carusos love the sounds and smell of her so passionately. But years ago, the wife of a Midwestern governor who came to New York to participate in the World's Fair expressed its challenge as well as anybody.

In accordance with prevailing custom, the mayor escorted His Excellency, the governor, in one car and I followed with the governor's wife. We traveled up the Westside Highway, passing by a new pier that was being built in preparation for the arrival of the *Queen Elizabeth*. We rode by foundations that were being dug for schools and hospitals, heard the riveting on the steelwork of the East River houses, mounted the ramp of the Triborough Bridge, made a detour to bypass sewer construction near Jackson Heights. Then turning our heads to the left, we watched an endless stream of trucks riding bumper to bumper, carrying land fill from the refuse dump at Riker's Island to the new North Beach airport shortly to become known as LaGuardia Field. When we had driven into the main entrance of the World's Fair, the governor's wife stepped down from the auto and exclaimed to me, "Oh, won't New York be a beautiful place—*if it ever gets finished!*"

CHAPTER 7 "Beauty Is Given a Home" off Broadway

THE founding of the New York City Center of Music and Drama is a unique chapter in the history of an American community. As it approaches the close of its eleventh season, giving the best in music, the dance and living theatre, I believe it can be said truthfully there is nothing quite like this institution dedicated to the performing arts anywhere in the world. Of course, it has its roots in the Old World, where a state or municipally supported theatre or opera house has filled an obvious need ever since the time when the sponsorship of the finer things of life used to be exclusively under the patronage of the nobles or the clergy. There is one essential difference between the European institution and the New York City Center. So far, we have operated without government subsidy of any kind.

Like any civic movement which has any validity, the City Center came as a result of a demonstrated popular demand. A set of unusual circumstances provided the opportunity for an experiment.

Shortly after I took office as president of the Council, Mayor LaGuardia asked me one day if I would like to take on the city operation of the WPA music project.

"You know, I am not a musician," I demurred.

"That is just why I want you to take this on. You're

'box office'; you know what kind of programs the average music lover wants to hear."

As with other extracurricular activities he assigned to me, I agreed to do it with the feeling that, perhaps, this would be an enjoyable and interesting experience. During the depression, the Federal Government was providing funds to help writers, musicians and actors, as well as bricklayers, plasterers and carpenters, keep bodies and souls together until opportunities for employment in private enterprise returned. These projects were not only necessary but were among the happier inspirations of the New Deal. There were 10,000 unemployed musicians in New York City and under WPA rules, 1,000 of them could go on a work-relief project. The city paid all the overhead costs of the project and one-quarter of the amount of the payrolls, whether the project was paving a street or giving concerts. I found this work already well organized, and entered into a congenial partnership with Horace Johnson, the federal director of the project.

I discovered that there were three WPA orchestras in New York, a symphonic band, a chorus of 100 voices, quartets and ensembles providing audiences in high schools and parks with good music. The remainder of the 1,000 men and women on the project were giving lessons to housebound children.

I attended a number of the concerts and one of the symphony orchestras appeared to be the best unit of all. One rainy evening in November, 1938, I listened to it playing in the auditorium of the Stuyvesant High School. A desultory audience was composed of a couple of hundred people who, of course, had come in free of charge. A few might have attended to get out of the rain.

After the concert I went backstage and talked to some of the musicians and, without much thought, I asked, "How would you like to play in a concert hall where people *pay* to listen?"

My question was probably put instinctively as a result of my Republican background. Perhaps, this project could be put at least on a partly self-sustaining basis. But what struck me most was the light which appeared in the eyes of these men and women replacing the haunted, baffled expressions which I found in my prior conversations.

Several of them had played in the premier orchestras of the world. The concertmeister, for example, had been a first desk man in the St. Petersburg Orchestra under the baton of Tchaikowsky himself; others had played in the symphony orchestras of Paris, Rome, Budapest, Philadelphia, Minneapolis, and the New York Philharmonic Orchestra. They had retired in order to take up teaching and were earning a decent livelihood when along came the depression! Now they were on relief.

After this little incident I felt impelled to do something to lift the spirits of these musicians and to restore their self-confidence. I called on Nelson Rockefeller, whose family interests had just completed the huge Center Theatre, at 49th Street and Sixth Avenue. I told him that I had understood that the theatre would remain dark until the film *Pinocchio* arrived in February.

"I would like to have the use of the theatre until then, if you will let me have it without rental. I will reimburse you for the heating, lighting, ushers and ticket takers."

He asked me what I wanted it for. I told him I wanted it for symphony concerts and recounted to him my meeting with musicians playing on WPA. I followed this up by expounding a theory of mine, that there were masses of people in the lower income groups who loved music but could not afford box office prices at the Metropolitan Opera House and Carnegie Hall.

"Well," said Nelson, "the acoustics are very unsatisfactory."

"Who said that?" I asked.

With a conclusive gesture he replied, "Toscanini."

"I'll bet that even Toscanini would say that the acoustics in your new auditorium are better than at the Stuyvesant High School."

We closed the deal.

From the Rockefeller Center I went to the Metropolitan Opera House, following a rehearsal of *Lohengrin*. Entering the dressing room of Lauritz Melchior, after the usual formalities I asked him when he last sang a "command performance."

"Oh," he replied brightly, "every year in Denmark His Majesty used to ask me to sing on his birthday and, of course, when my king commands me I perform."

Summoning all my courage I said, "Well, the People of the City of New York command you to sing as a guest artist with the New York City Symphony on the evening of December third at the Center Theatre." Unconsciously I had picked up LaGuardia's manner of "talking big."

His eyes opened wide. He wanted to know, "What is the New York City Symphony?" I replied that it was the second greatest orchestra in the city. Then I told him about the WPA music project, and his sympathy and understanding immediately came into play. He agreed to open a series of Wagnerian concerts.

With him lined up, the rest was easy. Madame Elizabeth Rethberg, Frederich Schorr and Rose Bampton of the Metropolitan and Maestro Frieder Weissman generously accepted my invitation to perform as guest artists, without fee, with the WPA orchestra. Joseph Lhevinne and Albert Spalding, among other instrumentalists, were obtained as soloists, to follow with a Tchaikowsky series on the second four successive Sunday evenings. Of course, all of these artists came down to City Hall to be photographed with the mayor and to help with the publicity promotion.

We ran advertisements in the New York City subways and spot announcements on the Municipal Broadcasting Station. One of our signs read *Mayor LaGuardia presents the New York City Symphony with guest artists as follows*: ****** *Tickets 25¢ to $1.00*. Then in small print down at the bottom were the added words *WPA Music Project,* an unintended slight; which, I heard, brought criticism from Harry Hopkins, the then WPA administrator.

I arrived at the Center Theatre, with some trepidation, a half hour before curtain time. A fire chief at the door told me that every seat was filled and all standing room taken. Outside there was a line stretching around the block. Traffic was at a standstill and thousands of people were still pouring out of the subways to join the ticket line which ran to Forty-eighth Street from Sixth Avenue. The entire series of Sunday evening concerts at the Center Theatre were sold out that night and the following day. I went to a telephone to let the mayor know that we were off to a fine start and he could safely come to the theatre with the knowledge that the opening concert would be a success.

Enough money was realized from these concerts to pay the city's overhead costs, including the carting and storage of instruments and the expenses of the house. On the last night I announced to the audience that we would have to leave this concert hall because the motion picture *Pinocchio* would arrive the following week. After waiting for murmurs of disappointment to subside, I added, "And here is good news; *next Sunday evening we open at the Metropolitan Opera House!*"

I shall never forget the "Met" that evening. Every box in the celebrated Diamond Horseshoe was crowded; but no glittering jewels, no low-cut evening gowns, no stiff-fronted shirts took anyone's mind off the music. Clothing workers, buttonhole makers, spongers, needleworkers filled every available seat. Perhaps most rewarding of all was the appreciative hum of voices during the intermission.

Following the run of the orchestra at the Metropolitan, we moved to Carnegie Hall, and continued these programs until WPA was ended by the executive order of the President, shortly before we entered World War II. The orchestra was used in war bond drives and various fund-raising movements incident to this world conflict.

In 1943 came an opportunity to try another experiment. A unique building came into possession of the city, known as Mecca Temple. It had been built by the Shriners at a reputed cost of $3,500,000 twenty years earlier. The depression hit this august organization hard and the building was in arrears in taxes. After three years of delinquency in the payment of taxes, under the law the city must foreclose. The property now belonged to the people of New York. We advertised for purchasers, but no private real estate firm seemed interested.

As Chairman of the New York City Board of Estimate Committee on the aquisition and disposition of property, accompanied by Lee Thompson Smith, the City Director of Real Estate, I visited the building and went through it with George Glasten, the building superintendent. I mention his name because he has played an important part in the backstage life of the institution all these eleven years. George provided me with a flashlight because, he explained, the electricity had been turned off long since. We went through the Fifty-sixth Street side of the building, nine stories high, stumbling up the stairs and poking into the three huge lodge rooms. Each one of these rooms, thirty feet from floor to ceiling, was fitted out with a magnificent pipe organ. Between each lodge room floor was an oak-paneled robing room where the members used to keep their properties for the mystic rites. I thought of each one of these lodge rooms as possibilities for schools of music, rehearsal and recital halls. The seventh, eighth and ninth floors could be readily adapted for executive office space. On the south side of the building on Fifty-fifth Street I found the huge auditorium with 3,300 seats. The orchestra appeared to provide for 1,000 persons, and the broad mezzanine reached out over the eighth row of the orchestra. Above the mezzanine was the balcony receding steeply until it almost reached the mosquelike dome of the great structure. In the basement I found the largest ballroom in New York. At least, it is the largest without columns.

The question before us was what to do with what looked like a "white elephant" on our hands. Some members of the Board of Estimate suggested it could be converted into a city-owned parking garage. One official suggested using it for a convention hall, another for a super laundry!

But I had an inspiration. I said to LaGuardia, "Fiorello, Athens, Rome, all the great cities of the past had a center for the holding of their great cultural festivals. Why not do the same for the American people? Here is the ideal building."

The mayor looked at me scornfully. "Newbold, the city can't go into the theatre business."

"No, of course we can't. But I'll form a nonprofit membership corporation that will take the building over. We can't *sell* the Temple to anybody. We've tried to and no one will take it. So let's operate it for the people."

LaGuardia continued to be skeptical. "You'll never raise the money."

"I'll get a hundred thousand dollars in two weeks," I promised.

Once I won LaGuardia over to the plan, I obtained enough votes in the Board of Estimate to permit the leasing of the building to a public corporation, to be set up like a public library or a museum. This corporation assumed financial responsibility, paid rent to the city, and operated without profit. I received $65,000 from the city to remodel the building.

Then I took my proposal to a cross section of New

York's leading citizens and organizations. I talked to Gerald Warburg, son of the great and generous music-loving Felix, to Mrs. Lytle Hull, who had had experience with the New Opera Company, Sidney Hillman of the Amalgamated Clothing Workers, David Dubinsky of the International Ladies' Garment Workers, Adolph Held of the Workmen's Circle, Marshall Field, Edmund Guggenheim, Howard Cullman, Mrs. Reis of the League of Composers, Macklin Marrow, who had been one of the conductors with the WPA music project, Mrs. Lawrence Tibbett and, of course, Jack Rosenberg and Bill Feinberg of the American Federation of Musicians Local 802. I had known Jack in the WPA days, and he and his associates were the first to see the possibilities of such an organization.

Working with me closely in all of the planning and budgeting was an old friend of mine in politics, Morton Baum. His indefatigability, retentive memory, and knowledge of music helped enormously in those days of preliminary organization, and we have had the benefit of his voluntary services all through the years. Within a short time I had a number of individuals and organizations signed up in an underwriting agreement, and in that way some $63,000 was pledged. Outright gifts brought the total up to approximately $95,000, which Baum and I felt would provide sufficient working capital to get going in the fall. The mayor and Comptroller Joe McGoldrick agreed, and the mayor's legal secretary, Frank Bloustein, who has acted as legal counsel for us without any compensation whatsoever and now serves as a member of our board of directors, prepared the necessary legal papers to incorporate under the Membership Corporations Law.

The old Mecca Temple was dedicated as the New York City Center of Music and Drama on December 11, 1943, by the Mayor of the City of New York, with a concert contributed by the New York Philharmonic Society with Artur Rodzinski conducting and Lawrence Tibbett as guest soloist.

John Golden, the famous Broadway producer, was one of the generous and public-spirited individuals who signed up as an incorporator and who agreed to serve on the board of directors; then put together with his own sets the hit production of *Susan and God,* which he revived for us, with the late Gertrude Lawrence. This play was a sellout and added cash to our working capital. Following that success, we relied on booking a number of plays or what our house manager, Ben Ketcham, calls "Outside Attractions," all of which paid us rent for the use of the four walls and again added cash to the treasury.

In the meantime, we were covering ground in many directions. Howard Cullman brought Jean Dalrymple into our lives as publicity director. Jean, in turn, knowing that the St. Louis Opera Company had failed and gone out of business, got in touch with the director of the company, Laszlo Halasz. Not only did he arrive, but brought with him the sets and costumes from his St. Louis repertory.

Mrs. Reis introduced us to Leopold Stokowski. The mayor was delighted to hear that he would be willing to assemble an orchestra and conduct it without any compensation as a contribution to the musical life of New York. LaGuardia, with his usual sense of publicity, had planned personally to announce the appointment of Stokowski as Director of the New York City Symphony, but Stokowski, who had the same flair, beat him to it. He invited me to come to his apartment one afternoon, and as I entered I found reporters from every newspaper waiting for him to enter the living room. I realized what was happening, and I thought that I might tell him that the mayor planned a statement from City Hall, but before I could interrupt, the maestro asked the reporters to come in and told them what he planned to do. He did it so beautifully that I sat spell-bound as he revealed his program, which would include a series of student concerts, a presentation of the Bach Christmas Oratorio, using the 100 voices from Bob Shaw's Collegiate Chorale. Robert Edmond Jones, the famous scenic designer, a friend of mine and a member of our board, was to design the costumes and the sets without charge. The next day the Stokowski story was on the front page. I realized I had met another person in the same class as Franklin Roosevelt and Fiorello LaGuardia when it came to the field of public relations.

Later, I got the musical members of our board, Mrs. Reis, Macklin Marrow and Gerald Warburg, to take a particular interest in the Stokowski concerts and to act as sort of liaison between us lay members of the board and the great artist himself. This brought us down to budget making, and I told Mr. Stokowski I didn't see how we could put on the Bach Oratorio because "it would leave us with a deficit."

"How much of a deficit?" he asked sharply.

"Well," I answered, "it looks as if it will be about $10,000 with only two performances at our low prices."

Without a word he pulled out a checkbook and wrote a check in the amount of $10,000. I realized that here was a creative spirit who refused to permit a paltry deficit to stand in his way, and I accepted his contribution gratefully.

I shall never forget Christmas Eve of 1943. As Robert Jones said in announcing it over Station WNYC:

> "We shall see The Annunciation, The Journey to Bethlehem, The Shepherds keeping watch by night, the Wise Men of the Orient as they journey toward The Star, the Adoration of the Infant Jesus, and, at the end, a host of angels moving in their glory. . . . There will be music and there will be singing, and a Voice will say again the words that are so old and yet so new. Let us go to this central place and watch and listen, and remember once more the promise made to us by the Prince of Peace."

In the early days we had to move quickly and fit various performances into what was already turning out to be a very crowded schedule. We had booked one musical production which failed on the road only two weeks before it was scheduled to appear at the City Center. But with Jean Dalrymple at the other end of the telephone, things started to happen. She put me in touch with Jed Harris, the Broadway producer. It was obvious something had to be put on the boards to keep our revenue coming in, but we couldn't build sets and design costumes on two weeks' notice. The obvious solution would be the revival of Jed Harris's hit, *Our Town*, by Thornton Wilder. Jed was drafted and telegrams crackled over the wires signed by Mayor LaGuardia. Martha Scott, who had originally played in the role of Emily Gibbs, couldn't stand the idea of anyone else playing the part. She got a leave of absence from her motion picture studio to come to New York. Frank Craven, who had played the part of narrator in the original production, was also telegraphed "in the name of the people of New York" to do the role once again. But having indicated he would accept, he found that his Hollywood contract would not permit him to make the trip. Again Jean turned up with Marc Connolly, the playwright. She coached me carefully, and I said to him:

"Marc, would you like to be in a revival of *Our Town?*"

He looked surprised and pleaded that he couldn't act.

"That is just why we want you for a narrator. He shouldn't be an actor. He should just be his natural self."

Marc learned the role in six days and was magnificent.

To play opposite Martha Scott, Montgomery Clift was cast in what, I believe, was his first important part.

At first, during rehearsals we had acoustical trouble. This was during the war and materials for amplification were not available. However, it came to my attention that the state legislature in Hartford, Connecticut, met every other year, and I had read somewhere that the members used microphones. I called up a friend of mine in Hartford and was told, "Yes, they're not in session this year." We borrowed several microphones. We hired a sound man to hook them up, and I listened to Marc

Connolly perform during rehearsals. He kept talking down into the mikes and you couldn't hear him. Jed would yell, "Marc, throw your head up and it will come out!"

Well, God bless the fellow. On opening night he did the most beautiful job, soft hat, pipe and all. I have rarely seen an audience moved so profoundly. And the Broadway critics poured out their superlatives on Marc.

For a time, it had looked as though *Our Town* might not open at all. The play calls for an organist to perform at a wedding and a funeral. We engaged the girl who had played the organ at the original production, but the night before the opening, the Union told me they wouldn't permit her to go on. It was impossible to find an organist who could learn the cues in time. It developed that this girl hadn't paid her dues to the Union for several years. I argued the point with Jack Rosenberg, the president of Local 802.

"I'll tell you why the girl hasn't paid her dues," I told him. "She got married to a lighthouse keeper and has been living in a lighthouse on the Maine coast. Surely you're not going to discriminate against a girl because she has been living in a lighthouse?"

"O.K.," he said. "Let her go on, but she's got to pay her dues for this year."

Of course, it was impossible to keep the theatrically minded mayor away from rehearsals. One late afternoon he interrupted the inimitable Gertrude Lawrence going through her lines in *Susan and God* to coach her.

Incidentally, LaGuardia was involved in one of the funniest off-the-record performances in the history of show business. Once when he was scheduled to appear before an organization of political writers, he called up Sophie Tucker and invited her to collaborate with him on a skit to be presented for the occasion. With only a half hour's rehearsal, the Little Flower and the Red Hot Mama appeared before their select public and brought down the house. I am certain that Broadway lost a comic genius when Congress gained a politician.

During the early months of our City Center, theatre space was at a premium in New York. Billy Rose found himself without a house for his production of *Carmen Jones*. Billy came to City Hall and tried to persuade me to rent the Center to him. We would book a hit, he claimed. We could take 10 per cent of the gross, about $3,000 a week, and build up our working capital. I felt, and the board of directors agreed with me, that it was necessary for us to build our own operating companies. We decided we must continue with our own theatre, ballet, opera, even if we faced deficits. Billy kept on arguing with me:

"Look, you've got a 'poor man's house.' Let me have it, and I'll carpet the joint!"

But we held to our original goal to build an institution with an audience. In fact, it wasn't long before we had a mailing list of 100,000 people who were so entranced with the project that they insisted on being posted "on what was going on at the City Center." Through the years this mailing list has constituted our box-office advance, and we have never dealt through brokers. This has caused annoyance to some of the carriage trade who merely have a secretary call up a broker and find two seats waiting for them at the box office. But we made the decision that you can't both have a loyal following eager to have a chance at the best seats by mail order and turn over your 800 choice seats to brokers, many of which ultimately reach the hands of scalpers. There have been plenty of performances at the City Center for which wealthy people would have been willing to pay $25 a ticket. We found a certain amount of hostility on Broadway, but we just continued on our way with 3,000 democratically available seats, outlandish décor and no carpets.

The city did provide sufficient funds to put the building in repair for its new tenant and has done a pretty good job under succeeding mayors. But the City Center with its working capital and surpluses from profit-making hits has spent one-half million dollars in one way or another in improving the theatre acoustically and providing the necessary properties.

Gradually the dramatic critics forgot our acoustical problems and concentrated on the artistic merit of the City Center productions. No longer did they refer to the building as "LaGuardia's Barn."

The next play that was presented was Sidney Kingley's *The Patriots,* with Walter Hampden. We booked Cheryl Crawford's *Porgy and Bess,* with Alexander Smallens conducting, and by February 21st the City Center's own opera company was launched. Harry Friedgut, who had had varied experience in community theatre organization, as first managing director took particular interest in this company. Mr. Halasz had auditioned singers tirelessly and perhaps his greatest triumph was a fresh and lively chorus of fifty voices. Young American soloists like Martha Lipton, Robert Brink, and Hugh Thompson appeared in the widely hailed English version by Vicki Baum of the opera *Martha*, presented for the first time in New York.

In recent years the Opera Company has produced new works, such as *The Dybbuk* by David Tamkin; *The Trial* by Von Einem; and *The Tender Land* by Aaron Copland.

Many of our Opera Company singers have gone on to the Metropolitan Opera Company, starting with Dorothy Kirsten. This at first upset some members of our board of directors, but I pointed out that it was the finest thing that could happen; for every one of those young people there are 100 more singing their hearts out in obscurity. It was the City Center's job to go and find them, and we did.

Halasz kept on auditioning, filing cards away against the time when he would need a particular voice. Regina Resnick, whom I had heard as a child in school long before, joined our company and made such a reputation that she soon disappeared into the vast recesses of the Metropolitan Opera Company. She comes back to visit us, and on the Tenth Anniversary of the Opera Company sang as a guest artist.

Camilla Williams, a young Negro soprano, was "discovered" by Halasz, and he made a note that someday we would offer a new production of *Butterfly*. Sure enough, this work was produced, Camilla was cast in the title role. This was the first time a member of her race was cast by a major opera company in a lead role; and overnight she became a star.

We had problems in temperament, and finally it became necessary, in the opinion of the board, to dispense with the services of the able Laszlo Halasz. He has been succeeded by Dr. Joseph Rosenstock, who stepped into the top position and gave the company an unruffled continuity.

Of course, a company loaded with youthful temperament sometimes has misadventures. In 1953 the newspapers were full of such an occurrence during a performance of *Carmen* in Chicago. The young tenor who sang Don José couldn't agree with the conductor of the orchestra on the tempo of the music, and as the opera progressed the tension grew. In the climactic scene, during which he was supposed to stab Carmen to death, the tenor threw down his hat and cloak and, shouting to the conductor, "*You* finish the opera!" walked off the stage. Another tenor who was in the audience rushed backstage and sang the concluding lines of Don José's role from the wings as the audience sat stunned. For the first time since Bizet rang up the curtain on his opera, seventy-eight years before, Carmen expired without being stabbed. As a matter of fact, her collapse was a genuine one. The poor girl was in hysterics when the curtain fell. Immediately after the performance our director announced that the temperamental tenor had, by his action, separated himself from the company. But I understand that he made a sensational comeback in the provinces, billed by his agent as the man who rewrote *Carmen.*

Maurice Evans became so interested in the City Center and its tremendous audience that he agreed to head a new City Center Theatre Company, playing the leads and directing, in many cases. Shaw's *Devil's Disciple, Captain Brassbound's Conversion* and Shakespeare's *King Richard II,* followed in later seasons by

the *Taming of the Shrew, Idiot's Delight, The Wild
Duck, Anna Christie* and *Come of Age,* brought the best
in drama to thousands of people who had never before
seen a legitimate stage production. Indeed, he tackled
the job of directing our theatre with gusto. Evans came
to us well versed in performing for the off-Broadway
playgoer. During the war, he had gone to the Pacific
as a major in charge of GI entertainment and he had
put together a production of *Hamlet* played by GIs that
was a masterpiece of improvisation. He staged *Hamlet*
on shell-pocked islands while Thunderbirds and Zeros
roared overhead and soldiers scrimmaged for positions
only yards away. During one performance, a fuse blew
and Hamlet had to die in darkness. For footlights Evans
used discarded coffee cans in which he placed electric
bulbs sealed over with gelatine. And the lamps for the
palace in Helsingfors were salvaged from the hulk of
a riddled naval vessel. For the City Center, Evans assembled a cast of players who worked at Equity minimum rates. He scrounged the neighborhood colleges
for old props, and put on a whale of a repertory season.

José Ferrer took over this tour of duty, when our
finances were at the lowest ebb in history. Joe's acting
in and directing *Cyrano, The Shrike, Richard III* and
Charley's Aunt, stage-directed by Margaret Webster,
left us with a new profit of more than $90,000. Jean
Dalrymple took care of all the details of production
and persuaded many other great actors to join Ferrer
in their free time between making motion pictures or
acting on Broadway.

One of the staunchest supporters of the City Center
Theatre Company is John Golden, an original incor-

porator and a member of our board since we first organized. When the discussion turns to ballet or opera, he always leaves, protesting that he knows nothing about these two media. I have talked a good deal with him in his picturesque office near Schubert Alley. John will speak of his own efforts to give the American showgoer a bargain deal. John is a fabulous character even by Broadway standards. He made a fortune as a songwriter even before he became a producer. One song he composed while washing up in the men's room made so much money that he was able to go into play production with the proceeds from a single check.

"Many a tidy fortune has been built upon Sullivan operas," he quips, "and I for one always knew where my next steal was coming from."

Golden contributed $100,000 toward the founding of a national theatre similar in spirit to our community theatre, and he has continually been financing unknown playwrights. It was Golden who took Frank Bacon out of obscurity and starred him in *Lightnin'*, the play that wrung the hearts of theatregoers for more than twelve hundred performances and held the record on Broadway until *Abie's Irish Rose* arrived. When the *Lightnin'* company finally quit New York and prepared to entrain for its Chicago opening, it paraded up Broadway to the music of four bands (one headed by Victor Herbert himself) and to the cheers of hundreds of thousands of New Yorkers. Mounted police had to be called out to prevent this demonstration of affection from turning into a riot. Nothing like it had been seen before—or since.

John Golden is fond of telling how he became the only Tin Pan Alley writer to collaborate on a song with a

President of the United States. It happened in 1916 while President Wilson was traveling around the country delivering speeches on preparedness. It struck Golden that the Chief Executive's prose had a lyrical tang to it. Golden took a line from a Kansas City speech, added a line from a talk Wilson delivered in Chicago, from one in Philadelphia, and so on, until he had put together a complete series of rhymes which he set to music. Then through his friend Bernard Baruch he submitted the song to the President. Not long afterwards, the President invited him to the White House to play the song on the piano. When Golden finished he said apologetically, "I don't suppose it's very good, is it?"

"I don't know about your music," answered the President, "but my words are great!"

Golden informed President Wilson that a publisher wanted the song and was willing to pay an advance on royalties.

"How much can you get?"

"At least a thousand dollars."

"Hmmmm," muttered the President, "I ought to have looked into this business before. I'll tell you what we'll do. Let's print it with your name and mine on it, make a lot of money and give it to the Red Cross."

And they did.

When the Ballet Russe de Monte Carlo moved on to the Metropolitan Opera House, we were fortunate to have Lincoln Kirstein and George Balanchine, the world-renowned choreographer and ballet master, come into our lives. The ballet repertory included ten works in its first City Center season. In 1954 there are thirty-two established ballets which have thrilled audiences, not only at the City Center, but on tour in other American cities and in all the countries of Western Europe.

George Balanchine is a transplanted Russian who was a student in the Imperial Ballet School and who left after the Bolshevik Revolution to work with Diaghilev and Nijinsky in Paris. Here he met Lincoln Kirstein, a young man out of Harvard and one of the heirs to the Filene fortune, who had dreams of founding a national ballet in America. Kirstein had no intention of transplanting an exotic art to America. He was determined to develop the home-grown variety. Americans are strong and graceful and are naturally fond of the dance. Why should Russia and France monopolize this plastic art?

Kirstein induced Balanchine to come to the United States, and the two opened a ballet school as a first step in training talent for a company. Once the school began to graduate students, the City Center Ballet Company was organized as a sister branch of our opera and drama center. The company became the first resident ballet in America and has developed into one of the world's most provocative ballets. We have Morton Baum to thank for bringing this new unit with Kirstein and Balanchine into the City Center.

George Balanchine is a premier choreographer and a chain smoker to boot. Nervous energy exudes from his every gesture. Before he came to America he had been a leatherworker in a harness shop, a circus performer and a piano player in a movie house. He once staged a ballet for the Ringling Brothers elephants dressed in pink tights. When he arrived in America, Hollywood claimed him temporarily as a choreographer. The movie producer with whom he worked had difficulty understanding his English and asked for an interpreter. Not to be outdone, the Russian informed the producer that he wanted an interpreter for his own convenience: "You speak unlegibly!"

Today America has caught the infectious enthusiasm of Balanchine and Kirstein in a big way. More than a hundred thousand students are enrolled in ballet schools throughout the country. And America has contributed her own brand of audacity to the long-haired art. Young Jerome Robbins joined City Center to develop his satiric and psychologically colored choreography for our boards. The New York Ballet has toured Paris, Barcelona, Florence, Zurich, Berlin and the Low Countries, London, Edinburgh, and has received ovations from fastidious audiences who ordinarily refuse to buy culture that isn't trademarked "made in Europe." Lincoln not unjustifiably considers the company an arm of the State Department. When our troops moved out of Trieste the Ballet Company moved in. American prestige was restored.

The City Center survived for ten years without having to resort to a campaign for funds from the general public. Each year's operations ended with a small surplus or an insignificant deficit which could be liquidated simply by passing the hat among the official City Center family. Just as we prepared to celebrate our Tenth Anniversary, however, all three operating companies produced deficits which left us with approximately $100,000 of unpaid bills, no cash with which to meet them and no working capital for the mounting of new productions. This required a gigantic effort, and I decided that if

$100,000 couldn't be collected from the public at large within the period of one month, we would have to announce that the City Center's doors would close forever. The City Center board asked me to undertake the leadership of this drive.

I left my office in the middle of April. I begged, pleaded and wept in some of the loveliest drawing rooms in New York and in the offices of industrial leaders. The Unions working in the theatre set up a special committee to cooperate. They realized that 1,500 individuals, not only performing artists but wardrobe mistresses, ushers, electricians, carpenters, stagehands and others, had a stake in the City Center. And I was interested in that audience which bought one-half million tickets each year. Surely those people "out front" would not let us down. I appeared before the curtain rose on the last act of whatever was playing each evening. Checks and money orders started to roll in from people not only in New York but from all over the country. I begged and obtained free radio and television time, telling the story as a guest of well-known commentators. Actors and actresses, singers and dancers joined me and members of the board in making appeals in many different directions.

By the middle of May $78,000 was in a special account. I racked my mind for other people of wealth to see and foundations which I hadn't approached and could think of no other source of generous support. The small contributions had started to peter out, and I just about made up my mind that we would have to refund the contributions and announce the end of this institution. I was ready to call up Morton Baum to tell him of my decision and to send out a call for an emergency meeting of the board when another miracle happened. I was told by the switchboard operator that my friend David Heyman was on the wire. His cheerful voice was asking me how I felt.

"Terrible, Dave," I groaned.

I had forgotten that at the suggestion of Frank Bloustein I had sent his foundation a fervid appeal, but I didn't think there would be much chance because I thought the foundation was dedicated to health programs. Dave said:

"I just wanted to let you know that my board met last night and voted a grant of $25,000 to the City Center."

Dave's voice seemed very far away. I managed to gasp: "Say that again, Dave. You mean $2,500, don't you?"

"No," he said, "$25,000."

Still unable to believe my ears, I asked if there were any strings attached, any restrictions. Was it to be used over a period of years? Again he reassured me that a check would be in the mail for $25,000 to be used for any purpose the board saw fit. A great sigh of relief was all I could muster, and I tried to mumble a few words in gratitude. It seemed as it a great cloud had suddenly been blown away and the sun had reappeared in all its glory. The City Center was saved!

By the time our efforts ceased, contributions, large and small, and grants totaling $284,734.66 had come in.

An important milestone in the history of the City Center was a grant from the Rockefeller Foundation in the amount of $200,000, to be expended over a three-year period. This grant was primarily made to encourage the commissioning of new works, new choreography, designing costumes and scenery, but under its terms could not be used for their manufacture and construction or for operating costs.

Because so many contributors had been under the misapprehension that the City Center was a municipally supported theatre, Morton Baum and I thought it was time that the city ought at least to have the power to make grants in aid to the City Center. So, Baum prepared and together we lobbied through the legislature a bill for this purpose. It was duly signed by the governor, and today the city is enabled to aid our organization as it does kindred educational institutions, such as the Public Library, the Metropolitan Museum and the Bronx Zoological Gardens. As this chapter goes to press, we are awaiting action by Mayor Wagner and members of the Board of Estimate upon a resolution which will cancel our lease with the city under which we must pay approximately $28,000, and let us occupy the premises at a nominal rental of $1 a year.

We have tried to keep the City Center on a self-sustaining basis. Surely it is not too much to find that at the end of ten years we were $100,000 in the hole. The Metropolitan Opera Company finds it necessary to raise three-quarters of a million dollars each year to balance its budget. It broke some of our hearts to have to abandon the most expensive unit of all, the orchestra which wound up its mission of giving concerts to working people at six o'clock in the evening so that they could get home early for their labors the next day.

Stokowski had handed over his baton to young Leonard Bernstein, who, at twenty-seven, typified the youthful optimism of the organization. Formerly the assistant conductor of the New York Philharmonic, young Bernstein had scored a musical sensation by taking over for the regular conductor, Bruno Walter, when the Viennese maestro suddenly fell ill before a performance. By the time he was twenty-five Bernstein had established himself as a conductor, a concert pianist and a composer of serious and popular music. Few composers rack up box-office hits on Broadway and win the acclaim of the long-haired critics with equal facility. But Bernstein has earned success as the composer of *Wonderful Town* and the *Jeremiah Symphony*.

As I write this chapter the City Center is winding up its eleventh year. A week ago there was a gap between our unpaid bills and liquid assets of approximately $50,000. Another miracle has happened in the last few days. A new unit, which we call the New York Light Opera Company, has been a dream of Morton Baum all through the years and finally became a realization under the direction of young Bill Hammerstein. The first two musical productions were running at deficits. Then the Rodgers and Hammerstein light opera *Carousel* opened with a box-office advance of $60,000. The first week it grossed $45,000. Popular demand justified a summer run. So, I feel as Stokowski did when he completed a great concert. He turned to the audience, raised his hands for silence, and then the words suddenly came strong and clear, "I love you!"

Four or five years ago I was invited to speak at a lunch of the Fine Arts Federation. I suggested that it might be a fine thing to have a gallery for the exhibition of the fine arts, as a new unit in the City Center. I told them that

we have what might be called a "captive" audience of
3,000 people attending the theatre. In intermissions
some of them might smoke on the sidewalk, tarry in the
lobby or go to a nearby bistro for a drink, but why
wouldn't some of them wander into an art gallery if it
was easily accessible? Here again was a gap which ought
to be closed—a gap between the unknown painter and
the ordinary man or woman who always thought works of
art were out of the reach of the average pocketbook.
I imagined a married couple standing before a painting
and the wife saying, "Oh, John, look at this beautiful
water color and its price is fifty dollars. Why, we spend
as much as that each year for flowers. Let's buy it."

Unknown to me at the time, my idea was "bought"
by the then president of the Fine Arts Federation,
Harvey Stevenson. To make a short story shorter, the
art gallery opened a year ago and unknown artists' works
have been submitted to juries for a fee of $2, hung with-
out charge and sold without the payment of a commission. What is most exciting, more than three-fourths
of those sold have been to members of the theatre audience who never thought of being connoisseurs.

So many people are mystified because I give so much
time to the City Center. But I am not the only one.
There are members of our board of directors and many
volunteers who in one way or another contribute experience, taste and time without any financial reward.

There is reward in abundance. For me it comes as
I mingle with the crowds in the lobby and in the street
during intermissions and listen to their enthusiastic
applause and as I stand in the side aisles of the theatre
during the performance watching the eager faces, so many

of them so young. The reward comes when I sit back and listen to the music of *Swan Lake* or *Lilac Garden* or *Interplay* or Tchaikowsky's *The Nutcracker;* see Maria Tallchief dancing, as John Martin of the *Times* writes, "like an angel," or witness a performance of young chic Tanaquil LeClerc, recently arrived as a première ballerina, and Diana Adams, a new star in the Balanchine constellation. The reward comes in reading the letters which come in from mothers of young children who have attended the performance as part of their regular school curriculum accompanied by their classroom teachers, students of music, students of the dance, and students of Shakespeare.

We have enjoyed having the superintendent of the High School Division of the Board of Education on our board, and he has assigned a high school teacher, Mrs. Ida Martus, full time to work out the schedules. The reward comes from little incidents, such as when I felt my sleeve plucked as I left my place during intermission. I looked down and saw a little old lady, crutches in her hand. She looked up at me with a radiant smile. It was the opening night of the New York City Opera Company.

"Oh, Mr. Morris," she exclaimed, "the City Center has been formed just in time."

"In time for what?" I asked.

"Well," she replied, "you don't remember the old Academy of Music where I used to buy standing room and I have been watching performances on my feet for years in the Metropolitan Opera House and Carnegie Hall until I became crippled with arthritis. But now for almost the same price as standing room I can find a good seat in this theatre."

Yes, the reward is there and in abundance. Not being a poet, I am going to take the liberty of quoting a dedication poem by Bonaro W. Overstreet:

Within these walls
Beauty is given a home—a place to live
Where it can be welcoming host to men and women
Who learn to turn down this street . . . to enter these
    doors . . .
Finding here the something they've always wanted,
But haven't known where to find: the immortal blessing
Lent by the True and Good and Beautiful
To private mortal lives . . .

Who are the people
Who have come here tonight?
Why . . . They are *people*
Not any special group. Not the best people.
Not even *the people* (that political fiction).
But *people:* fathers and mothers, husbands and wives,
Young men and women: people who've come from work
In offices, factories, colleges, homes, and shops:
People who've passed the word among themselves:
"I'm going to the opening, tonight, of the City Center . . ."

Little did I realize what forces were being unleashed with the flowering of the WPA orchestra in the dark days of the depression.

CHAPTER 8   The Return of the Natives

SOON after I was elected to a second term as president of the City Council, the Japanese attack on Pearl Harbor plunged the country into war. New York City put almost 1,000,000 citizens into uniform and produced vast quantites of material for the fighting fronts. It served as the vital transportation link in the war effort. In a sense, it is not too much to say that the war in Europe was won in the Port of New York.

LaGuardia, as director of the U.S. Office of Civilian Defense and as chairman of the U.S.-Canadian Joint Board, was out of the city for long periods. He appointed me the New York City representative on the U.S. Regional Civil Defense Agency. I also represented the city on the Metropolitan Defense Transport Committee which was responsible for setting up a secondary network of highways and secondary distribution points for commodities, in the event that the primary highways and distribution points were destroyed by enemy bombing. The mayor also assigned to me the job of chairmanship of the War Manpower Committee; it was through my office that applications for deferment of vitally necessary employees engaged in "essential" services went. But the mayor was very insistent that we should cooperate fully with Gen. Arthur McDermott, head of the Selective Service System in New York, in seeing that city employees, able-bodied and not vitally needed at home, were inducted.

Because of its interracial vulnerability, New York City had become the leading target of Hitler's propaganda. LaGuardia declared war on Hitler back in 1939 when he stated that he would have no exhibit at the World's Fair from a country which was directed by a "brown-shirted fanatic." He followed that up by saying that if Nazi Germany did have an exhibit at the World's Fair he would put a wax figure of Hitler in a chamber of horrors. This mayor of Italian-Jewish stock, who so dramatically projected the aspirations of America's racially "impure" minorities, was presenting a dynamic flesh-and-blood demonstration of democracy at work that could not be lost on the world. In fact on a world stage he was the antithesis of Adolf Hitler. Throughout the LaGuardia administration, Hitler's henchmen in America tried desperately to exploit the tensions of New York's racial groups. The Yorkville Bund and America Firsters and Joe MacWilliam's Brooklyn Christian Fronters came to grips with LaGuardia liberals and other shades of anti-Nazis in battles that were a replica of the world-wide struggle.

Even before the war the Nazis had been having a field day with LaGuardia's non-Aryan origins. Shortly after his first inaugural, the mayor had confessed to reporters, "My mother undoubtedly had Jewish blood in her veins, but I never thought I had enough in mine to justify boasting about it." Hitler's press returned LaGuardia's compliments to the Nazis by calling the mayor "a Jewish ruffian." Not long after this transatlantic exchange, a

Nazi delegation visited New York and its reaction was unprintable when it discovered that the mayor had assigned it an escort of Jewish policemen.

By the time of his second term in office, LaGuardia had become possibly the best-known political figure in America after Franklin Roosevelt. Curiously enough the two men had been born in the same year—1882— but under quite different circumstances. Whereas the Little Flower had begun life in a crowded tenement house, the Squire of Duchess County had been born on an estate. Yet despite the difference in origins, LaGuardia was able to say of Roosevelt, truthfully if a trifle facetiously, "He is a distinguished faculty member of my school of thought."

The President and the mayor were warmly disposed toward one another and they savored their little jokes. This correspondence was replete with humor. On one occasion LaGuardia wrote the President regarding a judgeship to be filled in Washington:

> If the endorsement of an obscure mayor of a town along the Hudson is of any value, may I state that I can highly recommend [the name of the candidate follows] for the office of Judge in the Juvenile Court. Of course this recommendation is entirely nonpolitical. I know nothing about politics (!) and live in the midst of millions of voters while [the candidate] is pretty keen but lives where good people have no votes. That makes it about even.[1]

While Roosevelt trusted LaGuardia, he did not trust the Democrats in New York State, to say nothing of the

[1] All the letters quoted in this chapter have hitherto been unpublished. They have been selected from the LaGuardia private papers.

Tammany organization. And this added up to a curious situation. In February 1937, nine months before the gubernatorial election, he asked LaGuardia (a Republican!) to make an off-the-record survey regarding the chances of the various *Democratic* candidates for governor, the public reaction to each individual, etc., and to evaluate the material for him. I have before me as I write a hitherto unpublished letter from LaGuardia to Roosevelt illustrating how closely the two men worked politically at times.

> Dear Skipper: Recalling our talk a few days ago, I sent out feelers and spoke to several people concerning the gubernatorial situation in our State. I am sending along the reaction, which is accurate, and my conclusions which, of course, are of no value, knowing less about politics than anyone else in this City [*sic!*].
>
> Strange as it may seem, Jackson [Robert Jackson, the late Supreme Court Justice] is not at all known. From the ordinary man of the street to people who are generally well informed, he is not identified with any particular achievement or standing. He varies from "the man who did something about the President's Court Plan" to "the man that they gave a dinner for a few weeks ago." He would require a great deal of building up, handshaking and getting around in the meantime. As to getting by a Convention, I find that the ordinary variety of politicians, the kind that would be delegates, do not take to him at all. Naturally, Tammany and affiliates know of your interest in Jackson. . . . The mere discussion of Jackson among politicians before and after cocktails, brings out possibilities of Herbert [Lehman].

The Governor is doing a great deal of speechmaking
and acts like a candidate, even if he is not one.

Bennett has quite a following. Al Smith would use
Bennett as first shock-troop. There is talk of a com-
bination between Tammany, the O'Connells of Albany, the Machine in Rochester and Erie County.
In that event, after the first skirmish, a compromise
they may have in mind today is Mayor Thatcher of
Albany. Tremaine is liked by some of the people
who are rather friendly to you, but they frankly admit he would not be a very attractive candidate.
Graves is politicianing around and has hopes of
being a compromise candidate. . . . Personally I
believe that Lehman is very much in the race. . . .
And so much for that.

During the dark days of the war, LaGuardia passed
along to the President a suggestion for softening up the
morale of Italy that, while it undoubtedly had its practical side, could also have come from the pen of Mark
Twain.

Dear Skipper: A matter that I think should be
decided real soon is a joint statement that Rome
should be an Open City and not bombed. . . . The
Fasciste heads are all well furnished with money and
if Rome is declared an Open City, there will be the
darnedest rush to that City now overcrowded, and
all the war profiteers and big shots and politicians
will be vying with each other for apartments and
food. This will make a profound impression on the
rest of the country, and we can rub it in on our radio
talks.

The versatile mayor felt free enough with the President to offer him (for what it was worth) a geopolitical

strategy for defending America at the time that France
fell to the Nazis.

> Dear Skipper: I was talking to Colonel ——. After
> we got through all official business we naturally dis-
> cussed the existing world crisis. He pointed out the
> strategic location of Cape Verde Islands and the
> Azores. They are really key positions. Should we
> not be thinking about acquiring the Cape Verde
> Islands, perhaps jointly with Brazil, and getting by
> purchase the Azores? The latter islands, as you
> know, are now being used as a by-station by the
> Pan-American service. That would be rather good
> justification for seeking to acquire them. I thought
> I would pass this on to you.

Always LaGuardia's correspondence was stamped
with his inimitable brand of audacity. Here, for instance,
is a wire to Roosevelt on the eve of the visit of King
George and Queen Elizabeth of England to New York
in 1939.

> Everything the Department of State says about
> the arrangements to receive their majesties . . . is
> not only true but let me say [it doesn't] even com-
> mence to describe the situation. Instead of twenty
> thousand people to receive their majesties we will
> have at least one hundred thousand people. If we
> had followed their [the State Department's] stupid,
> inane, indifferent suggestions the reception would
> have been a dud—dead and almost offensive. I think
> I know your views and I am carrying them out to
> give the King and Queen a real, rousing, living,
> enthusiastic American reception. I don't know much
> about the protocol, thank God, but I do know some-
> thing about human nature. . . . Leave it to me and

their majesties will be happy and you will be satis-
fied. Further the deponent saith not. Signed F. H.
LaGuardia, *Still* The Mayor Of The City Of New
York.

At one stage the friendship of these men cooled somewhat. When America entered the war, LaGuardia was
eager to get into the army. The President, I was told,
promised him a commission as a general officer. But at
the last moment, rumor had it that Secretary of War
Stimson vetoed the commission. He rebelled at the idea
of having the unpredictable LaGuardia on his hands.
He probably had visions of the mayor suddenly popping
up on some foreign shore and shooting off his pistol in
advance of the American army, throwing the carefully
laid plans of the diplomats into confusion. LaGuardia
was deeply disgruntled by this rejection. But he carried
on like a good soldier on the home front.

Both Roosevelt and LaGuardia attempted to translate
American progressivism into action according to their
lights. But LaGuardia was able to succeed in various
areas where the New Deal failed. New York provided
a much richer soil for social experiment than the country
as a whole. Although the New Deal's relief program
was sabotaged by innumerable communities that fattened
on the handouts without putting the unemployed to
socially constructive work, LaGuardia rebuilt his city
and expanded its services, getting a hundred cents'
worth of results out of most of the dollars he spent. La-
Guardia had the money-tightness of the peasant in his
make-up, not the money-lavishness of the Hyde Park
aristocrat. He never saw eye to eye with Roosevelt's
policy of deficit financing.

The New Deal was largely frustrated in its attempt to turn art into a socially useful force for the country as a whole. The LaGuardia administration got very encouraging results in this direction, as I have related in the previous chapter. The Roosevelt Administration was plagued by a rash of violent labor disputes in Chicago, Detroit and other industrial centers. LaGuardia was able to keep the nation's largest city remarkably free of labor violence. He enforced lawful picketing, substituted negotiation for skirmish lines and succeeded in safeguarding the interests of private capital to an extent unattained by conservative politicians elsewhere who persisted in calling him a "radical."

The President and the mayor were greatly disturbed over the split that occurred in labor's ranks when the A.F. of L. showed the industrial unionists in its family (C.I.O.) the door. And both Roosevelt and LaGuardia, sympathetic as they were to rank-and-file labor, were not blind to the effect labor politics was having on the nation's well-being.

"I need not remind you," wrote LaGuardia to the President in 1938,

> of the deplorable situation organized labor is making for themselves. It is a cause of worry for every one of us. It is for the friends of labor to bring them to their senses. The present division of labor is causing not only consternation within their own ranks, but uncertainty in industry which adds to the real and imaginary difficulties regarding the resumption of normal activities. . . . Miss Betty Hawley [his labor adviser] and I have been talking over the situation and it occurred to us that the moment is propi-

tious for you to call the two factions together. At
this very time after you have gone through hell to get
substantial appropriations to aid industry and labor, no one, not even a Liberty Leaguer, can question your sincerity and desire to stimulate business
and provide work. . . . To aid in bringing this
about and for purposes of consultations, in order to
relieve you of the details, there are many outstanding friends of labor at your call who would be very
glad to cooperate. Needless to say I would do anything you would ask in the matter.

While on the subject of labor, it is interesting to
record that LaGuardia was the first government official
to establish a fact-finding board as a mechanism for set-
tling management-labor disputes peacefully.

In a letter to Roosevelt he discussed how he came to
use the board. It was first employed to avert a strike
on the Brooklyn-Manhattan Transit line.

From my experience with the procedure worked
out in the National Railway Labor Act, we borrowed the notion of a fact-finding board, with no
express powers to conciliate, mediate, or arbitrate.
As you know; no such board or body is provided for
under our local law. Both sides readily accepted the
proposal. . . . The Fact-Finding Board began its
sessions at once. As all the facts came clearly to the
fore, mediation loomed nearer. Mr. Arthur S. Meyer,
as chairman, together with Dr. William Leisersen
and Professor J. P. Chamberlain, worked with extraordinary skill, while hearing the facts, to bring
the parties together. The final agreement reached—
of a 10% increase in pay and a minimum wage of

$25.00 a week, would have seemed a miracle two weeks before.

Between the one-time inevitable chaos of industrial disputes, and the peace-of-the-grave achieved by dictatorships, through the suppression of trade unions and the outlawing of strikes, we in this country have found methods more in keeping with a democracy. Without compulsion, and merely with the aid of the light shed by public disclosure of all the facts, the instrumentalities for mediation and conciliation created by government, can act as the bridge between opposing forces, to bring them to a voluntary agreement. . . . A strike which did not happen is not a spectacular thing. But to have averted the suffering in countless obscure homes, which would have otherwise ensued, is a rewarding thought.

There was ample evidence that a social experiment was having its flowering in New York. Just to mention several examples: During the LaGuardia administration, the health department of the city became a model for the nation. Hospitals were largely rescued from the rule of politics and placed under the administration of experts.

It was once a political axiom that a police department could break a mayor. Until LaGuardia it had occurred to too few politicians that a mayor could *make* a police department. Under LaGuardia, not a single promotion was made in the department through political influence. A sound actuarial pension system was established. Equality in pay in the higher ranks was established. A laboratory of scientific detection of crime was put into operation.

LaGuardia found the Fire Department badly run down in equipment. He discovered that the specifications for equipment were being provided by manufacturers who had the inside political track. LaGuardia changed all that—and not singlehandedly. He joined a group of mayors all over the country to break the conspiracy of the fire hose manufacturers. Under LaGuardia's direction, greater emphasis was placed on the training for scientific fire fighting. Young men with the necessary educational background on the force were sent to engineering schools and colleges. The educational requirements for new entrants were raised.

Until LaGuardia entered City Hall, nothing at all had been done in public, low-rent housing. Slum dwellers were occupying firetraps by the thousands. As LaGuardia himself has put it, "It was not pleasant to live through the nights of those early years of my administration when a fire call would come in. Every winter scores of lives were needlessly lost in tenement fires." LaGuardia did not race to fires for fun. They were his job, and they provided him with a liberal education. When LaGuardia left City Hall, he had built fourteen housing projects accommodating 17,039 families. At the laying of the cornerstone of the very first project—the Williamsburg Houses in Brooklyn—LaGuardia placed in the box a copy of Jacob Riis's classic book describing slum conditions in America, *How the Other Half Lives*. Thirty years before, while recuperating from a siege of influenza in the Consulate in Trieste, LaGuardia had first come across this book. And now he was able to bring about the realization of Riis's dreams. Public housing for low-income groups—something entirely new in

municipal government—meant more than the trans-
formation of the old railroad-flat tenement into a beautifully landscaped housing development. It transformed
the sadness of a mother's face into a smile, the look of
apathy of a child into an expression of hope.

The philosophy of the LaGuardia administration was
a very simple one. LaGuardia acted on the premise that
the well-being of the individual was just as much a concern of our government as the protection of his property.
"I once dreamed of a city called Heaven," said the mayor,
"and I tried to make it my New York."

LaGuardia found almost complete freedom from
political interference. Franklin Roosevelt, as President,
seemed to find it necessary to play ball with Frank Kelley
of Chicago, David Lawrence of Pittsburgh, Frank Hague
of Jersey City. Unlike Roosevelt, LaGuardia carried on
for long stretches with very little support in the legislature.

LaGuardia's administration suffered a reverse in his
first year. A capable, dynamic young veteran, Arthur
Cunningham, who was elected comptroller on the La-
Guardia ticket, died of a heart attack in 1934. This
tragic loss of a city-wide officer with three votes on the
Board of Estimate was followed the following year by
the death of Bernard S. Deutsch, president of the Board
of Aldermen. That meant the loss of another city-wide
officer with three votes on the Board of Estimate. In two
years LaGuardia lost control of that governing body of
the city. Tammany candidates filled these two vacancies
for the balance of the term. LaGuardia with his three
votes on the Board, Borough President Raymond Inger-
soll with two votes and George Harvey, president of

Queens, with his uncertain one vote, were deadlocked by Tammany.

LaGuardia's renunciation of commitments to the political groups that elected him was remarkable even for a reformer. Before he left office, the radicals became as exasperated with him as the conservatives. Shortly after his first election, he stood before his Fusion supporters who had carried the ball so single-mindedly for him and declared, "It has not been easy for our Fusion government to say after the successful campaign, 'Sorry, there is nothing in it for you workers who have made our success possible.' But that is the way it must be."

Three days after being sworn in for his second term, he told the American Labor party whose votes had given him the margin of victory, "I hope our relations continue pleasant, but I wouldn't be surprised if by the Fourth of July you were damning me as the Republicans did. I am going to continue to administer the city as I did the past four years. . . . My attitude toward political parties will be what it was in the past." When told that the Communists, engaged in their "popular front" tactics of jumping on the bandwagon of liberalism, were supporting him for mayor in 1937, LaGuardia answered, "They will get no aid or comfort from me." LaGuardia hated the Communists with the intensity of a true liberal and a sincerely religious man.

Incidentally, the American Labor party, which was created by liberal groups to support Roosevelt and La-Guardia, was, as time went on, infiltrated and finally dominated by the extreme left wing.

Of course it was Roosevelt's New Deal that made La-Guardia's independence from machine politics possible. Tammany had for generations kept its voters in line with handouts of coal and food to the underprivileged. But it was completely overwhelmed by the high-powered relief methods of the New Deal. And LaGuardia, as chief magistrate of the city, was in charge of unemployment relief in New York.

The business partnership between the Son of the Revolution and the Son of the Steerage (as the mayor chose to classify the President and himself) over the howling protests of Eddie Flynn and the Tammany political bosses is one of the most provocative episodes in American politics. It was the manifestation of a trend that LaGuardia himself believed would ultimately revolutionize American politics. He was convinced that it was only a question of time before a political shake-up would alter the alignments of the two major parties.

During Roosevelt's first term, Al Smith and his Liberty Leaguers and the Dixiecrats had begun to make common cause with the Hoover-Landon Republicans. And to LaGuardia it seemed that the informal association between the New Dealers and the progressive Republicans would eventually solidify into a party alliance. Bob La Follette, Jr., Hiram Johnson, George Norris and Bronson Cutting had crossed party lines to work with Roosevelt (although they did not agree with him on every issue), and LaGuardia in 1937 joined these progressives to endorse Roosevelt for a second term. These "Roosevelt" Republicans called a conference of progressives in Chicago and formed a committee through which they could work for Roosevelt's re-election without becoming involved with the Democratic party machinery.

From this time on, LaGuardia's political career was committed to the fortunes of this working coalition of independent voters who had nothing in common with the parasites living off the major party machines to whom an election victory meant a fat public pay check or a lucrative slice of real estate. The independent voter is and has been the most potent force in American politics when he has realized his strength. LaGuardia hoped that this voter would continue to serve as the bread-and-butter support of his program long after he personally had left the scene.

When World War II broke out, Roosevelt offered LaGuardia a series of assignments that challenged even the Little Flower's powers of resiliency. In addition to his duties as Mayor of New York, U.S. Director of Civilian Defense, and President of the United States Conference of Mayors, he accepted the chairmanship of the American Section of the U.S.-Canadian Permanent Joint Board on Defense.

And in the early stages of the war, when it was necessary to dramatize to the American people the problems of preparedness against possible air attack by the enemy, Roosevelt appointed LaGuardia head of the Office of Civilian Defense. LaGuardia was as busy as the proverbial beaver building the nation's dams. He started and ended one typical day in New York, flying to Washington, Cincinnati and Chicago to deliver speeches. He flew to Washington weekly to attend Cabinet meetings at the White House. And he kept his finger—more accurately, his whole fist—upon the pulse of City Hall. As before the war, he insisted upon attending to details. When Paris fell, he sensed that New York would become the fashion center of the world. And, to pictorialize this opportunity to the people, he designed a dress that was worn by a pretty model who was photographed launching a new patrol boat. (Fashion married to the war effort—everything was grist for his mill.) He arranged for a radio program to publicize a plan for distributing federal food stamps. But when none of the scripts met with his approval, he wrote one of his own and acted in it. He snatched time from his war duties to promote a scheme for restoring New York as the nation's movie capital. He succeeded in luring private money for two major film productions. But Hollywood successfully withstood the Little Flower's competition.

Just to be certain that he would be active on Sundays as well as during the rest of the week, the mayor instituted a series of Sunday broadcasts from his desk at City Hall, speaking to New Yorkers over a municipal station the city had purchased for such purposes. His chats were typically unorthodox. He told women how to buy economically under wartime conditions. He broadcast recipes of inexpensive dishes (many of which he had sampled himself; he was an excellent cook); he advised the home owner how to save on fuel; he informed tenants that their landlords were required to paint the premises (war or no war)—"Just tell me if they don't!"; he advised housewives how to get rid of cockroaches in the kitchen. When a ban on racing went into effect during the war, he hurled a challenge at the professional gamblers over the air waves, lapsing into Yiddish. "I don't know what the firms of . . . *Gonovim* [crooks] Unincorporated are going to do, but we are going to watch. If you try any monkey business, we will grab you by the seat of the pants and throw you out, do you hear?"

When LaGuardia's political opponents, taking a look at his soaring Hooper rating, charged him with using the municipal radio as a political plaything, he retorted that he didn't need free time for politics. He declared that he had been flooded with offers from sponsors to go on commercial stations, and he sent the Board of Estimate a letter he had received from a cosmetics firm offering to sponsor his talks at a thousand dollars a week. This stopped the politicians cold.

As the war drew to a close, the deep-seated animosity of the machine Republicans to the LaGuardia administration crystallized into serious opposition. Indeed, as early as the Republican primary of 1941, LaGuardia had had a bitter struggle to win the nomination for the third term. Republicans were angry at him because he wouldn't give them the jobs they wanted. District leaders were irritated because they had not been appointed commissioners. A group of Republicans put up John Davies, a very respectable old-guard politician, to oppose La-Guardia for the nomination, and the mayor, as has already been mentioned, barely squeaked through the primaries.

As LaGuardia's third term approached an end, leading Republicans and Democrats in the city and state, starved for patronage for twelve years, met privately to discuss the possibility of putting up a bipartisan candidate to beat the mayor. As early as 1937, elements of both parties had been plotting this strategy. But at the time shrewder heads warned that the spectacle of Tammany and the Republicans openly crawling into the same bed would infuriate the public. The Seabury investigation was still fresh in the people's memory. The year 1945, however, was another matter. The politicians were convinced that people had by that time forgotten the Walker scandals and, riding the boom of a war prosperity, would put up with a return to the old political practices in City Hall.

This bipartisan conspiracy to gang up on LaGuardia was a dramatic illustration of a curious situation that has always existed in New York. Far from opposing one another in a genuine two-party struggle, leading elements of the Republican party have often collaborated behind the scenes with Tammany Hall to perpetuate the rule of machine politics in city government. This tacit alliance between the political bosses of both major parties has been true not only in New York, but in most American cities, and is the greatest single obstacle to the achievement of democratic, representative government.

For instance, in New York it is a notorious fact that for years the Republican bosses of the Bronx and Staten Island had been on the payroll of the Democratic bosses. One held a ten-thousand-dollar-a-year job as Commissioner of Records in the Bronx Surrogate's Court, and the other was Richmond Borough Works Commissioner. Both jobs were controlled by the Democratic machine. The adoption of the New York City charter and the county reform bills—the leading measures advocated by reform groups—were opposed by both major parties and became law only when they were overwhelmingly voted by the people in a popular referendum.

While the bosses were busily hatching their bipartisan conspiracy, the mayor decided not to seek re-election. He had once said to me in a moment of depression that one year of being mayor took five years off a man's life. He had served in City Hall for twelve years, the longest of any New York mayor, and he had put more bounce into the job than any of his predecessors. In the spring of 1945, he was a very tired man. I know that he was frequently in great pain. He would sit in his chair holding onto his back. The mayor seemed to have the premonition that he wouldn't last long.

For years LaGuardia had resisted the pleas of many leaders in good government who urged him to build a hard-knit, dedicated political organization that would carry on his program after he had retired. With his prestige as mayor, he could certainly have developed a hard corps of supporters formalized into a single party. But he refused to do this. He was afraid that some of those who assumed responsibility in such an organization would demand favors and political appointments—that he would in fact be creating a political machine; and as for designating a successor to carry on, he remarked emphatically to me, "In a democracy a public official cannot designate his crown prince."

LaGuardia's problem—how to keep alive the reform movement without turning it into a political pressure group of its own—is the dilemma faced by every municipal reformer. His decision *not* to solidify his following into an organization had profound consequences for the city.

When it became known that LaGuardia would not seek re-election, many of my associates took it for granted that I would be nominated by the Republican party for mayor to carry on LaGuardia's program. As a matter of fact, the young Republican Club actually came out for me. Certain liberal Republican leaders declared me as their first choice. And I read in the newspapers that Thomas J. Curran, my county chairman, announced his support. On the very day I read this announcement, I attended a luncheon of the Brooklyn Sunday School Union. After the meal, we gathered in Prospect Park Meadow to view the Sunday school parade, at which a hundred thousand Protestant children marched under a banner and the cross while the band played "Onward Christian Soldiers." During the activities I noticed Governor Dewey, who was present, talking animatedly with John R. Crews, the Republican leader from Brooklyn, and looking in my direction. Afterward, Johnny came over and asked me if I would run for re-election on the Republican ticket as president of the City Council.

I asked, "Who's running for mayor?"

"Goldstein."

I was sitting next to Nathaniel Goldstein, the very able Attorney General, and I said, "You mean Nat?"

"No, I mean Jonah Goldstein."

I was astounded. Goldstein the Republican candidate for mayor? Had I heard correctly? Goldstein had been a lifelong Tammany Democrat. He had been appointed to a judgeship by Mayor Walker. *Until the eleventh hour, Goldstein had been a leading candidate for the present Tammany nomination, vying for the prize with Bill O'Dwyer, who had been defeated by LaGuardia in 1941.*

The next morning the Republicans publicly announced they had chosen Goldstein for mayor, Mc-Goldrick for comptroller, and Morris for president of the Council. That afternoon I bolted the Republican ticket with explosive words.

In bolting the ticket, I had not solved my own political problems. The question was what would I do next? Would I run as an independent? If I did, I would at least give the people an alternative to voting, in an election staged between two Tammany candidates.

During the brief period in which I was trying to reach a decision overtures were made to me by mutual friends of mine and Bill O'Dwyer to join his ticket and run with him for re-election as president of the Council. The Flynn group supporting O'Dwyer were worried about the aggressive candidacy of Judge Jonah Goldstein on the Republican-Liberal ticket. I thought about this for about two minutes. If I have a choice of being on a ticket with one of two Tammany Democrats why not pick the one with the best chance of success! O'Dwyer was having trouble selecting a ticket satisfactory to him. For unknown reasons he announced that he would not consent to having Assemblyman Irwin Davidson as his candidate for president of the Council nor would he accept Lawrence Gerosa as a candidate for comptroller. It is interesting to note that the latter is comptroller of the City of New York today. The former, who was always known as one of the great wits of the legislature, has been "elevated" to the City Court. It has been reliably reported to me that Flynn's first choice for president of the Council was Jonah Goldstein. But Jonah was boiling mad at having lost the Tammany nomination and told them that he would lick O'Dwyer as a Republican candidate. It was into that vacuum that my well-meaning friends were attempting to push me in order to keep me in public life. O'Dwyer's advisers, particularly the late Lester Stone, for many years secretary to Mayor La-Guardia, told me that if I ran with Bill it would bring the LaGuardia legend of good government into the Tammany camp.

But I realized I could not possibly support O'Dwyer. I think it was at that point I decided to offer the voters of New York an independent ticket.

Just for fun I put the O'Dwyer possibility up to three friends. Bob Moses encouraged me to accept; Judge Seabury, the archangel of good government and archfoe of Tammany Hall, said that no matter what I ran for he was for me.

When I put the proposition up to LaGuardia, the Machiavellian flavor of it warmed his soul. His eyes flashed. Here was a twentieth-century political version of the Trojan horse strategy. "What an idea! I would jump at the chance to do this myself if I were twenty years younger. You can thumb your nose at the Republicans, and you'll surely be elected." Then his face fell, and he looked at me and said quietly, "No, Newbold, *you* can't do it. *You couldn't live with those people!*"

Then we went to work to put together a ticket. Judge Levine of the Bronx agreed to run for comptroller, Magistrate Peter Horn of Queens was drafted to run for president of the Council, Lt. Commander Byrnes Mac-Donald, with the U.S. Navy, radioed his acceptance as a candidate for president of the Borough of Manhattan, from the Third Fleet in the Pacific. Judge John F. X. Masterson joyously joined the team as candidate for president of the Borough of Brooklyn, and Tom Gray, a quiet, gentlemanly lawyer from Queens, ran for president from that Borough. Colonel Woodward of Staten Island completed the ticket, which was called the "No Deal" ticket because we were beholden to no bosses. That was LaGuardia's idea. Then came the problem of signatures to the independent nominating petitions to place our names on the voting machine. Dorothy Schiff, publisher of the New York *Post,* espoused our cause personally, editorially, and with many ideas. On the front page of the *Post* she ran a "box" daily, directing people to come to my office at City Hall for the purpose of signing the petition. I stayed at City Hall every night until ten o'clock while people lined up for this purpose. John Masterson recruited a group of friends and admirers in Brooklyn; I shall never forget the last day before the petitions had to be filed, when John and a few of his friends came in staggering under the burden of twenty thousand valid signatures from his borough.

O'Dwyer himself had difficulties in putting together a ticket. When Lazarus Joseph, a Jewish candidate from the Bronx, was selected for comptroller, it became desirable according to tradition to place on the ticket a candidate of Italian extraction from Manhattan. The question before Tammany Hall was "Where do we find an Italian from Manhattan?" This blending together of the various racial appeals is always figured out as scientifically by the politicians as a distiller blending his drinks. Everyone scratched his head over this one. No one came up with the answer. Time was running out. The hard-pressed politicians picked up a volume of the Official Directory of the City of New York, known as

the "Green Book," and thumbed through the listing of
city officers and employees until they stopped at the
name of Vincent Impellitteri, secretary to Supreme
Court Justice Gavagan. He was drafted as president of
the City Council. Within six years he entered City Hall
as mayor.

LaGuardia came out for me immediately, lending
his prestige to the "No Deal" ticket. He put his whole
heart and soul into the fight. Every morning during the
campaign he had breakfast with me and my running
mates at the Yale Club. I had my quarters there, largely
because we needed a quiet spot away from the political
hubbub to check our nominating petitions. The election law is full of technicalities on this point. If the
election district was listed incorrectly after any signature,
it was thrown out. We had literally to use a microscope
to read the numbers on the election board maps. I was
assisted by a couple of hundred friends who practically
wore out their eyes examining those petitions. Eventually we filed forty-six thousand signatures. We held
strategy meetings every morning from the middle of
September until election day. I was still working in
City Hall, and I put in a full day there, taking to the
campaign circuit nights.

I selected as my campaign manager Barent Ten Eyck,
one of the chief racket-busting aides of Tom Dewey
when he was district attorney. Influential backers of
Wendell Willkie during the 1940 election came out for
me; chief among them was Russell Davenport, Willkie's
leading aide.

I shall always remember Elsa Maxwell for her generous support. Glamour is a necessary ingredient of any

campaign to arouse the citizenry. But where was I going to get glamour? In early October, Elsa telephoned inviting me to a party she was giving at the Waldorf for me. When I arrived, I found among her guests Dorothy Thompson, Katherine Hepburn, Vincent Sheean, John Gunther, Ray Massey, and a number of other writers and actors. Elsa appealed to all of them to be available for radio broadcasts on my behalf. And then and there she collected a fund to arrange a series of programs on the air. These were the days before television, and Manya Novik was a volunteer in charge of production.

A few days afterward, Dorothy Thompson hired a sound truck, and together we toured the city stopping off at strategic locations. This resourceful and utterly charming journalist would gather the crowd and hold it with her oratory and then turn the meeting over to me. These were heart-warming incidents in an otherwise bleak campaign.

LaGuardia fought tooth and nail for us, delivering the most inspired addresses of his career, but deep down in his heart he knew that if I won out against the machines, it would be the political miracle of the century. Even the "splinter" parties gravitated into the orbit of the major political machines. The American Labor party joined Tammany in backing Bill O'Dwyer, and David Dubinsky's Liberal party allied itself with the Republicans. Organized labor which had united behind LaGuardia was split, but neither wing supported the candidate LaGuardia pleaded for as the only one who stood for his kind of government.

When the election returns came in, the era of reform was over, the experiment was at an end. O'Dwyer was elected the mayor of New York. But although I was a candidate without a party, running in an election rigged by the political machines, I received 21 per cent of the vote, considerably more than the polls had predicted. I received 408,408 votes for mayor, almost a hundred thousand more than the Republicans cast for Goldstein.

I have spent time dealing with the personalities of this election, not because the names are of intrinsic significance. The scars of the campaign have healed. I consider Judge Goldstein to be personally an able man and a good friend. I have told the story only because the bipartisan conspiracy employed to destroy bossless, liberal government in New York City is a classic instance of a pattern that continues to repeat itself throughout our municipal life.

As for LaGuardia—the rest of his story is brief. When he stepped out of City Hall on January 1, 1946, he had twenty months to live. Practically till the end, he remained active, stumping for causes. Shortly after leaving office, he was appointed by President Truman Director General of UNRRA to succeed Governor Lehman, and he tackled the job of distributing food to starving Europeans with typical gusto. He toured Europe, charming the natives with his optimism and flamboyancy. At home he warned farmers to stop hoarding food and to make available 700,000 tons of wheat monthly for transshipment. "We can plant wheat every year, but people who are starving die only once."

Upon leaving UNRRA, he was signed by commercial sponsors to continue the radio chats he had carried on so successfully as mayor. But LaGuardia, disregarding the sensitivity of his sponsors to advertising revenue,

ripped into certain vested interests with such energy
that one sponsor dropped him within six months.

Even after quitting City Hall, the ex-mayor refused
to run from a fight. Early one morning shortly after
O'Dwyer had been inaugurated, LaGuardia phoned
me. "Newbold, have you read the newspapers?"

It seemed that one of the New York daily tabloids
had run an editorial accusing him of having destroyed
certain records just before leaving office, to obliterate
traces of graft in his administration. I bought a copy of
the tabloid and read the editorial. It was a real mud-
slinger. One would think LaGuardia had been the very
devil shoving damning documents into a bonfire with a
pitchfork. The writer ended up by saying, "Up until
now we have accused 'Butch' of many things. But this
is the first time we have challenged his personal honesty."

When I phoned LaGuardia back, he said, "I'm going
to sue the sheet for two million dollars libel damages.
I want you to be my lawyer."

"We'll never get two million," I said. "Let's sue for
a more realistic sum, say three hundred thousand."

Shortly afterward I called on LaGuardia in his office.

"Fiorello, *have* you by any chance destroyed records
of your administration?"

"No," he returned emphatically. Then, after a pause:
"Wait, there was one time when I did. A letter reached
my desk from a correspondent informing me that a well-
known multimillionaire had crossed the state line into
New York with an actress for the purpose of sexual inter-
course. The informant asked me to start an investigation.
But I didn't care to poke my nose into the affair. I tore

the letter up and threw it into the wastepaper basket.
That is the only time I have destroyed a paper that has
crossed my desk."

He died before the case could be heard so I tried the
action for libel without him as a witness. The jury
brought in a verdict for us. The award was for six cents.
But LaGuardia had been vindicated.

In June of 1947, LaGuardia was hospitalized. It was
cancer. He lingered on during the summer in his home
in Riverdale, writing the early stages of his autobiography
and delivering his weekly broadcasts. However, during the final weeks he had no strength for the broadcasts, and I and other friends filled in as guests. When I
subbed over the air, LaGuardia lying upstairs in his
bed would listen to every word. After the program was
over he'd say, "No, no, Newbold! Put more hell into
your talk!"

His last days were exceedingly painful. When I
dropped in to visit him toward the end, I scarcely recognized the wasted little bundle of a man whose arm had
once been as strong as a blacksmith's and whose grip
could send a wince of pain through one.

After LaGuardia's death, accompanying Marie his
widow, I opened his safe deposit box, and was astonished
to discover that his total investments consisted of $8,000
in war bonds. It has been estimated that a Democratic
district leader in Manhattan takes in about a hundred
thousand dollars a year in "side business." There have
been few mayors who have been insensitive to the even
greater opportunities that come from operating out of
City Hall. But this man who had been chief of a multi-

million-dollar government for the longest period in New York's history, after his medical and funeral expenses had been paid, left as his sole, tangible property, and as an amazing testimony to his integrity, *some $8,000 in war bonds and a mortgaged house in Riverdale!*

CHAPTER 9   A Touch of Jimmy Walker with a Dash of FDR

WILLIAM O'DWYER, the new mayor of New York, his friends have told me, was able to discourse for hours on Byron, Keats and William Butler Yeats. And like Jimmy Walker before him, he was the victim of a political system that raised him to prominence. His career symbolizes the tragedy of a man caught in the Tammany way of life. Born in County Mayo, Ireland, Bill rose from the lowliest circumstances. He studied for the priesthood when he was sixteen. Upon landing in America, he took a job in the building trades, then became a bartender, and eventually entered the police department, pounding the toughest beat in Brooklyn, the gangster-ridden water front. In his free hours he attended law school, gained his degree and entered politics through the Tammany gateway. One of his early law partners was an alderman from a district dominated by the hoodlum Joe Adonis. In those days Adonis ran a restaurant patronized by bootleggers, gunmen and ward politicians of both major parties. Bill O'Dwyer got to know people that he was unable to shake off through the years. When he was appointed to a magistrate's bench, he had the backing of a district leader who, according to the Kefauver Committee Report, was a close friend of Adonis. O'Dwyer rose to be a county judge, and then in 1939 ran for the office of district attorney of Kings County. He was elected; and he chose for his confidential assistant James J. Moran, a man who possessed no legal training whatsoever for the post. Moran had been a good-natured attendant in Brooklyn courtrooms. The O'Dwyer-Moran collaboration produced some peculiar results in regard to the Brooklyn water-front situation. John Harlem Amen, a special investigator appointed by Governor Dewey, had uncovered evidence that mobsters held top offices in the water-front unions and extorted millions of dollars from the workers. At O'Dwyer's request, Amen turned his evidence over to the district attorney's office, *whereupon the water-front investigation was abruptly stopped.* After Pearl Harbor, O'Dwyer left office to serve in the army, where he rose to be brigadier general and was assigned by President Roosevelt as head of the Economic Division of the Allied Control Commission in Italy. Meanwhile he had been re-elected district attorney during his absence and, resuming the office in 1945, he resigned to run for mayor of New York.

Governor Dewey appointed George J. Beldock to succeed him as district attorney. Beldock discovered that conditions on the water front continued to be deplorable. He immediately dismissed O'Dwyer's appointee, James J. Moran. Beldock uncovered evidence of extortion and embezzlement of union funds that had previously been made available to O'Dwyer's office by union members, but upon which O'Dwyer had taken no action. Beldock convened a special grand jury. When O'Dwyer was called before it, he explained that he had dropped the water-front investigation because a more important matter had engaged his attention and needed the full deployment of his staff. This was the investigation of Murder Inc., a national crime syndicate that had organized murder as a big business. While O'Dwyer broke up the syndicate, he prosecuted none of the top leaders.

Furthermore, O'Dwyer had what he himself admitted was a "perfect murder case" against Albert Anastasia, chief lieutenant of Joe Adonis, and rumored to have been one of the chief killers in Murder Inc.

On the morning of May 25, 1939, an aged man, Moshe Diamond, was shot dead on a Brooklyn street as the result of an underworld feud. O'Dwyer placed in "protective custody" Abe Reles, a member of Murder Inc., who confessed that the murder had been planned in his house. He implicated Anastasia and a trigger man named Parisi. Yet this star witness, the man who could have sent Anastasia to the chair, was himself silenced in a most amazing manner. On the morning of November 12, although six policemen were keeping him under guard on the sixth floor of a Coney Island Hotel, the body of the gangster was found dead on a roof below the hotel window. Police Captain Frank C. Bals, in charge of the guard, claimed that Reles had leaped to his death. How he got away with six policemen watching him has never been satisfactorily explained. Indeed, millions of New Yorkers, the Kings County Grand Jury, and the Kefauver Committee that later investigated the case, wonder whether Reles hadn't been *pushed* out of the window by a person or persons interested in quashing the case against Anastasia. O'Dwyer, who had not taken the precaution of bringing Reles before a grand jury to record his testimony under oath, now dropped the case against Anastasia for lack of evidence. Six months later, it was discovered that the "wanted" cards of the men involved in the Anastasia crimes had been removed from the police files. Elwood J. Divers, a police sergeant in charge of them, swore under oath that he had been ordered to remove them by James Moran, O'Dwyer's ubiquitous assistant.

Much of this information concerning O'Dwyer's background previous to his being nominated by the Democrats for mayor was gradually revealed to the people of New York after he was elected to office. It was brought out, for instance, by the Kefauver Committee, that shortly before the 1945 nomination, while O'Dwyer was still in the army, he visited Frank Costello, prime minister of the underworld, at his Park Avenue apartment. Michael Kennedy, the boss of Tammany Hall, was present at this meeting; and also the remarkable Mr. Moran, along with several other Tammany politicians. One of O'Dwyer's associates testified before the committee that a politician had to get Frank Costello's okay before he could receive the Democratic nomination for mayor of New York.

"I saw no impropriety in going to Costello's home, and I see none now," O'Dwyer informed the committee. He admitted that he had been friendly for years with one Irving Sherman, whom he knew to be a friend of Costello and Joe Adonis. Sherman visited James J. Moran frequently in City Hall, always, it was said, being announced as Dr. Cooper. Sherman, upon being called before the committee, conceded that he knew Louis "Lepke" Buchalter and Jacob "Gurrah" Shapiro, members of Murder Inc., who died in Sing Sing. A telephone repairman testified under oath that when O'Dwyer entered City Hall, Sherman asked him to examine the mayor's wires to determine whether they were being tapped. He performed the same chore for Frank Costello.

This, then, was Bill O'Dwyer, whom fate and Tammany had tapped to bring New York back to a regime of business as usual. One must bear in mind the political background against which O'Dwyer emerged into prominence. There was a direct nerve connection between the political happenings in New York and Washington.

In April, 1945, Harry Truman had become President of the United States. To few public men could the adage be more justly applied than to Truman, "I can defend myself against my enemies, but God protect me from my friends!" When Truman nominated Ed Pauley, a California oil lobbyer, to become Secretary of the Navy, the Senate Naval Affairs Committee, remembering Teapot Dome, rebuked the President, and Secretary of the Interior Ickes quit his post. Truman named William Boyle, an old Pendergast associate, to be chairman of the Democratic National Committee and, in opening the post to this man, he boosted the former incumbent, J. Howard McGrath, into the office of Attorney General of the United States. McGrath had been governor of a state that had been wide open to gambling, whose police force was riddled with influence-peddling and graft. McGrath may have personally been no more responsible for this than Governor Dewey, for instance, was personally responsible for corruption in Saratoga Springs. Nevertheless, why couldn't the ex-governor of a state in which citizens were machine-gunned on the streets have

been given a less sensitive post than that of chief law enforcement officer of the nation?

Mr. Truman's political troubles were further multiplied when on another level the Republicans achieved
an overwhelming victory in the congressional elections
of 1946. Thenceforth, a coalition of the Dixiecrats and
right-wing Republicans in Congress was able to block
any legislation disagreeable to it, and all pretense at two
parties battling genuinely over issues was at an end. Of
course the Republican and Democratic organizations
continued to shadowbox with one another for the edifi-
cation of the voter who still had old-fashioned ideas about
democracy. But anyone at all sophisticated knew that the
boys were living together.

It was against this background of negativism in Washington that the O'Dwyer satellite operated in New York.

Incidentally, this suspension of bipartisan government on Capitol Hill was, as we have pointed out before,
a well-recognized phenomenon locally. O'Dwyer's administration was at one point saved from an investigation similar to Walker's by the intervention of the
Republican leader of the state senate who was a close
friend of O'Dwyer. The Democratic assembly leader in
Albany carried on a business, on the side, with the Republican leader of Nassau County. The Republican
chairman of the powerful Ways and Means Committee
in the state legislature was the board member of a firm
with which a leading Democrat was connected. One
prominent Democrat was a law associate of the Republican leader of Manhattan. When I was politically wet
behind the ears, I used to be shocked to find at social
gatherings, Democratic and Republican clubhouse pol-

iticians huddling with their arms around one another.
And then I came to realize that there was nothing illogi-
cal about this. These boys were in the same business.
Just as suit and cloakers from Bridgeport, Jersey City,
and the Bronx fraternize at conventions to drum up
business, politicians do the same. This fools nobody but
the American voter.

This collusion between the parties not only breeds
corruption, but illiberalism. For there is a definite connection between the two. Government officials up to
their necks in machine politics cannot possibly provide
the people with a forward-looking administration. They
are too busy keeping the machine well oiled to look out
for the interests of the people.

Personally, O'Dwyer is a man of charm and is an
extremely likable person. When he entered City Hall,
he set out to cultivate a good many well-meaning citizens.
Even former LaGuardia supporters and personal friends
of mine were captivated by him during his "honeymoon"
period in office before his past began to catch up with
him. One person went so far as to inform me that
O'Dwyer had the wit of Jimmy Walker and the soul
of Franklin Roosevelt.

Shortly before leaving City Hall, LaGuardia appointed
me to serve an unexpired term on the New York City
Planning Commission, and on a number of occasions I
met and talked with Bill O'Dwyer. The first time I saw
him after the 1945 campaign was at Grover Whalen's
home. The mayor-elect put his arm around my shoulders.
"We have so many friends in common, Newbold, we
ought to get along pretty well together." My term expired in 1947, but Mayor O'Dwyer did not appoint a

successor until February of 1948. After my retirement
from the Commission, he gave me a farewell party at
Gracie Mansion, his official home. He invited the borough presidents, the commissioners of borough works,
the chief engineer of the Board of Estimate, the planning
commissioners, and various people with whom I had
worked for many years. When he invited me for seven
o'clock in the evening, I said, "Bill, I hope you won't
mind if I am a few minutes late. I have a radio broadcast at N.B.C. which is over at exactly that hour."

Just before the program got under way in the studio,
the announcer told me that I could slip away at two
minutes to seven before the commercial. I took off my
wrist watch and placed it by the microphone to make
certain that I would depart promptly. And in my hurry
to leave the studio, I left my watch behind.

The mayor greeted me at the door of Gracie Mansion.
"You're late, Newbold, do you realize what time it is?"
I looked at my wrist and discovered that my watch was
missing. I told the mayor I must have mislaid it and that
occasionally I was careless about watches. I related that
when I was president of the Council, I once had put my
grandfather's gold watch and chain in my desk drawer
before going upstairs to a Board of Estimate meeting.
Upon returning to my office, I opened the drawer and
found it missing. I never recovered the watch although
the police searched every pawnshop in town.

Shortly after my arrival, we sat down to dinner. While
I was engaged in conversation with Jim Lyons, borough
president of the Bronx, I heard the sound of a siren outside. The door opened and a motorcycle policeman
walked up to the mayor, saluted him, and handed him a

package, which he put in his pocket. Then the mayor rapped on a glass for quiet and rose at his place. He declared that he had invited his guests to dinner to say good-by to me since I was retiring from the city payroll after fourteen years in public office. He added that some friends of mine, learning of the occasion, had gotten together and sent something to be presented to me as a token of their affection. At this point, the mayor reached into his pocket and handed me a package—it was my wrist watch!

"One thing I want to tell you friends of Newbold," added the mayor. "He is very careless about his personal belongings. Some years ago he lost a valuable heirloom at City Hall, and under a reform administration he never recovered it. Tonight he left his wrist watch somewhere, and he got it back in twenty minutes—and under a Tammany administration!"

This was Bill O'Dwyer in action. Is it any wonder it took the people of New York so long to get angry at him?

CHAPTER 10   God Made So Few Republicans!

LIKE Jimmy Walker before him, Mayor O'Dwyer entered City Hall on a boom of war-induced prosperity. During his term in office, industrial wages over the country went up 85 per cent over depression years. Everything went up, including real estate valuations and consequently taxes. Hotels, restaurants and night clubs were packed. Sales of luxury items reached a new high.

However, despite this flow of easy money, New Yorkers and indeed all Americans were entering a period of anxiety. The world had been launched into the atomic era. Communist Russia had gobbled up the countries of Eastern Europe and had imposed a blockade on Berlin that threatened momentarily to develop into a third world war. New Yorkers made merry with the desperate urgency of children who whistle as they pass a graveyard in the night. On the one hand they danced to the clattering tunes of *Annie Get Your Gun;* on the other hand they sought comfort in Rabbi Liebman's *Peace of Mind* and an outpouring of similar books.

In Washington, Whittaker Chambers had stunned a congressional committee by accusing Alger Hiss of being a Communist spy. President Truman startled the world by getting re-elected. He had lost the right wing of the Democratic party because he couragcously espoused a civil rights program in an election year. He lost his left wing which flocked to the standard of Henry Wallace on the Progressive party ticket. At Columbia University, General Eisenhower was preparing for a greater assignment.

In the meantime, while New Yorkers were busy scanning the international horizon, the bosses took over City Hall under their noses. Bill O'Dwyer inherited vast powers. But, as time passed, he made some very curious appointments. He appointed to the post of Seventh Deputy Police Commissioner Captain Frank Bals, the man who had chosen the six cops who watched over gangster Abe Reles in the Half Moon Hotel, the morning Reles was killed and the case against Anastasia vanished. After the appointment, O'Dwyer confessed that the post which had been vacant for some time had no particular function and needed no occupant. He admitted that the appointment of this cop who was under heavy suspicion was a mistake. He dismissed Bals after two and a half months of service—and retired him on a deputy commissioner's pension, providing $1,000 more salary per year than he had earned on active duty!

Mayor O'Dwyer appointed as deputy commissioner of the Department of Hospitals Philip Zichello, whose brother-in-law was Willie Moretti, one of the leaders of Murder Inc. In October 1950, Moretti was killed by two gunmen in a Newark saloon. When O'Dwyer was asked by the Kefauver Committee whether he couldn't have found someone more suitable than Zichello for the hospital job, he replied, "I could have found a hundred. But there are some things you have to do politically if you want cooperation."

Some years previously, New Yorkers were shocked to learn that Judge Thomas Aurelio, upon being made a judge, phoned Frank Costello to express his thanks to the racketeer for swinging the nomination to him. "Now," added Aurelio, "we have to take care of Joe [Loscalzo]." O'Dwyer appointed him to the magistrate's court.

But the shining appointment was O'Dwyer's elevation of his Man Friday, James J. Moran, to the profitable office of First Deputy Fire Commissioner. Moran became the presiding genius over a system of graft and extortion that would have warmed the cockles of old Boss Tweed's heart. It was brought out after his arrest that Moran, among other things, had shaken down New Yorkers to the tune of half a million dollars for the approval of new oil-burner installations.

Before Moran was indicted and ousted from public office by O'Dwyer's successor, O'Dwyer had given him a presumably lifetime job as water supply commissioner. Moran was found guilty by a jury on twenty-three counts of extortion and one of conspiracy. And he was convicted of perjury on five counts. His prison sentences totaled a maximum of twenty-eight years.

Under Bill O'Dwyer, the gangsters returned to town again, taking up where they had left off twelve years before. Some of them, like Costello, moved into the swankiest apartments, attended the Metropolitan Opera and first nights at the theatre, and generally behaved like members of the international set. Two of them actually sent their sons to West Point through the recommendation of a puppet congressman. But the sins of the fathers should not be visited upon the sons.

And the lower echelons of the Big Fix worked busily and smoothly. During O'Dwyer's term in office, the general cost of living rose 57 per cent above the level of the LaGuardia days. But the cost of city government went up more than 100 per cent. New Yorkers paid millions of dollars a year for the padded salaries, the graft and the pay-offs of the politicians and gangsters operating in and around City Hall.

Housewives were systematically victimized by the Big Fix along the water front which sent up the price of food imported into the city to unprecedented heights. Gullible wage earners were fleeced of their take-home pay and their bank savings by the organized gamblers who ran a city-wide bookmaking circuit directed by the underworld. The narcotics business throve and claimed for its customers more juveniles than ever before in our history. Money that could have been spent for education was sluiced away mysteriously into the gravy train. A substantial number of the city's children were sent to public schools that were firetraps; even the better schools were overcrowded.

Forgotten were LaGuardia's plans, worked out in great detail before he retired, to renovate and remodel and expand the city's public hospital system. Forgotten was his project for erecting a wholesale terminal market in Manhattan which, operated by the city, would reduce the cost of overhead, handling and transportation of food, and bring edibles right to the breakfast table at a savings of millions of dollars to the consumer.

Most tragic of all, the whole educational system was shot through with dirty politics. The key posts in the Board of Education were being held by Tammany stooges, and these had hired as their assistants former political district captains at $3,500 a year and up. Striking evidence of this tie-up between education and politics was forthcoming when O'Dwyer ran for re-election. Advertisements appeared in the newspapers urging teachers to visit their Tammany district leaders immediately to bargain for an increase in salary with the votes they could deliver in the election. It is a sad comment that any of these teachers were compelled to strike a deal with Tammany in their struggle for financial security. Just as shocking were political contributions from Police and Fire Department organizations—the first time in history.

The corruption of our educational system is a symptom of the antiliberalism that lies at the heart of the political machine. There were specific impulsive actions of O'Dwyer's, too, that illustrated that a man who is bossed politically is not a free agent in any sphere. When the Prime Minister of Ulster visited New York, O'Dwyer refused to welcome him at City Hall, permitting his personal (and quite understandable) prejudices with regard to Irish national affairs to interfere with his judgment as an official of New York City. When a Hollywood producer attempted to shoot a film in New York whose theme was personally distasteful to the mayor, he banned the producer from using the city as a background, exercising a petulant dictatorship over the project. Bill O'Dwyer, basically a well-meaning fellow, was vulnerable to the mood of the witch hunt that had begun to possess so many Americans, because he had already been corrupted on other counts. The tragedy of this stampede to the right is that it sweeps along, not only the anti-social, but the well-intentioned as well.

As Mayor O'Dwyer's first term came to a close, many of my friends urged me to oppose him for re-election. The matter required careful thought. Having run once for the office of mayor, unsuccessfully as an Independent, I felt strongly that whoever was to be the anti-Tammany candidate should be able to command the confidence, enthusiasm and support of all the forces of good government. Naturally, I hoped that my party would return to a position of leadership in organizing a Fusion movement. I knew that there were two aggressive candidates for the Republican nomination and both were personal friends of mine. One was Congressman Jacob K. Javits and the other was Edward Corsi, Commissioner of Labor of the State of New York. Partly because of my personal esteem for these two men and partly because I was skeptical about the possibility for the Republican nomination since I bolted the party municipal ticket in 1945, I decided to make no overtures for any nomination. Not having been abroad since 1931, and without a vacation for many years, my wife and I left for a two-month trip to Europe.

By the time we returned, a committee composed of Republicans and Liberals under the chairmanship of Charles H. Tuttle was in continuous session, making an effort to bring about a coalition of the two parties behind a Fusion ticket. When we landed, a number of reporters told me it looked as if I were the only candidate for mayor that both parties could agree on. Out of these conferences finally came a ticket for the three city-wide offices. I was to be designated for the office of mayor; Harry Uviller, member of the Liberal party and an impartial chairman in the Ladies' Garment Industry, was designated for the office of comptroller. For the office of the president of the Council, the nominee was to be Judge Matthew Diserio, a LaGuardia appointee to the Court of Domestic Relations, and a good Republican. From then on it became increasingly difficult to find agreement between the two parties on the candidacy for presidents of the five boroughs. It was my hope that young Oren Root would be acceptable to both parties for the office of borough president of Manhattan, but Robert Wagner, Jr., was the Democratic choice and the Liberal party decided to support him. The two parties came together for a choice of Abe Stark for the office of president of the Borough of Brooklyn and with Abe, Fusion ceased. Each party went its own way in the Bronx, Queens and Richmond. This lack of cooperation greatly weakened the bold united Fusion front.

A forlorn little incident ocurred shortly after I learned that I was to be a candidate for mayor. I called my old friend Tom Curran, Republican Chairman of New York County, to thank him for his confidence in me. He was forthright in telling me that his first choice had been Ed Corsi but that the organization would work hard for my candidacy. I thought to myself perhaps it was Johnny Crews, Republican Chairman of Kings County, who had pushed me through as a Republican candidate. Johnny was equally frank, explaining that his first choice was Corsi. The other county chairmen had the same response and I wondered how I could possibly have been acceptable to the Republican party if every Republican leader had preferred Corsi. Ed's turn came, only a year later when a special election was held following the abdication of Mayor O'Dwyer. This favorite son of the Republican organization received but a little more than 382,000 votes, out of a total vote cast of more than 2,500,000, and with a Republican enrollment of 566,000 voters.

With this response from the Republican leadership my spirits were understandably not lifted. In an effort to show my appreciation for the nomination, I wondered if perhaps it was Governor Dewey's intercession which had brought about my candidacy. But a couple of months later when I had a conference with the governor I asked him how it was possible for me to have been designated when the Republican organization had indicated preference for another. Although Dewey and I have never been intimately associated, we had both originally been elected to high public office in 1937. Before that we had served as idealistic young Republicans on the board of governors of the Young Republican Club. We dreamed of a brave new world with a progressive Republican party, calling for new blood in the ranks. I did not think that Tom could have held it against me that I came out for Wendell Willkie for the Republican nomination in 1940. He was always a good trouper and even if he did harbor resentment, he certainly remained friendly. At least on the surface. He and the late Kenneth Simpson also had differences of opinion and of course Simpson was entirely responsible for Joe McGoldrick and me being nominated on the various party tickets in the city election of 1937. After that meeting with the governor I realized that the enthusiasm and support for my candidacy must have come from Adolf Berle, David

Dubinsky, president of the Ladies' Garment Workers Union, and Alex Rose, president of the Hat, Cap and Milliners Union. These three members of the Liberal party opened up their hearts to the ticket in the campaign and poured forth resources which matched their enthusiasm. Dubinsky is a tough-minded idealist, a man who had come up the hard way, subdued the Communists who attempted to take over control of some of the locals in his union.

Once I visited Unity House, a vast resort in the mountains where workers in the garment industry could spend a summer vacation. For extremely low rates all kinds of activity were provided. Shortly after I arrived on a hot summer evening, Dubinsky took me through the new dining hall in which five thousand people could eat at a time, showed me the tennis courts, the bridle paths, the lake where there was swimming, boating and fishing, and, on its banks, a natural amphitheatre in which symphony concerts were held. As a fresh breeze coming off the water rustled through the pine boughs, he looked up at me and said with an infectious grin, "You have had the world for a long time. Now it is *our* turn." I couldn't help smiling as I wondered whether in Dubinsky's mind I loomed as a feudal lord, a master of capital, or (perish the thought!) a manufacturer of ladies' apparel. Well, I suppose it was true. For generations we had had "our turn."

The campaign for mayor was a bitter one, and it was waged against the backdrop of a turbulent senatorial campaign. Ailing Senator Robert Wagner, the sponsor of Roosevelt's labor legislation, had retired and left a vacancy in the office. The Democratic party prevailed upon Herbert Lehman to run for this seat in a special election. The Republican party nominated John Foster Dulles, now Secretary of State.

The odd-numbered years were reserved for municipal campaigns. This special election deprived the people from focusing attention upon municipal government. I decided on the outset to resist every attempt on the part of the Democrats to be drawn into the Lehman-Dulles fight. Obviously the mayor would use the Lehman candidacy to the utmost in order to further his own re-election.

Before the municipal campaign reached intensity and bitterness there was a prelude with a very human note. I was about to hold one of my early press conferences when the telephone rang and I recognized the voice of Gertrude Keane calling from City Hall. She was a career secretary and I knew her when she was on LaGuardia's staff. I was astonished when she said the mayor would like to talk to me. In a moment Bill's voice came over the wire, bluff and hearty as usual. He told me that he had just heard about my wife's illness and that he would like to send up an iron lung to help her.

Somewhat surprised, I told him that an iron lung is not used in the treatment of tuberculosis. "Oh," he answered, "I heard it was the dreadful polio. Well, I would like to help out no matter what it is." I thanked His Honor and told him that his offer brought tears to my eyes—an embarrassing situation since I was about to go downstairs for a press conference at which I was prepared to "knock his block off."

"Keep punching, Newbold," he answered. "After it is all over we will get together and have a drink."

Well, I never did have that drink. The campaign got too hot and I suppose it ended whatever was left of our beautiful friendship. The waters which I stirred up in the campaign rose to spill over the dam when the Kefauver Senate Committee came into New York shortly after.

I do not believe I have ever had any personal feeling against O'Dwyer. He just couldn't buck the rules of the game. It saddened me to realize that here was a man who commenced in adversity and reached the pinnacle of success. Up to a point his life could well have fitted into the American dream of any boy seeking to emulate Horatio Alger. Starting with nothing in the world but good health, a sense of humor and ambition, he finally was elected mayor of his city by an overwhelming vote. But he never could shake off the sinister forces which helped him on his way.

In the campaign I hit hard at organized gambling. The extent of gambling in the United States is almost unbelievable. When LaGuardia entered office, he discovered in a survey that the sum of money white-collar and working-class New Yorkers were spending on slot machines *in a single month during the depression* was equal to the money kings and millionaires gambled away at Monte Carlo *during the entire boom year of 1928!* And slot machines were merely one outlet for gambling in New York.

I knew from friends on the police force of the extent of bookmakers' operations. As a private citizen there was nothing I could do to prove charges; yet I knew there were thousands of "horse parlors" throughout the five boroughs. In fact, as I toured the city of New York, speaking on street corners while I indicated with my thumb that a bookie ran an establishment around the corner, everyone laughed—they realized what I meant. Brooklyn is known as "the City of Churches" and I knew a number of clergymen from the borough. I asked a few of them if they would go to some of the addresses which I received from a police captain, just to see for themselves. But they were not inclined to get involved, particularly during a political campaign. So, my friend Leon "Buck" Sachter, a veteran of World War II, enlisted a group of young veterans. He brought me back sworn statements that they had visited 165 betting establishments in Brooklyn alone. It was possible to take only a sampling. I announced the addresses publicly and, looking back on it, I am amused to remember the comment of Police Commissioner O'Brien. He said the list was out of date! Of course it was. As soon as I announced it the bookies moved.

One of these bookmakers came to see me at my headquarters at the Hotel Astor. He told me that he operated a small cigar store and that his wife's illness had run through his savings. In order to pay the bills, he decided to do a little business on the side as a bookmaker for just a short time. It wasn't long, he said, before the big shot mobsters moved in to make him join the "syndicate." The bookmaker must pay the "banker" $500 a day in order to stay in business, "or else."

I have never been against bookmaking for blue-nose sentiments, but for very practical reasons. I don't worry about the millionaire playboy who can afford it. But the average gambler who bets on horses through the corner bookie can't win over a period of time. The take-

home pay of the average wage earner who plays the
ponies isn't sufficient to absorb his losses. Sooner or
later, gambling means no milk for the children of the
house. It means a new victim for the loan sharks and the
thugs who collect on the IOU's. The morning after I
went on the air to attack bookmaking in New York, I
received dozens of letters from widows, wives and children of men whose passion for playing the ponies had
wrecked their homes.

Later, Miles McDonald, the courageous District Attorney in Brooklyn, began a comprehensive investigation
of the situation. The top brass in the police department
resisted him, but he painstakingly documented what I
had declared to be a fact—that there was a widespread
partnership between organized gamblers and some of
"New York's Finest." He went even deeper and uncovered a rags-to-riches story that was a shocking per-
version of the American fable. He introduced the public
to Harry Gross, a stumpy little smart aleck from Brooklyn who, eleven years previously, had opened up a horse
parlor in a private garage. Gross was a go-getter and in
order to stay in business, he learned that he would have
to cut the police into his operations. Before Harry was
retired from business, he had taken in twenty million
dollars, had acquired thirty-five horse parlors, employed
four hundred in help, and paid the police one million
dollars a year for protection. Key police from inspectors
down to the cop on the beat and platoons of detectives
were cut in on the "ice." Gross, under McDonald's questioning, charged that a former police commissioner and
a former chief inspector received the top salaries. The
others received monthly wages according to their rank.

Whenever Harry wished to add a new parlor to his chain, he contacted police headquarters and gave the location of the proposed place so that the cops could investigate and see if he would be hampering the business of any other bookie in the neighborhood. And if the okay was given, he would open for trade. On one occasion, Gross lost heavily in gambling and he couldn't pay off his horse customers. He fled to California. But the cops had no intention of being separated from their gravy train. When Harry returned to New York, the police advanced him money to go back into business, and soon everybody prospered again.

When the cops got wind that Gross was "singing" to McDonald after his arrest, a hundred and fifty of them resigned suddenly or went into retirement hoping to avert personal investigation. But a number of cops were indicted and brought to trial. After posing as a cooperative witness, Gross suddenly balked and refused to go through with his testimony on the stand. Because of a constitutional provision which protected the accused from being tried twice on the same charge, the cops had to be freed.

Eventually a large number of them were dismissed from their jobs as a result of departmental trials. But the law had been successfully flaunted.

During the campaign I hammered away at Frank Costello over the radio. I charged that Costello was a power behind the government; that no Democrat could get a nomination to city office without his approval. Costello's slot machine empire had been cut to pieces by LaGuardia, and he had been kicked across the Hudson clear down to New Orleans, where he opened for new business. But with LaGuardia's retirement Costello had renewed his lease on City Hall.

Costello, disliking the publicity I was giving him, suddenly slipped out of town and made a beeline for Hot Springs, Arkansas. Before he left, however, a friend ran into him. "What's eating Morris?" he is reported to have asked. "I'm only a businessman. If he wants a financial contribution I'll give him one." In addition to Costello's trying to quiet me, unsuccessfully, a Costello emissary offered a reporter on a New York newspaper $1,500 to stop writing about him.

This man Costello certainly got around. In 1948, during his race for Congress on the Liberal party ticket, Franklin Roosevelt, Jr., had charged that Costello had used his influence to prevent him from being nominated by the Democratic party. "When we have a situation where a Costello can tell a Roosevelt that he can't run on the Democratic ticket," young FDR declared heatedly, "I, a Democrat, thank God for the Liberal party."

Throughout the campaign, I challenged Mayor O'Dwyer to a public debate. I offered to meet him any place, on the steps of City Hall, in Carnegie Hall, the Copacabana Club, or even hanging on the strap of a crowded subway train, to put certain questions to him face to face. His Honor refused the invitation. While I couldn't meet the mayor in a personal match, I continued to pound away at his record. I dramatized to the people instances of how special privilege was making suckers out of them. I told, for example, the story of one Bronx Democrat who bought a garage for a cash outlay of $35,000 and parlayed it into $200,000. Although the city director of Real Estate had stated that the property was assessed at $220,000, the Tammany Board of Estimate authorized its sale to a corporation controlled by this Bronx Democrat for $35,000. The police cooperated by handing out parking tickets all over the area to force automobiles into this fellow's garage. And his enterprise prospered exceedingly well.

Before the campaign was over, President Truman turned a state visit into a whistle-stop appearance for the mayor. He had scheduled a "nonpolitical" appearance to preside over the laying of the cornerstone for the new United Nations building. To enable the greatest number of people to see him, it was first proposed that the President would ride up Seventh Avenue through the heart of the garment district. But O'Dwyer's advisers pointed out that Dubinsky, the president of the International Ladies' Garment Workers, was one of my supporters and that a huge "Vote for Morris" banner was strung across Seventh Avenue. So, I heard, the President's advisers rerouted the procession to pass up Fifth Avenue instead.

During the closing stages of the campaign, O'Dwyer was invited to a beefsteak dinner at the National Democratic Club. One of the guests was Frank Erickson, the gambler. LaGuardia had driven Erickson along with Costello out of town. (He had investigated the gambler's finances and had found that, among other things, he had banked millions of dollars in eleven years.)

When O'Dwyer entered the club for dinner, Erickson held out his hand to greet him. As the news cameras got set to snap pictures, the mayor's aides swarmed in to block off the view. O'Dwyer walked quickly by the outstretched hand to a dinner that was unquestionably not easily digested by him.

The president of the Democratic Club "couldn't understand" the excitement this episode stirred up in the press. "Erickson has been a member of the club for fifteen years or more. He has the same privileges as the other guests. There is no reason why he shouldn't have attended the dinner." (Shortly after this remark, Erickson was sent to the penitentiary.)

O'Dwyer won the election. He received 1,266,000 votes. I received 956,000. Vito Marcantonio, Labor party candidate, polled 356,626 votes.

Under O'Dwyer's administration City Hall was no longer the seat of government. It was a political headquarters. The law of the jungle prevailed. District leaders who supported him loyally were doled out patronage. District leaders who did not support O'Dwyer were not "recognized." Recognition means that the district leader thus smiled upon is able to obtain jobs for the faithful who in turn support him. Since the days of Andrew Jackson this system has been known as the spoils system. Our fellow citizens accept this as inevitable, shrug their shoulders and become preoccupied with their own personal lives and problems. It is not confined to any party and those in public office who defy this system almost inevitably find themselves retired to private life.

The patronage system of course is employed by high-minded statesmen as a club with which to push through legislative programs. Roosevelt used it with dexterity; he punished and even "purged" members of Congress who rebelled against party discipline. President Eisenhower will doubtless find the effectiveness of the patronage system a means to finding support for his policies. The appointment of forty thousand postmasters in the United States is quite a source of power in the presidential hands. Of course such a weapon is unheard of in modern times in Great Britain. Every government job is in the career service. One great advance in our own Federal Government was the placing of Collectors of Internal Revenue under Civil Service. At least this field has been removed from the huge reservoir of political "spoils."

The method of electing Council members by proportional representation was abolished during the O'Dwyer administration and the first Council elected from districts gave the city a legislative body with twenty-four organization Democrats and Stanley Isaacs, the lone minority member who was elected with the support of the Republican and Liberal parties. Back to the old Board of Aldermen!

The Republicans always have expressed one compelling explanation for continuing as a minority party in New York City. So many Republicans leaders in New York City have told me through the years that there just aren't enough voters who enroll in the Republican party. In 1949, for instance, when Mayor O'Dwyer defeated me by a margin of some 300,000 votes there were but 484,722 enrolled Republicans out of 2,775,636 registered voters. It seems that mortality is constantly taking its toll of the Republicans and the Lord just doesn't make enough new ones to fill in the ranks! Of course, I cannot agree with this rationalization. I don't believe that the future of reform depends solely upon the birth of staunch Republicans. LaGuardia's twelve years in City Hall can be offered in rebuttal, and of course we cannot begrudge Tammany its talent for tabbing three out of four babies born in the city. Perhaps the climate upstate agrees with Republicans. They thrive better in rural areas!

I cannot judge the Republican party's performance in serving the cause of good government without recalling that it was that party which launched an investigation of New York City when Franklin Roosevelt was Democratic governor of New York but when the legislature was in the control of the Republicans. I also will not forget that it was the Republican party which, having set the stage for the great reform movement of 1933, nominated LaGuardia and a Fusion ticket that resulted in cleaning Tammany out of City Hall, restoring the city's credit with the bankers and even more important giving New Yorkers a feeling of pride and elation in the knowledge that it was not only the largest but the best-governed city in the United States. Of course, it was a disappointment to realize that the Republicans in Albany did not assert this leadership and that they maintained a curious hands-off attitude with regard to the O'Dwyer administration. It remained even more difficult to explain to the bystander that it was the Democrats, Senator Kefauver, District Attorneys McDonald in Brooklyn and Hogan in Manhattan, who lifted the lid for a glimpse of what went on behind the scenes during the Tammany renaissance. Sworn statements, under oath, and projected on television, shocked the city. Equally mysterious was the O'Dwyer deference and kid-gloves attitude toward the powers that be in Albany. Without the facts before me I can only surmise upon this state of affairs and reflect upon the vagaries of politics in the Empire State.

A month after the election, and before his second inauguration, O'Dwyer entered Bellevue Hospital in a state of thorough exhaustion. The public learned many months later—though the secret was well kept at the time—that while at Bellevue, O'Dwyer had made out an application to retire from office. Close friends got wind of this and promptly interceded. They pointed out to him that he would be breaking faith with the voters (to say nothing of his political associates) if he were to quit right after he had been elected to a second term.

O'Dwyer listened to these arguments and withdrew the application. To newsmen who had heard the grapevine reports and asked him point-blank about retiring, he replied, "It is utterly ridiculous. It touches my sense of humor."

Suddenly the resourceful Mr. Flynn appeared in the role of O'Dwyer's good angel. He had long known of the mayor's wish to retire. He made an unpublicized trip to the White House and prevailed upon President Truman to hand O'Dwyer a one-way ticket out of New York. On August 16, 1950, the President announced that he had nominated O'Dwyer to be the United States ambassador to Mexico.

To reporters who besieged him for elucidation, the mayor was the soul of discretion.

"Why did you resign as mayor?" he was asked.

"I wanted to."

"Will you elaborate?"

"That speaks for itself."

"Is there any particular significance in your resigning at this time?"

"I am resigning."

This exchange took place after O'Dwyer on eight previous occasions had stated publicly that he would never quit office. Vincent Impellitteri read in the papers that he had become acting mayor.

Eddie Flynn (may his soul rest in peace; he has left us since), had as usual wangled things for his dear old alma mater, the Democratic party. Nineteen hundred and fifty was the year of the state gubernatorial race. Tom Dewey was certain to run for re-election. Eddie realized that if he got O'Dwyer out of office (before September, the deadline for such matters), a special mayoralty election would bring out a heavy Democratic vote in the city, and this might be the decisive factor in putting the Democratic nominee for governor into office. As things turned out Dewey won the election anyway, with a tremendous vote of confidence. The Flynn candidate for mayor was defeated by Impellitteri, the president of the Council and acting mayor, who ran as an "independent" and earned an unexpected victory. I don't think I am unjustified in putting quotation marks around the term independent. The voters little realized, although I tried to tell them, in my support of poor Ed Corsi, that the "Impy" candidacy was nothing more than one side of an intraparty dispute; that the Flynn forces supported Judge Pecora and the anti-Flynn forces supported Impellitteri. So huge is the Democratic party in New York that the bosses can afford to commit mayhem on each other and yet Tammany has almost always survived—except in our own time when a little man with a stout heart and a shrewd sense of politics kept them and their underworld allies from plundering the city for twelve years.

As I forecast publicly in the campaign of 1949, O'Dwyer had abdicated shortly after his re-election. This man who defeated my effort ran out just in time. His Tammany supporters went out of power. A new set came in. He said good-by to whoever cared to listen on a hot August day. Grover Whalen, the perennial greeter, presided at his first and only farewell function. Seven bands led columns of wilted policemen, firemen, sailors and soldiers up Broadway into City Hall Park and stood before a reviewing stand banked with the consuls of fifty nations, the perspiring political bosses of the five boroughs, and His Honor himself. It was reported that seven cops and an elderly deputy fire commissioner collapsed from sunstroke.

When Myles McDonald and Senator Kefauver proceeded to place our ambassador to Mexico on a hot seat, of course the President came in for criticism of his nomination of O'Dwyer. But Truman stood by the man from County Mayo as tenaciously as though he had been born in Independence, Missouri. This is old history.

As I write this chapter my own mood and message to anyone who reads this is best expressed by a quote from the late Heywood Broun. "When a good cause has been defeated, the only question is, when do we fight again."

CHAPTER 11 "One Fork, One Wife, One Million Dollars"

Except for my campaign against O'Dwyer in 1949, I had been almost completely retired from politics since 1945. There were still activities which kept me in touch with the public and which occupied all of my spare time; some of which took me away from my law office on a part-time basis. Although I was no longer in City Hall, a part of me was left behind. On December 31, 1945, LaGuardia had appointed me to fill a vacancy on the Planning Commission, and many a late afternoon I would walk from the Municipal Building, where the Commission operated almost literally from an ivory tower. I used to cross the street to City Hall and wander nostalgically through its dignified rooms again. My successor as president of the Council, Vincent Impellitteri, always made me feel at home when I stepped into my former office. I was happy to see that he had followed my advice and took good care of the John Adams furniture and my great-grandfather's portrait that hung upon the wall. But he did ignore my plea to keep the old faded and tattered but beautiful brocade curtains which had hung there ever since 1815. He also had an attractive new carpet. That was all right with me. The LaGuardia economy-minded administration would not permit recarpeting anywhere and I used to try frantically to cover spots on the frayed rug left from some of the hilarious parties given by my predecessors.

I also kept my fingers on the pulse of life in the most congested section of the city: the lower East Side. As president of the Henry Street Settlement I deepened and ripened a beautiful friendship—begun many years before—with Helen Hall, who succeeded the late Lillian Wald as director. My first meeting with Helen occurred on one of my first trips to Albany in 1934. She was on a mission to secure the passage of an amendment to the Multiple Dwelling Law requiring landlords to provide a toilet in every apartment. This did not seem like a very revolutionary doctrine to me. The LaGuardia administration was supporting the bill and I joined Helen in speaking on its behalf. I was surprised to find so many of my prosperous friends in the real estate business on the other side of the argument.

Another time, Helen organized a trip through some of the old lower East Side tenements for a special committee from the Constitutional Convention working on a housing amendment. I recall following the chairman of the committee up the steep stairway. He was a rather bewildered upstate political leader whose gruff voice I heard say: "I don't see any rats here." Playfully I reached up and grabbed his ankle with my fingernails and for a brief moment I think he believed there were rats at large!

Since I had served on the New York Public Library Board *ex officio* for eight years while I was president of the Council and had become exceptionally interested in its work, the board very graciously elected me a regular member, and one of my greatest pleasures has been not only in sitting with the gentle, refined and erudite scholars that are on the board, but also traveling through the various boroughs inspecting branch libraries with such dedicated people as Morris Hadley, president of the Library and son of the late great president of Yale, and Henry Bruère, who built the Bowery Savings Bank into the largest institution of its kind in the world. These men are the type who, without any compensation or glory, give time and imagination to making life in our city a little less drab. Of course the City Center of Music and Drama required a great deal of time, and Hampton Institute at Hampton, Virginia, organized to provide opportunities for education and training for life to Negroes, elected me a life member of the board of trustees. In mentioning Hampton I look forward to the day when there will not be any Negro colleges. In fact that day is dawning; the Supreme Court of the United States has determined that "equal but separate" facilities is no longer the law of the land, so someday perhaps the halls of Hampton will be open to all.

Before leaving City Hall in December, 1945, and shortly thereafter, I received offers for further public service.

The City of Yonkers sent a representative to find out if I would be interested in serving as its city manager by appointment of the Yonkers City Council. I declined. I also received an invitation from the late Robert Patterson, the Secretary of War, to accept an appointment as a sort of "Ober President" to supervise the reactivation of the Democratic processes in the three German states under occupation by our armies. I had a hard time in turning down the offer because it would have given me an entirely novel experience. But I felt under an obligation to stay with the Planning Commission and to stay home with the family while the little children were still at school.

That May, 1946, I was asked by the Norwegian delegate to the United Nations, in charge of organizing the Emergency Famine Relief program to feed little children—to take over the administrative post in that work. But the U.N. had decided not to appropriate its own funds for this purpose and I was expected to raise millions of dollars all over the world to provide an adequate fund. I did not see how this could be done and pointed out that the only effective way to do the job was to assess each member nation.

However, I did agree to head a fund-raising campaign for the New York areas on President Truman's emergency relief drive.

An amusing incident occurred when I went to the committee to secure the cooperation of the mayor. Bill O'Dwyer asked me to come in alone before the committee entered his office. Somewhat flushed, he told me that the President had not consulted him before appointing me. He declared angrily, "Who does Truman think is mayor now?" I tried to mollify him. "Bill, let us forget that. We need your help as the mayor."

"Well, the President didn't consult me, but if he had I might have appointed you anyway." I couldn't help making a friendly jab, for the mayor had just returned from one of his many vacations on his brother's ranch. "Bill, he couldn't have consulted you, because he couldn't find you when you were in El Centro, California."

Few knew where El Centro was at that time, but the mayor with his vacations, as the years went by, certainly got it on the map!

The opening gun of the famine emergency relief drive was held at City Hall. Missing was the LaGuardia genius for showmanship and organization. I arrived to preside at the speaker's stand. The principal speaker of the day was to be the U.S. Secretary of Agriculture, Clinton Anderson. Mr. Anderson had not yet arrived and I kept listening for the motorcycle sirens with which LaGuardia used to expedite high cabinet officials' trips from the airport to City Hall. The walls were not even decorated with the traditional flags of the United States and the city and of the U.N. All we had at twelve noon when the program started was free time which I had secured from the networks to carry Secretary Anderson's speech and the mayor's address over the air to all parts of the country. This precious time was used up by the Department of Sanitation band playing "The Halls of Montezuma" and other popular tunes. In the meantime I was fretting. *At long last I saw a dilapidated-looking taxicab make its way through the crowd. Out stepped the Secretary of Agriculture, representing the President of the United States!* Of course I had wanted the mayor to speak first. I sent messenger after messenger to City Hall; but it was about 12:30 P.M. before the mayor emerged—in the middle of the Secretary's speech. I got to thinking of the majesty of the people of the City of New York and the fervor that had bound all of us eight million souls together when LaGuardia presided.

The National Association for the Advancement of Colored People, the American Jewish Congress, and the

Urban League had not been satisfied with the work of the state commission against discrimination in employment. They invited me to head a committee to look into it. Investigation showed that Negroes seeking employment would be rejected even though they possessed adequate training or skills. Filing a complaint with the commission, the person discriminated against would have to wait months or years while individual members of the commission attempted to change patterns of employment rather than enforce a single individual right. This job seeker would then have to accept employment at a lower skill in order to avoid starving. Several members of the committee wanted to issue a fiery public statement but I persuaded them that perhaps we could accomplish the same purpose by an interview with Governor Dewey. We traveled to Albany and found His Excellency not only sympathetic but interested and many steps were taken to accelerate and improve the work of the commission.

I have always become outraged when little people get pushed around, particularly because of the accident of birth. To me it is not important where we were born or from what race we spring. It makes no difference when we came to America, whether we landed at Plymouth Rock more than three hundred years ago or arrived yesterday at International Airport at Idlewild as refugees from the hatreds of the Old World. The important thing is what we did for America when we got here.

It is a challenge to live with our neighbors. No matter how sympathetic we may be, we do not always understand them. In attempting to praise, we may end up by being patronizing. I have fallen into an old habit, which is best described by recounting an incident: I once addressed a class in an elementary school which was discussing minority rights as part of its curriculum. I happened to remark to them how impressive it was that despite the fact that the American Negro arrived here in chains and had been subjected to indignities ever since, they could still laugh, sing, and express artistic talent.

One little Negro girl with bright eyes, her hair done up in two pigtails and a blue ribbon in each, half-stood up at her desk, with her hand in the air. "Mr. Morris," she blurted, "I think you misunderstand. Some Negroes are like Bill Robinson and Marian Anderson; sure they can laugh and dance and sing, but there are lots of Negroes who are tone deaf and can't sing a note. Others have no sense of rhythm and can't dance a step. Yes, and there are Negroes who never laugh. They have tears in their eyes. We are just the same as everybody else."

I had tried to excuse the misery inflicted on these people by saying that they were basically different— more happy-go-lucky than whites. I shall never fall into that misunderstanding again, and if I find myself thinking that way I close my eyes and remember that little girl (she is grown up now and has children of her own), with the bright eyes and the pigtails with the blue ribbons, saying to me, "We are just like everybody else."

LaGuardia had told me that he believed his greatest accomplishment had been that he had set an example of decent government for the rest of the country to follow. Just three months after his death, I had gotten together with a group of his friends to form the LaGuardia Memorial Association to commemorate his crusade for decent government. We decided that each year we would make an award to an individual, newspaper, or voluntary organization that had made an outstanding effort to bring about a reform of municipal government anywhere in the United States. As president of the association, I was in a position to keep alive the LaGuardia tradition.

Our first award was not given until 1950, three years after the founding of the association, and then it was awarded jointly to an individual and to an organization. It was given to L. Perry Cookingham, the city manager of Kansas City, and to the Greater Philadelphia Movement. Cookingham had become city manager in 1940, when the voters turned against the Pendergast Machine and sent Boss Pendergast to the penitentiary. In ten years Cookingham had established a climate of decency in government that was the envy of civic leaders throughout the Middle West.

The Greater Philadelphia Movement was an organization of more than a hundred business, political and financial leaders who, disgusted with the corrupt practices of the GOP machine, took matters into their own hands and forced through the adoption of a new city charter, clearing the air for more decent government in the city of brotherly love.

In 1952, we presented the LaGuardia award to Edward G. Conroy, director of the Bureau of Governmental Research in San Antonio, Texas. In 1953 the award winner was De Lesseps Morrison, mayor of New Orleans who, with the support of leading businessmen and civic leaders, rescued his city from the Huey Long machine.

In discussing the efforts of individuals to improve

their city government—in marked contrast to the situation in New York—I don't wish to overwork the word "reform." Reform like patriotism (with apologies to Samuel Johnson) can be the last refuge of a scoundrel. But the story of how the people of Kansas City, Philadelphia and San Antonio rose up and threw the boodle boys out of City Hall proves conclusively that Americans can be shaken loose from their traditional apathy toward political skulduggery, and, what is more, can develop techniques to eliminate it.

The Kansas City story, for example, is an excellent illustration. The government for forty years had been the private property of "Uncle" Tom Pendergast, one of the most notorious political bosses in history. Built along the lines of a gorilla (he weighed 225 pounds), Uncle Tom had started out as a saloonkeeper in the North Side slums, and his dynamite-packed fists had advanced him to the front rank of street-corner toughs. Monopolizing the votes of his friends and neighbors for the Democratic machine, he systematically gobbled up the other local bosses and became top political dog in the city.

During his rise to power, a large number of local Republicans collaborated with him—so obsequiously, as a matter of fact, that they became known as the Democratic Aid Society. Under Pendergast, the judgeships were prize political plums because of their control of patronage. Pendergast's judges knew as much about the law as Uncle Tom did. One of them who had completed his schooling at the age of nine boasted, "I don't know what's in the book, but I can read a man's face as good as the Chief Justice of the Supreme Court." Indeed, these judges spent most of their time doubling as boxing referees, seeing to it that the litigants who threw punches at one another in front of the bench fought an honest match.

In 1924, progressive elements in Kansas City joined together to put through a new governmental charter that would usher in an era of reform. Uncle Tom, who took a back seat to nobody in cunning, pulled a fat trick out of his bag. He actually joined the reform movement and became its most vocal spokesman. He had studied the proposed charter and had spotted loopholes in it that he could exploit to obtain an even tighter hold over the city. The charter provided for the abolition of the two chambers of thirty-two aldermen in favor of a single nine-man council. It proposed that all candidates drop their party labels and enter nominating primaries as "independents." It called for the election of a city manager (chosen by the council) who would assume practically all the powers held by the mayor.

Uncle Tom liked the idea of a nine-man council. He realized that it would be cheaper to buy nine politicians than thirty-two. As for the idea that "independents" could be successfully entered to run for office without the backing of any party organization—that conception brought a belly laugh from him. Moreover, he realized that the new city manager could become far more powerful even than the old mayor, if Uncle Tom controlled simply five out of the nine councilmen!

So Pendergast the wolf slipped into sheep's clothing and saw to it that the "reform" charter was adopted. He ran his henchmen as "independents" in the "nonpartisan" primaries. However, the opposition turned out to be more stubborn than he had anticipated, and in the election of November 3, 1925, he gained control of the new council (five to four) by less than three hundred votes—the margin of victory by which the fifth Pendergast councilman was elected.

Shortly after the election, Pendergast's council met to name a city manager. It had been the reformers' intention for the council to hire an administrative expert, preferably from outside the city. But the Pendergast boys, appealing fulsomely to civic pride, decided to hire one of Kansas City's own. They named Henry F. McElroy, a real-estate dealer. And the experiment in "reform" government was launched.

Henry F. McElroy introduced into City Hall a curious system of bookkeeping. Each year he announced that there was a surplus in the treasury while behind the façade of his homespun bookkeeping he was actually running up a deficit of millions. Little by little he usurped the ceremonial functions of the mayor (a Republican), which were practically the only duties that individual had retained under the charter. When Queen Marie of Rumania stopped off in Kansas city, McElroy drew up the plans for the reception, and His Honor had to hustle to obtain a place in the parade. When Amos and Andy came to town, the mayor waited at City Hall for hours to receive them. When the procession finally arrived, Henry McElroy was in the first limousine sharing the bows with the radio stars. The city manager even seized the mayor's office, assigning him to a room behind the city clerk's. He took over the mayor's automobile, elbowed him out of the seat of honor at Chamber of Commerce luncheons, and delivered all the major speeches. Finally, goaded by state Republicans to assert himself, the mayor got his revenge. At the opening of the American Association baseball season in 1927, he beat the city manager to the gun, racing to the mound with the pitcher's mitt. McElroy, casting him dagger looks, put on the catcher's mask and glove and signaled for a waist-high pitch over the plate. His Honor threw a curve that broke wickedly and struck McElroy, almost breaking his kneecap.

Not only did McElroy rule the city with an iron hand, but once a week the "nonpartisan" city manager reported punctually to Tom Pendergast in his lavish residence on Ward Parkway to take new orders.

Uncle Tom's home was the unofficial seat of power. But his official headquarters were at the Jackson County Democratic Club, a few blocks from the Red-de-Mixed Concrete Company and the wholesale liquor business which he owned. On the second floor of a shabby little building which thousands of citizens passed daily on their way to work, above a linen shop and a luncheonette, Uncle Tom put in a solid day's work, directing his machine under a picture of Woodrow Wilson. He had developed a block-by-block control of the voters—one worker for very five citizens—throughout the entire city. He had installed an espionage system that included thousands of volunteer workers spying on one another. The machine received a kickback from the salaries of city employees, who were compelled to sign applications requesting a reduction in pay. Furthermore, several thousand Pendergast henchmen were on the payrolls of private business firms whose owners were in one way or another obligated to Uncle Tom.

As the new "reform" government gathered momentum under McElroy, the Kansas City underworld rode high, wide and handsome. In a typical year—1928—eighty-eight murders were committed, thirteen of the murderers were caught, seventy-six went unpunished. Over 2,300 holdups and burglaries took place—more than seven crimes a day. This was a percentage of crime that was higher in relation to the population than Chicago's.

"Ransom bandits" moved in from all parts of the country, and a wave of kidnapings took place that shocked the nation. One wealthy owner of a chain of drugstores was kidnaped on a busy street in the middle of the rush hour. A height of irony was reached when out-of-town bandits moved in and kidnaped the daughter of Henry F. McElroy, and the parsimonious city manager had to pay a ransom to get her back!

The proconsul who, together with McElroy, ruled Kansas City on behalf of Uncle Tom, was Johnny Lazia, a North Side gangster who had done time in the Missouri penitentiary for highway robbery. Pushing himself forward as spokesman for the duped immigrants of the North Side, Johnny Lazia delivered block votes with monotonous regularity to the Pendergast machine, and became a powerful political ally. A mild-looking fellow with rimless glasses and a shy smile, Lazia was affectionately known as "Brother John" to the immigrants who received coal and old clothes and job handouts from him. As the vice lord of the Kansas City underworld, he was one of the three politicians who named men to the police department.

Johnny had his headquarters in the Cuban Gardens, a fancy night club and gambling casino across from the

Riverside Race Track, owned by Pendergast. Armed guards patrolled the entrance, letting in only the "right" people. Trigger men in evening clothes supervised the roulette and blackjack games that were held inside.

In 1929 Uncle Tom intensified his grip over the city when he elected all nine members of the council. And three years later, he extended his control to Jefferson City when his candidate became governor of Missouri. Henceforth, the State Capitol was known as "Uncle Tom's Cabin."

Meanwhile the thievery in Kansas City continued at a merry pace. The president of the Chamber of Commerce was convicted by a federal jury of pocketing almost a half-million dollars in a charity swindle. When he returned to the city on bail after his conviction, the council engineered a tremendous municipal welcome. "There would have been an even greater crowd at the station if the lobby could hold it!" one of the dignitaries assured him as he was escorted from the train.

City Hall officials publicly defended the city-wide slot-machine racket, although school children were spending their lunch money on the "one-armed bandits." When a grand jury was summoned to investigate the gambling, it was so overwhelmed by phone calls and notes threatening physical violence that it had to meet secretly. One crusading judge, beyond the grip of the machine, told the jury members: "If something should happen to any of us, we would only be making the sacrifice that thousands of American soldiers have made in order that this country might be a decent place in which to bring up our children."

Such was the nightmare through which Kansas City

was passing when a number of individuals shook themselves loose from their apathy and banded together to put an end to it. One of the first to speak out against the reign of terror was a Jewish rabbi, Samuel Mayerberg. Beginning in 1932, he attacked Pendergast from the pulpit and prodded ministers of other faiths to organize for action. He called upon the city government to permit a public audit of its books. And when it refused to do this, he called upon the district attorney of Missouri to begin ouster proceedings against the key officials. Although the immediate results were nil, many people offered the rabbi their support. When he received phone calls and mail threatening him with violence, a former chief of police, disgruntled with Pendergast, organized a bodyguard for him. Mayerberg was given an automobile equipped with bullet-proof glass. (He was actually fired on during a trip.)

Once the rabbi and his fellow ministers started the ball rolling, other groups took up the fight. One called itself the National Youth Movement. It began its work underground, in 1933, using various tricks of psychological warfare. To give the impression that they had several thousand followers, NYM leaders passed out to their personnel metal discs beginning with the number 2,301. Members would sneak up to a local businessman, a teacher, a worker on a busy street and hand out ten cards—one to be filled out with the individual's own application for membership; the others for nine of his friends. After more than a year of secret maneuvering, the NYM came into the open, revealed that it had four hundred members, and announced that it would enter a nonpartisan ticket in the election of 1934. People were

astonished to discover that the NYM was not a movement of wild-eyed radicals, but of well-to-do young men
recruited from the property-owning families of the
South Side. They were rising young executives in their
thirties and early forties, who had graduated from Harvard and other Ivy League colleges, who had played golf
on the fashionable courses and driven their wives to
country club dances. Until a year or so ago, few of them
had given much thought to local politics, but shocked
at last by the steadily deteriorating situation in City
Hall, they had begun to make a study of Henry McElroy's
financial magic and were astonished to discover that the
city had been maneuvered into a position of bonded
indebtedness which would result in their having to pay
off the debts for years to come.

As the NYM movement intensified its activity for the
coming election, the parents of the members joined in,
business leaders, independent Republicans, anti-machine
Democrats. These various groups united in a Citizens-
Fusion ticket. The NYM continued to act as the publicity
arm, training speakers, raising funds, contacting various
religious and cultural groups.

The Pendergast machine managed to squeeze through
the election, winning the mayoralty by less than 60,000
votes. It kept seven of the council seats. The Citizens-
Fusion party gained two. The election was one of the
bloodiest in the city's history. A Kansas City *Star* reporter
who drove up to the polls with a Citizens-Fusion candidate was chased all the way back to his office by gangsters
who peppered his auto with bullets. A Negro precinct
captain was murdered by thugs; a Negro chauffeur was
shot for driving a carload of independents to the polls.

In the wake of this election, the Pendergast machine suffered a series of blows that finally brought it apart. On July 10, 1934, at three in the morning, Johnny Lazia turned into the driveway of a hotel. As he stepped from his automobile to let his wife out of her seat, a sub-machine gun opened up on him, and four assailants sped away into the night. Lazia died several hours later in a hospital, after a battery of physicians, ordered to the scene by Pendergast, and three transfusions failed to save him.

Johnny Lazia's murder was never solved. Pendergast, McElroy, and the chief of police rode in the funeral procession.

That same year, the vice-president of a leading insurance company asked Uncle Tom to influence the Missouri state legislature to abandon its attack on proposed increases in insurance rates and to break up the impounded premiums that had been accumulated during the controversy. The insurance executive proposed that 80 per cent of the ten-million-dollar premium plum be handed over to the company. This little matter was attended to, and Uncle Tom received $315,000 for his services.

The FBI got wind of the deal. But before it had completed its investigation, a second scandal wafted its smell into Washington. The 1936 Kansas City elections resulted in a vote that was larger than the population figures gave it a right to be. An investigation by the Federal Government disclosed that sixty thousand "ghost votes" had been cast by Uncle Tom's machine. The revelations showed to what a tragic extent the machine had corrupted the ordinary American. The majority of the people who had voted fraudulently were not crooks, but small jobholders, ordinary housewives, workingmen who had been terrorized by the machine into doing its bidding because of the economic power Pendergast wielded over their lives. Over two hundred of these people were indicted.

From 1936 on, Pendergast was a marked man. Kansas City buzzed with FBI agents unraveling the maze of his past. The Government finally decided to prosecute him on a count of income tax evasion. In the spring of 1939, J. Edgar Hoover and Attorney General Murphy flew to Kansas City, and three days later Pendergast was indicted for evading $830,000 in taxes.

It was a very sick Uncle Tom who stood trial. He had suffered a coronary thrombosis—and this was followed by an abdominal ailment. Because of his illness, the sentence was light—fifteen months in the penitentiary.

Pendergast's political demise lifted the lid off the cesspool. The FBI uncovered a narcotics ring that had been wringing twelve million dollars a year from addicts, many of whom were juveniles. A federal grand jury uncovered a garbage scandal involving members of Uncle Tom's family. Otto Higgins, the Chief of Police, was sent to Leavenworth for evading close to seventy thousand dollars in income taxes. The secretary-treasurer of seven of Pendergast's companies jumped into the Missouri River before he could be called to trial. The successor to Johnny Lazia as vice lord was sent to jail. The city manager, McElroy, resigned and while under indictment died of a heart attack.

In the spring of 1940 the Pendergast Democrats were finally driven from City Hall, and the Citizens-Fusion people, now calling themselves United Campaigners, took over the government. John B. Gage, an Independent Democrat and a lawyer and cattle raiser, was elected mayor. But the most significant event was the selection of a new city manager, who, as the inheritor of the real power of government, proceeded to make history in municipal administration.

Perry Cookingham was not a politician, a lawyer, or a businessman, but a professional administrator with a background in municipal science. For twenty years, after receiving a degree as a civil engineer, he had made an intensive field study of city government. By the time the Pendergast crowd was turned out of City Hall, Cookingham had achieved a reputation as manager of Saginaw, Michigan. He had held a similar job in two previous towns. Members of the new Kansas City Council traveled to Saginaw, took a look at the job Cookingham was doing, and hired him for their own city.

He reported to City Hall in 1940, and he is there today. When he entered the administration, he went over each department with a fine-tooth comb. He staffed each with experts, installed up-to-date accounting systems and engineering techniques, provided for a constant audit of records. He reduced the size of the city payroll, increased wages, cut taxes on real and personal property, placed the community on a sound financial basis. By 1946, the city was twenty-two million dollars richer than when he arrived. When he came to Kansas City, the water department had 862 workers on the payroll. Within two years, he had the department running efficiently with half that number, lopping off nearly a half million dollars annually that had been paid out to political loafers.

Cookingham cracked down on every detail of corruption, even petty graft. Today, the city's fire engines average as much mileage as under the Pendergast regime, but on half the amount of gasoline. Cookingham insists that fire captains keep their mileage and expenditures of gas at a proper ratio. "Fire engines are no longer acting as filling stations for people's automobiles."

Under Pendergast, the city had been paying money to a private contractor to dispose of garbage from city hospitals and from vegetable stalls at the markets. Cookingham changed the system. Today, city prisoners haul the garbage to a city farm where a pressure cooker converts it into food for livestock. The city has invested in pigs, cows, chickens. Pork is provided for the farm prisoners, milk and eggs for hospital patients. An up-to-date canning plant, operated by the prisoners, puts up tens of thousands of tins of vegetables each summer for the general consumer.

Cookingham has the answer to the age-old argument voiced by apologists for the political machine. Al Smith used to present it to me frequently. "In the old days, Newbold, the poor could take their problems to their district leader and always get a hearing; if they were hungry or cold, they would receive a bag of groceries, coal for the furnace. To whom does the little fellow go today, when the government is run by nonpolitical administrators who, in many cases, were born and raised a thousand miles away from his precinct and do not give a damn for him?"

Cookingham's answer is an effective one. The Kansas City Department of Public Welfare sends out trained social service workers into the city precincts. They are warmhearted, dedicated men and women who, unlike the ward politician, do not seek primarily to help out the unfortunate *after* he has gotten into trouble, *but to prevent him from getting into trouble.*

Cookingham is one of approximately twelve hundred city managers doing a job today in the cities and towns of thirty-six states. While these are heartening statistics, it does not follow that the forces for good will necessarily live happily ever after. The spirit of Uncle Tom is by no means dead in Kansas City or in other places where the machine has received a setback. But the revolt against Pendergast is striking evidence that the American people are capable of cleaning house when they are aroused to the issues.

The story of what has happened in Philadelphia is additional evidence of this. For eighty years the GOP in Philadelphia has offered living proof that Tammany Hall is not confined to the Democrats of New York. However, unlike the chiefs from lower Manhattan, the Republican bosses of Philadelphia have been recruited from Harvard, Yale, and Princeton. They have been aristocrats whose social standing and eminence in the financial world have given their machine rule a gloss of respectability that the graduates of Fulton Fish Market never could acquire.

Significantly, like Uncle Tom Pendergast, the top Republican boss in Pennsylvania, Boies Penrose, in 1919, pushed through his puppet legislature a "reform" charter to gull the public. It called for a revision of the electoral law, providing for a stagger system of elections that made it virtually impossible for any opposition movement to upset the machine. The mayor was to be elected one year, the comptroller, the treasurer and county officers the next, and the judicial officers the third year. In this way, any successful revolt against boss rule could deprive it of only one-third of the city machinery in any single year. For the next thirty years—as well as for the fifty previous years—the only political struggles in Philadelphia were between the factional heads of the machine. The Democrats were as influential here as Republicans in Mississippi. They quietly took orders from the Republicans and were permitted to name minority party members of various commissions and to maintain a small organization. To illustrate how tight was the GOP death grip around Philadelphia—of the *fifty* members serving on the Republican City Committee (a committee consisting of district leaders from each of the city's fifty wards) during one typical period, *forty-six* held jobs on the public payroll ranging up to $15,000 a year. The machine paid eight million dollars annually out of the city treasury to ward leaders. All public employees under control of the machine had their salaries assessed for political expenses. On the day before each election, the Republican City Committee met, and the ward leaders received their orders and their campaign funds. Men who by reason of large families and numerous relatives were able to deliver thirty or more votes were hired as "watchers" and were paid out of the city funds. The Republican vote remained at practically the same level election after election, regardless of what candidates were running, or what issues were involved.

So notorious was the vote-buying that two Republican senators from Pennsylvania were actually refused seats in a United States Senate controlled by their own party. A few days before an election one of the candidates summoned the ward leaders to a meeting and ordered each man to rise and state the majority he would deliver for him at the polls. Then the candidate bought full-page ads in all Philadelphia papers, arrogantly announcing the total vote he would be elected by. The final results were almost exactly what he had predicted. This was too much even for his fellow Republicans on Capitol Hill. They disgorged him from their midst.

Even the depression and the New Deal couldn't shake Philadelphia loose from the stranglehold of the GOP machine. Although Roosevelt swept the city in 1933, the machine, thanks to the staggered system of elections, lost control of only one-third of the administration. The mayor and judges remained in power, and ultimately the GOP won back control of the city council.

Needless to say, under the eighty-year rule of a machine all political ethics become calcified. In Philadelphia, an ancient, civilized community, containing a high proportion of native American aristocracy, under the very shadow of Independence Hall and the Liberty Bell, political conduct had plummeted at times to a low that was unattained even by the sewer morality of Kansas City.

The contrast between the level of Philadelphia community culture and the caliber of her public officials was absolutely astonishing. One representative mayor carried a neon sign to public functions. He would plug it into the nearest electric outlet and place it at the center of the speaker's table, from which it modestly advertised his name to the guests. Another mayor spent only an occasional hour in City Hall. He was the full-time superintendent of a cemetery.

Through it all, Philadelphians remained indifferent. Fifty years previously, Lincoln Steffens had called their attention to the fact that they were completely disenfranchised; that they had no more actual rights at the polls than Negroes down South. Until 1948, when a series of scandals finally shocked them into political action, the majority of Philadelphians accepted the condition of one-party domination as though it were an act of God.

In 1948, the suicide of a minor official touched off an investigation that finally separated the parasites from the blood stream of government.

On May 28, the collector of amusement taxes stepped into the cellar of his home and hanged himself to the water pipe. He left behind a note revealing that he and members of his staff had been tapping the city treasury for years, dividing the money every Saturday afternoon. Three days later, one of his assistants was found dead in his home. He was listed officially as the victim of a heart attack. A grand jury investigation brought out that the city comptroller couldn't have uncovered this larceny even if he had been disposed to, since, despite his official title, he had no knowledge whatever of accounting. Then the Department of Supplies and Purchases came under scrutiny, and the director ended up with an indictment on ten counts of forgery, two of embezzlement, nine of falsifying city records, twenty-eight of doing business illegally with the city through his own florist firm.

Subsequent disclosures touched the depths of low comedy. Employees in the city morgue were found to have stolen shoes and gold rings from the corpses and to have conspired with undertakers to bill the city for padded expenses. The fire marshal went to prison for shaking down hospitals and orphanages. The chief of detectives was charged with foul play in forcing a man to confess to a murder he didn't commit. The superintendent of the city's water-distribution system admitted that he had taken a bribe to tap a pipe outside an industrial plant, and had diverted thousands of gallons of free water into the factory daily. A city plumbing inspector jumped into a river; the head of the vice squad put a bullet through his head.

Actually there had been sporadic attacks on the machine by a minority over the years, and these had found a newspaper to rally around ever since J. David Stern had bought the Philadelphia *Record* from the Rodman Wanamaker estate and turned it into the leading competitor of Annenberg's Republican-inspired *Inquirer* until the *Record* ceased publication.

But in 1948, for the first time, important elements of the community entered the political arena, from which they had hitherto remained aloof, to compete with the politicians on their own terms and to get bloodied up in the process. And, as with the case of the NYM in Kansas City, the new movement was sponsored by individuals with a blue-ribbon rating. The leader of the 1948 revolt was Richardson Dilworth, who came from a family of industrialists. Dilworth had been a schoolmate of the younger Mellons, and had left Yale to join the marines during World War I. Although his left arm was shattered by machine-gun bullets, he returned to Yale, played football and rowed on the crew. During World War II, he fought on Guadalcanal where he received the Silver Star.

Dick Dilworth threw every ounce of his tremendous energy into political campaigning from 1948 on. The machine found in him not another milk-and-water reformer who expressed pious sentiments in the parlor, but an aggressive, brawling opponent who descended upon a precinct with the impact of a leatherneck landing on a Pacific Island. He ran for mayor in 1948, and though he failed to be elected, it was apparent that it would only be a matter of time before his tactics paid off.

Dilworth was joined early in his campaign by Joe Clark, a blue-blood from Chestnut Hill and Harvard, whose great-great-grandfather had founded one of the city's oldest banks. And other individuals rallied to their support. The president of N. W. Ayer and Son, one of the country's leading advertising agencies, met with the president of the First National Bank and over a hundred other business and civic leaders to launch the Greater Philadelphia Movement. This group appointed a committee of twenty-five directors headed by three chairmen, a Republican, a Democrat, an Independent, to direct the campaign. The movement, in the true Fusion spirit, refused to play politics with national issues, but exerted a powerful influence on the more enlightened elements of both major parties to unite in the local house cleaning.

This serious threat to the machine provoked a typical reaction. The bosses themselves tried to jump on the band wagon of the good-government movement by endorsing a phony version of reform. As an aftermath to the 1948 scandals, William F. Meade, a former newspaper reporter who had emerged as the leading spokesman for the machine, was elected chairman of the Republican City Committee. He tried to take the wind out of the GPM sails by pushing forward his own bills to "reform" the city charter. Examination by the GPM revealed that the proposed legislation would leave the machine unimpaired. While Meade planned to consolidate city and county offices, he proposed to exempt from the reorganization the Board of Revision of Taxes which controlled the assessments and choice of patronage. And the president of this board was, strangely enough, William F. Meade! He had intended that the new city charter would be written by men who were appointed by the machine-controlled mayor and council. But the GPM, taking up Meade's challenge, decided to compel the writing of an *honest* charter. It moved in on the mayor with the names of fifty community leaders of the highest integrity and demanded that the membership of the commission be substantially recruited from this list. The pressure GPM applied got results. Six of the fourteen members chosen were GPM directors.

The charter that was adopted by the voters in 1949 can serve as a model for American cities. It provides for the continuous participation of private citizens in municipal affairs. The city's chief financial officer and its civil service commission are appointed jointly by the mayor and by private citizens grouped in nominating panels. A petition signed by 25 per cent of the voters can recall from office at any time the mayor or any other elected official. The mayor appoints a managing director to direct all service departments. This official can be fired only with the consent of the Civil Service Commission. A bureau of information and complaints has been established. Any citizen can report to it on corrupt practices by city officials and employees and get speedy action through the mayor's office. A commission on human relations has been set up to protect people against job discrimination by reason of color or creed.

In the election of 1951, the machine tried desperately to assume a respectable appearance by running a minister for mayor. But he was soundly beaten by Joe Clark, who became the first Democratic mayor to enter City Hall since 1880. Dick Dilworth was elected district attorney in the new administration.

Shortly after his election, Joe Clark announced that he would serve only a single term to relieve himself of the necessity of playing politics for re-election. He has eliminated patronage from his important appointments. And he has staffed the city departments with nonpolitical experts from California, Colorado, Wisconsin, Vermont, and New York.

As in the case of Pendergastism in Kansas City, the GOP machine in Philadelphia is down but not out. It remains to be seen whether Boies Penrose and company have been permanently exiled from Independence Hall. In the meantime, however, we have experienced a deep satisfaction in presenting the LaGuardia awards to Laurie Perry Cookingham and to GPM for achieving the very finest type of American action in this imperfect world.

A third municipal revolution I studied in connection with the LaGuardia medals took place in San Antonio,

Texas, in the spring of 1952. The typical political elements in the people's struggle against disenfranchisement were present here, played out against the background of a southern community.

For generations, San Antonio (the nation's leading gateway into Mexico) had been an assembly point for international cutthroats, bail jumpers, convicts on the lam. Behind the exotic beauty of its rich residential areas festered the slums of Italian, Chinese, German, and Mexican immigrants. The four-square-mile region in which ninety thousand Mexicans were herded together has been called the worst slum area in the United States. Here entire families were packed into tenements that were simply wooden crates, not quite six feet high, in front of which prostitutes solicited their wares for twenty-five cents, and children ransacked the garbage cans for food. From this miasma of filth was bred the nation's highest incidence of tuberculosis and venereal disease. Here rats and fleas were fattened to spread typhus over the city almost annually.

Until recently, it was inevitable that the city government, ruled by a Democratic machine, would do nothing about the slums and the terrible disease rate. San Antonio operated under a charter providing for a mayor and four commissioners, who served at one and the same time as the elected officials and as the heads of the city departments. They not only appropriated the money to be spent, but did the actual spending; in other words, like Poobah in the *Mikado*, they took the money out of one pocket and put it into the other.

Actually one mayor was indicted for a misappropriation of funds, but the judge, his colleague, found a technical error in the indictment and freed him.

The Department of Health existed primarily to shake down streetwalkers for regular financial contributions, compelling them, moreover, to surrender to the police periodically and pay fines to line political purses. It was widely rumored that the Health Department for a "fee" gave clean bill-of-health cards to syphilitic prostitutes, enabling them to pick up wages shelling pecans (to be shipped all over the nation). When a federal grand jury attempted to issue an order enforcing state anti-gambling laws, 1,500 slot-machine operators marched on the courthouse demanding with threats that the order be rescinded. This mob was described in partisan newspapers as being composed of "local merchants."

The city police were regarded with contempt by the public, who felt that the law could be enforced only when the state troopers were called in on emergency missions.

One political boss, Charlie Bellinger, was a Negro who betrayed his long-suffering people by manipulating their votes until he actually held the balance of power in municipal elections for his own aggrandizement. A fellow Negro, a Baptist minister, finally exposed Bellinger and helped drive him to cover. This minister became one of the pioneers of the reform movement that scrubbed San Antonio clean.

Maury Maverick, the New Dealer, gave reform its first solid impetus when he left Congress in 1936, and became the mayor of San Antonio. Then, in 1940, the business leaders who had long regarded the politicians with a cynicism punctuated by fits of exasperation, finally decided to take action. At first they expressed themselves simply as businessmen, contributing money to renovate the city physically.

There were several painfully obvious situations to be corrected. The sewerage system was poor. Streets were pockmarked with pools of water after every rain. Streams running into the financial and residential areas had degenerated into open cesspools. The banks of the San Antonio River winding through the heart of the city were littered with dumped garbage.

Money was raised to build storm drains, to fill in the channels of the river and bury the refuse. Twenty-one downtown city blocks were beautified, and the river was turned into an attractive waterway. On one spot a theatre was built, with the seats on one bank, the stage on the other. Every detail was exploited to advantage. The overflow from a cooling system, instead of being poured into the river, was turned into a cascade.

Once definite progress had been made in improving the city physically, the business leaders took steps to clean up the *moral* climate of their community. They crossed the line into politics even as their compatriots in Kansas City and Philadelphia had done, and they devised strategy to beat the vote getters at their own game. Twenty of them formed a committee, putting up five thousand dollars apiece, to launch a campaign for a new city charter and to educate the people to the issues. With part of their funds they set up a bureau of governmental research and hired Edward G. Conroy as director, to make a study of city administration and to recommend the type of charter San Antonio should adopt. Conroy proposed a city manager-council form of administration. When, before the 1949 elections, the committee of twenty presented this recommendation to the mayor, a typical party hack (one of Maverick's successors), he attacked the committee for mixing into politics. In the heat of anger, he flung a challenge at them. If any businessman didn't like the way he was managing the city, let him step forward and run for mayor.

His Honor, who had spoken in haste, was flabbergasted when Jack White, the president of the Chamber of Commerce, took him at his word and announced his candidacy for mayor. Leaving the management of his three hotels in other hands, White conducted a vigorous campaign and beat the mayor by a four to one majority. It was the greatest landslide in San Antonio's history. For the very first time, a mayoralty candidate carried the polling places in every precinct.

White's victory in 1949 was the opening wedge. When he stepped into City Hall, he was the only reform official, surrounded by machine commissioners. However, in 1952, the reformers, calling themselves the Committee for Council-Manager Government, ran a complete ticket pledged to charter revision. White was re-elected by a two-to-one majority and the reformers swept all nine council seats. The new charter was adopted by the voters and the twelve-year struggle against the machine had ended in victory. San Antonio became the fourth largest city in the nation to adopt the council-manager system of government. Charles A. Harrell was hired from outside the city to be manager. The spoils system was replaced by a personnel management system. The dean of the School of Criminology at the University of California came to San Antonio to overhaul the police department.

Not so long ago, San Antonio had been the pesthole of the nation. But now, whenever the incidence of polio becomes menacing, the entire community, aided by press, radio, and television, unites in an impressive effort to protect its children. During one polio epidemic, the city rushed TIFA fogging machines into service, coating the entire city block by block with DDT. No one pretended to know whether insects and flies could carry the disease, but the people were taking no chances. Whatever the reason, the number of polio cases rapidly dropped, and the wholesale extermination of insects led to a striking decrease of diarrhea, especially in children under two—an illness that had previously caused fatalities.

San Antonio has become the sixth city in the nation to establish a "free port" similar to the one I have described in New York City. Although San Antonio is only the thirty-sixth largest city, it has developed a symphony orchestra that is rated by the National Music Council on the same list as the New York, Philadelphia, and Boston symphony orchestras. The people have held grand opera festivals at which leading Metropolitan Opera stars have performed with a chorus recruited from the natives.

The story of American democracy is not merely the record of what is happening on Capitol Hill, but, more importantly, what is taking place in American municipalities where people are able to exert a more immediate control over their political destinies. Our community politics provide the roots of our freedom with their basic nourishment—or their lack of it, as the case may be.

In 1938, when I had just become president of the New York City Council, I received an invitation from Charles P. Taft, the brother of the late Senator Taft, to come to Cincinnati and address the League of Women Voters. The GOP machine, which had been eliminated from power when Cincinnati adopted a new charter in 1926, had launched an all-out drive to repeal the system of proportional representation by which the city council was elected. The method of electing members on a round-robin basis, rather than by machine-dictated primaries, is as I have remarked elsewhere the most practical solution for avoiding the evils of a one-party domination.

Fresh from my own experiences with the Board of Aldermen, I pleaded with Charles Taft's audience to fight for the retention of PR. "It seems impossible that serious-minded citizens of this city, having once recaptured their government from a predatory political machine, could consider for a moment returning their government to a machine. . . . Don't let Tom Pendergast into Cincinnati."

Well, Cincinnati didn't let Tom in. The 1926 charter, which had freed Cincinnati from the grip of the Cox machine and had resulted in giving this city the most advanced municipal government in our history, was retained by the voters.

When the Cincinnati reform government was first launched, not even its well-wishers expected it to last beyond two or three elections. Today, after twenty-nine years, it is still in effect. It has even survived the test of defeat, and has staged a comeback with a resiliency usually possessed by the machine. Unlike other reform movements in the United States which are still in a period of innovation, the Cincinnati government has become a permanent feature of political life. It has long since been accepted by everybody in Cincinnati but the hardcore machine politicians, the "Bolivars." Two men who have served the city as managers, Sherill and Dykstra, have won a national reputation for their work. But I came away from Cincinnati pondering upon the story of two brothers. It seemed strange to me that the political machine that supported Bob Taft should have been so bent upon destroying Charlie's good government in their own home town.

The group that first organized the government was a temporary alliance of Independent Republicans, nonpartisans, and Democrats. But this coalition solidified into a permanent party, the Charterites. They became the city's largest political organization. Cincinnati is the only city in the nation that has a municipal party that outnumbers the Republicans and the Democrats. The majority of Charterites vote Republican in national elections, but in city affairs they function as a nonpartisan unit.

However, the permanency of the Cincinnati reform movement is a phenomenon, not the rule. Everywhere else the outcome of the struggle between the reformers and the bosses is still very much in doubt. In Kansas City, for instance, the machine after the 1940 debacle, when it lost the mayoralty and every council seat but one, has made a comeback under the leadership of Pendergast's nephew Jim and other politicos. While Cookingham still holds the reins in City Hall, the boss politicans have steadily increased their voting strength in recent elections. One local politico, Charlie Binaggio, appeared to be following in the footsteps of Uncle Tom in his rise to supremacy when he was suddenly murdered in his political clubhouse in 1950.

In Philadelphia, Bill Meade, who was retired from leadership of the Republican National City Committee when the machine surrendered City Hall in 1951, has already resumed his position as top boss in the city. He says quite candidly, "Don't think we're not going to return. These amateurs that are in there now will make a lot of mistakes, and the people will get fed up with them. They'll send for the old pros again. That's what has happened before."

Time will tell whether he is correct. In the meantime, the political bosses need not despair prematurely. The opportunities for political knavery are as ripe as ever. Politicians need by no means surrender the philosophy so modestly expressed by one of their tribe recently: "A man really doesn't need much to be happy in this world—one fork, one suit of clothes, one wife, one million dollars!"

CHAPTER 12 The Spirit of Dissent

Today, I am enjoying the rights, privileges, and immunities of private life. As a Tammany friend put it, my political future is behind me. For me there are no longer any political rallies or street corner meetings. Behind me are the conflicts presented in legislative and governing bodies. Of course, I still get mad when I hear of injustice or read of some little guy's getting pushed around. But, by and large, the old feeling of restlessness has gradually given way to an inner serenity.

Most of my friends who twenty years ago were so active as young Republicans are now in responsible state and federal office. I follow them with interest. Some have disappointed me; the performance of others has exceeded my expectations. Sometimes I toss in bed at night as I ask myself whether I would play it the same way if I were to start out in politics again.

I suppose my greatest political failing has been that I have never discovered the "art of compromise." My failure in this respect sometimes resulted in my differing even with Mayor LaGuardia. This great liberal was sometimes quite baffling to liberals.

In 1939, for instance, the New York City Board of Higher Education appointed Bertrand Russell, the philosopher, to a chair in a city college. LaGuardia, bowing to a segment of popular sentiment that was shocked by Russell's espousal of free love, asked the Board to dismiss him. It refused to do so, expressing resentment at executive interference with education. LaGuardia, however, played a trump card. He moved, on the Board of Estimate, to strike out of the budget the position and funds for Dr. Russell. While I did not agree with some of Dr. Russell's doctrines, I couldn't help but dissent and I cast my three votes in support of my belief that education must be kept free of political interference.

A few years later, I cast those same three votes against another proposal. The Metropolitan Life Insurance Company came to the Board of Estimate with a plan to build a large housing project for the middle-income group. In return for agreeing to a ceiling on rents, the Metropolitan would obtain tax exemptions of approximately twenty-five million dollars; city streets would be closed and deeded to the company, and the city's powers of condemnation would be available to enable various parcels to be acquired by the company at fair value.

One aspect of the project kept me awake at night. The president of this great insurance company who already had LaGuardia committed to the plan frankly declared that the project would accept no Negroes as tenants. To me the fact that some $25,000,000 in government subsidy was involved, that powers were to be delegated by the city, meant that *all* of the taxpayers were making this possible, not just white people or Gentiles. I felt that selection of tenants should be on the basis of *desirability* and not racial origins. I knew that "good tenants" and "bad tenants" could be found in every

284 LET THE CHIPS FALL

race. As a public official in the most democratic city in the world, the idea of applying "white supremacy" to a housing project was insupportable. I could not compromise with LaGuardia and I cast my votes against the project. It went through, but subsequently a law was introduced into the City Council preventing such a thing from happening again.

LaGuardia did not argue with me about either the Bertrand Russell incident or the Stuyvesant Town business. And I did not chide him. His forty-one years of public service left so much greatness in the balance that he will be remembered for that.

I have on occasion been known as an insurgent Republican. I have been criticized by my fellow Republicans for "irregularity." I can only reply that on those occasions when I disagreed with the party, I didn't leave the party, it left me.

When my father entered the Republican party during the last century, it seemed in many respects to be closer to the spirit of Abraham Lincoln than it is today. *Republicans,* not Democrats at the turn of the century, fought the battle of the people against entrenched privilege. The elder La Follette battled against the monopoly of the railroads; Teddy Roosevelt struck out against the big trusts; Norris fought to preserve the people's forests and rivers from exploitation by the utilities. Republicans pushed through the first social ordinances in state legislatures; demanded that the Federal Government protect the welfare of the forgotten man.

The men and women who met in Wisconsin in 1854 to found the Republican party might well be turning over in their graves at the antics of some of the present-day Republicans who profess to speak in their names. They were, to a great extent, people who toiled in the prairies and planted the farms and slept on pallets of straw. They were, in the words of Senator George Aiken, one of their spiritual descendants, "people who . . . wielded the ax and followed the plow until darkness fell and who, after supper . . . by the dim light of a candle did the chores . . . until weariness overcame them."

But as time passed, the party organization moved so far from its grass roots that George Norris, who had grown poor in the service of his country, was finally ousted from the Senate by GOP political bosses, young Bob La Follette was replaced by the present junior Senator from Wisconsin, and LaGuardia complained that he couldn't even get a gallery seat to a Republican national convention.

Once the Republicans provided the brains in American politics. But over the past thirty years, they have been under the paralysis of an inferiority complex, a virtual psychosis against imaginative leadership. The political descendants of Teddy Roosevelt have allowed Franklin Roosevelt and the New Deal to steal their thunder.

In the early twenties when I and numbers of other young men just out of college joined the Republican party we recognized that it had to press forward in its finest traditions if it were to thrive. It could best preserve the interests of private enterprise by providing leadership for the masses of Americans—the worker, the farmer, the average American consumer, as well as the enlightened businessman. American business, as a whole, has made tremendous steps forward in social responsibility since the days of the robber barons, and it was up to our party to reflect its civilizing influence, not to distort it. We young Republicans worked hard and enthusiastically, won our little victories and stood up to our defeats in the belief that we were helping to build a more humane society. The philosophy we shared had no foreign ideological taint. Nothing we proposed was nearly as radical, for instance, as Abraham Lincoln's Emancipation Proclamation which, at a stroke of the pen, divested an entire class of Americans of their property rights. We young Republicans believed in the party. And I believe in its destiny today.

But my party has changed color in certain respects over the years. When I first enrolled, it was the party of strong, centralized federal government. The Democratic party insisted stubbornly upon its outdated and obstructive states' rights philosophy. The Democrats just didn't make sense to me. One can imagine my disappointment, and that of like-minded people, when, with the election of Franklin Roosevelt, the party roles were reversed. Republicans embraced a states' rights philosophy, while the new President invoked the federal power to help the American people climb out of a devastating depression.

Today I am bewildered and saddened by some curious notions of my colleagues—their contempt for the New Deal "brain trusters," for instance; their scorn of professorial brains. I, for one, would be proud to see Republican "brain trusters" in Washington. Why shouldn't we have Republican "eggheads"? Wendell Willkie was not afraid to be classified as a thinker, and he stampeded a convention away from the know-nothings.

In pooh-poohing bold, imaginative leadership among the Roosevelt Democrats, and in stifling independent thinking in our own midst, we now find ourselves on the spot. The chickens have come home to roost. We are the "ins"—and we face a crisis in Republican leadership that has become the crisis of the American people.

Not long ago, I had tea with an old friend who has spent a lifetime in professional social work. She told me that organized society was either going Communist or Fascist or would blow itself up. I replied that there is a fourth alternative. Fortunately, Democracy still has a chance. Franklin Roosevelt, despite the erratic nature of some of his tactics, accelerated the social development of America half a century in twelve years. The Roosevelt Administration has been called by its detractors socialistic. These critics should be aware that an American government is never any more radical than the majority of the people desire it to be. Americans weren't "manipulated" by Roosevelt. They had been waiting for him to come along, to translate their dreams into action. So far no responsible Republican in power has repealed the basic Roosevelt social program. In New York, the Republican-controlled Constitutional Convention wrote collective bargaining, subsidized housing, social security into the organic law of the state during the nineteen-thirties. Although it has publicly spoken out against the welfare state, the Eisenhower Administration has seen fit to broaden the basis of social security.

Whether we like to face the fact or not, Roosevelt's ghost has not been laid. He has been running against the political reactionaries in every election since 1945.

Eisenhower was elected because millions of Americans believed that he would be a strong executive in the Roosevelt fashion, carrying on his policies of world leadership, even though he might differ from Roosevelt in his economic philosophy. Unless a Republican President is willing to lead the American people forward from the social positions they have attained during the last twenty years, his term will be limited to four unhappy years in the White House.

For decades there has been a bitter struggle between two classes of Republicans who have conflicting conceptions of public duty. One group, the Stalwart Republicans, believe that issues should be decided on the basis of what is good for the Republican party; that, if necessary, principles should be sacrificed for the sake of party unity; that social programs are merely a means to political power. The second group, the Progressive Republicans, have maintained, since the days of the Theodore Roosevelt "Mugwumps," that the party is simply an instrument through which to achieve social goals; that principles are more important than partisanship; that it is important to attack evil as evil, not as another name for the Democrats.

This struggle is going on today, not merely in political clubhouses and in Congress, but in the very nerve center of our government, the Executive branch. Upon its outcome depends the well-being of the American people, and indeed of the entire free world.

The Republican party, if it is to survive, must remain true to its origins. And its origins *are* inspiring. After all, this was the party that preserved the Union, guiding it safely through the agonies of the Civil War. It was a

Republican administration that placed the immortal thirteenth, fourteenth and fifteenth amendments in the Constitution, outlawing human slavery and guaranteeing civil rights to all citizens regardless of race, creed or color. Republican statesmen were the first to launch a vigorous foreign policy for this nation based upon their awareness of our global responsibilities. John Hay, a Republican Secretary of State, instituted the Open Door policy for China. A Republican administration liberated Cuba from the reactionary rule of Spain. Teddy Roosevelt was an ardent advocate of the Hague Tribunal; he reached halfway across the world to mediate a settlement of the Russo-Japanese War. The Grand Old Party has certainly *not* been bred in the traditions of isolationism, although the antics of present-day isolationists obscure this historic fact.

Unfortunately, however, the Republican party today is very largely dominated by reactionary politicians who have been boosted into their perches of power by virtue of years of grubby party service and seniority rights. They have successfully stifled all independent thinking, preventing it from rising to an expression of leadership within the hierarchy.

These reactionaries can by no stretch of the imagination be called responsible conservatives. They have no vision of unity, no sense of national destiny that is concerned with the welfare of all classes, characterized by a Winston Churchill in England. They are not of the breed of great American conservatives, Alexander Hamilton, John Jay, Henry Clay, Charles Evans Hughes, for example, who possessed an intelligence and integrity that qualified them to govern a nation, even if they expressed a philosophy with which one may disagree. The outlook of our present-day reactionaries is unworthy of the label of a philosophy. These mossbacks reason with their bellies, not with their minds. Their chief article of faith is the divine right of negativism. They believe passionately that it is their holy duty to shout, like Molotov and his associates, *"Nyet! Nyet!"* to any program put forward by the opposition, simply because it *is* the opposition.

In their fanatical desire to turn back the clock to the days of McKinley, they are considerably to the right of responsible conservatives in most other democracies. The British Conservatives, for instance, have had the common sense to realize that *laissez-faire* economics must be modified to keep up with the Hydrogen Age. But our reactionaries luxuriate in fantasies of a social order that vanished fifty years ago and which all their wishful thinking and their angry, petulant decrees can never recall.

In foreign policy, they are the political descendants of the negativists of 1920 who, blinded by their hatred of Woodrow Wilson, and pledged to destroy everything he supported, sabotaged America's entrance into the League of Nations, betraying their own party's high traditions of world leadership and making Hitler's aggressions and World War II inevitable. Then, in 1941, when England stood battered and alone in defense of the free world, these isolationists bitterly resisted every attempt of our government to sustain her. They voted against lend lease, surplus destroyers and other aid. They announced that Hitler's aggressions were none of America's business. Some even behaved like a Nazi Fifth Column in the United States.

Within recent years they have fought the Marshall Plan to contain Communism as bitterly as they resisted lend lease to contain Hitlerism. When President Truman sent American troops into Korea to stop the spread of Communism in Asia, they called his venture "Truman's War" and tore at the heartstrings of American mothers by speaking of the "needless" and "shameless" spilling of the blood of their soldier sons. If this cowardly exhibition does not come close to being treason, then Benedict Arnold never lived.

If these reactionaries continue to have their way, they will lead the Republican party, if not the American people, to suicide. We Republicans should take heed of the melancholy fate of the Whigs, our political forebears, who were buried as a party by the American voter without a tear, not long after the leadership passed out of the responsible control of Webster and Clay into the grip of the Know-nothings.

To halt the creeping aggression of today's Know-nothings, Progressive Republicans in large numbers will have to overcome their aversion for politics. They will have to roll up their sleeves and plunge squarely into the "dirty business." They will have to lick the reactionary politicians at their own game, reinvigorate the party machinery from the grass roots up, so that responsible liberal Republican thinking can again be reflected in political action, not just in dining-room conversations. We must rescue the party from the *cul de sac* into which it has stumbled since the days of the Versailles Treaty

and move it forward in the policies set forth by Teddy
Roosevelt. We have no future as the party of Warren
Gamaliel Harding.

Today the liberal Republican, and indeed the liberal
of every faith, is undergoing a great testing of his mettle. He is under a bitter crossfire from the totalitarians of the right and of the left. Throughout the country,
as is well known, there are self-appointed groups of
vigilantes who go around investigating the "Un-Amer-
icanism" of their neighbors. Wendell Willkie once said,
"Whenever we take away the liberties of those we hate,
we are opening the way to loss of liberty for those we
love." Without in any way wishing to underestimate the
danger of totalitarian threats from abroad—and indeed
because of this danger—I suggest that local governments
would do well to appoint citizens in each county to go
around making Democracy *work*. If Americans must
investigate, let them pry into intolerance and slum conditions and racial discrimination; let them be present
to speak up wherever there is persecution and suffering; let them examine, for instance, the records of some
of our Congressmen who are the most vocal anti-Com-
munists to find out how they voted on money and supplies
and armies to hit Communism out on the battlefield
where it hurts.

The history of American freedom has been the triumph of reason over human suspicions and fears. Not
long ago Judge Learned Hand remarked in a speech at
the University of the State of New York: "Our nation
is embarked upon a venture, as yet unproved; we have
set our hopes upon a community in which men shall be
given unchecked control of their own lives. That com-

munity is in peril; it is invaded from within, it is threatened from without; it faces a test which it may fail to pass. The choice is ours whether, when we hear the pipes of Pan, we shall be stampeded like a frightened flock, forgetting all those professions on which we have claimed to rest our polity. God knows, there is risk in refusing to act till the facts are all in; but is there not greater risk in abandoning the conditions of all rational inquiry? Risk for risk, for myself, I would rather take my chance that some traitors will escape detection than spread abroad a spirit of general suspicion and distrust, which accepts rumor and gossip in place of undismayed and unintimidated inquiry. I believe that that community is already in the process of dissolution where each man begins to eye his neighbor as a possible enemy; . . . where faith in the eventual supremacy of reason has become so timid that we dare not enter our convictions in the open lists to win or lose."

I like to feel that democratic institutions *can* meet any totalitarian concepts in the open market place and not only survive but gain strength from one year to another and from one generation to the next. Only by our willingness to live the democratic way of life, to fight for the rights of minorities with whom we may have not the slightest sympathy, and to see clearly the difference between dissent and disloyalty will we survive as a people who began life on a new continent without fear.

I realize that I was politically active during an era that is no longer with us. Today, the hard-boiled politician seems to be more in demand. A great American once said that the sins of the cold-blooded and the warmhearted are weighed in different scales. The American people demand of their government leaders today that, however numerous their sins, they be of the warm-hearted kind. We hope these gentlemen will keep our country strong and free and continue to provide prosperity for all who labor with their brains and hands.

Above all, let us not be frightened by those who would stifle the truly American spirit of dissent. They and their political progenitors have laid it to rest time and again, only to have it return to breach the ramparts of their smug complacency and lead the people forward to new achievements. They buried it with Roger Williams and the early American Quakers; they sang a joyous dirge to it when Thomas Jefferson left the White House; they thought they had laid it away for all eternity when Andrew Jackson departed from the scene. But it has returned to haunt them again and again. For it has more lives than the destroyers can hope to cope with. And even during periods when it seems to have been utterly stilled, it is simply slumbering quietly, unobtrusively in the hearts of the people awaiting the arrival of leaders who will harness its vigor into the realization of bold new American dreams.

APPENDIX

The following controversial document was what brought an end to my mission to Washington in 1952. It was printed in the Pentagon, with the approval of the President, and 20,000 copies were sent to my office for distribution. The first flight of them went out to the Department of Justice and the questionnaires when filled out and returned would have been classified as confidential. I had conferred with the Secretary of the Treasury. The next flight would have gone to that Department.

(To economize space, the blank lines of the original document for the answers have here been omitted.)

OFFICE OF THE SPECIAL ASSISTANT TO THE ATTORNEY GENERAL

Questionnaire

GENERAL INSTRUCTIONS

1. Please print plainly or typewrite all answers. Leave no spaces blank. If the answer is "Yes" or "No" or "None," so indicate in the space provided.

2. Use additional sheets where necessary, identifying on same the related question by number and attach them securely to this statement. Place name, address, title, agency and office to which attached at the top of each such additional sheet.

3. Initial the lower left-hand corner of each page of this questionnaire and of each additional sheet attached hereto.

4. For the purpose of this statement, wherever the term "immediate family" is used, it means spouse, children and other persons dependent on you or your spouse for support.

5. Upon completion, the original of this form should be returned to this office in the enclosed envelope.

6. The original must be notarized.

7. The duplicate copy of the statement should be retained by you for your records.

Date ———————————

1. Name ——————————————————————

            First   Middle   Last

2. Address ——————————————————

             Home Telephone Number ———————

3. Agency in which employed ——————————

     Where Assigned: City —————— Bureau ————

                                 Unit ————

     Telephone number and extension ———————

     Name of your superior officer, if any ————

4. Present Position

     Title and grade —————————— Salary ————

     Date of appointment ———————————

     Description of duties ————————————

     ——————————————————————

5. State all federal offices or positions held, specifying the agencies and dates of employment.

			Period	
Agency	Bureau	Unit	From	To

6. Date of birth ——————————————————

               Month   Day   Year

7. Marital status

     (a) Single ———————— Married ————

     (b) Name of wife ————————————————

                    First   Maiden   Last

     (c) Is your wife employed or engaged in any business? ——————————

         If the answer is "Yes" give the information required in (d) and (e):

     (d) Her occupation ——————————————

(e) Her employer, if any

Name	Address	Type of Business

(f) State amount earned by her in:

1947	1948	1949	1950	1951
$	$	$	$	$

(g) Children

Single

Name of Child	Age	School or College Attended		Employment, if any
		Name	Fees, Tuition or Charges	

Married

Name of Child	Name of Wife or Husband	Address

(h) Other Dependents

Name	Relationship	Extent of Support

8. List all persons contributing to the support of your immediate household:

Name	Relationship	Extent of Contribution

9. Net Worth

(a) Give the following information with respect to the net worth of yourself and your immediate family during the past five years or during the period of your federal employment, if less than five years:

	On Entering Federal Employment or Dec. 31, 1947, whichever is later	December 31, 1951
Assets *	$	$
Cash—In banks		
Elsewhere		
Loans Receivable		
Automobiles		
Securities:		
Stocks		
Bonds		
Other Securities		
Real Estate		
Mortgages		
Life Insurance Equities		
Personal Effects:		
Jewelry		
Furs		
Other Personal Effects		
Household Effects		
Other Assets		
Total Assets		

* State costs if purchased: if otherwise acquired state market value at time of acquisition.

	On Entering Federal Employment or Dec. 31, 1947, whichever is later	December 31, 1951
Liabilities	$	$
Current Obligations		
Notes or Loans Payable		
Mortgages Payable		
Other Debts		
Other Liabilities		
Total Liabilities		
Net Worth		

(b) Are any assets held in behalf of yourself or any member of your immediate family (a) by any person, firm or corporation, or (b) under a fictitious name, or (c) through a nominee, trustee or escrow agent? _____.

If the answer is "Yes" give the information required in the following schedule:

Designate Method by Which Held *	Name	Address	Type of Asset

* Specify whether person, firm, corporation, fictitious name, nominee, etc.

10.

(a) Give the following information with respect to the annual income of yourself and your immediate family during the past five years:

Year	Self		Wife	Dependent Children	Total
	Federal Salary	Other Income			
1947					
1948					
1949					
1950					
1951					

(b) Give the following information with respect to the total annual expenditures (including purchases, savings, investments, etc.) of yourself and your immediate family during the past five years:

Year	Amount
1947	
1948	
1949	
1950	
1951	

11. List all the bank accounts, such as, but not limited to, savings, checking, trust, postal savings, Christmas club, building and loan account, etc. of yourself and every member of your immediate family, and all such accounts held, in your behalf or in behalf of

any member of your immediate family, (a) by any person, firm, or corporation, or (b) under a fictitious name, or (c) by nominee, trustee or escrow agent, during the past five years, or during the period of your federal employment, if less than five years:

Bank   Address
Account _____
Opened   Closed   Number   Type
By Whom Held _____ Balance _____

12. List all safe deposit boxes held, during the past five years or during the period of your federal employment, if less than five years, in your name, your wife's name or in the name of any member of your immediate family, and all safe deposit boxes held in your behalf or in behalf of any member of your immediate family (a) by any person, firm or corporation, (b) under a fictitious name:

In Name of _____
Depository _____
Name   Address
Box Number _____ By Whom Held _____
Period in Possession _____ Contents _____
From   To

13. List all your gainful employment or business activities other than your federal employment during the past five years or during the period of your federal employment, if less than five years:

Employer or Business Association _____
                            Name
Address _____ Date _____
                            From   To

Nature of Business ⎯⎯⎯⎯⎯⎯⎯⎯⎯⎯⎯⎯⎯⎯
Nature of Your Association with Business ⎯⎯⎯⎯⎯
Nature of Your Work ⎯⎯⎯⎯⎯⎯⎯⎯⎯⎯⎯⎯⎯
Amount of Annual Earnings ⎯⎯⎯⎯⎯
Time Devoted to Such Work Per Annum ⎯⎯⎯⎯⎯

    If you are an attorney answer Question Number 14.

14. If you handled, or were associated, directly or indirectly in any manner whatsoever, any matter, other than in direct connection with your federal office or employment, during the past five years or for the period of your federal employment, if less than five years, give the following information:

  (a) Have you been associated with any lawyer or law firm under any arrangement whatsoever? ⎯⎯⎯. If the answer is "Yes", list below the names, addresses and nature of association with such persons or firms:

Name ⎯⎯⎯⎯⎯⎯⎯ Address ⎯⎯⎯⎯⎯⎯⎯
Period ⎯⎯⎯⎯ Nature of Association ⎯⎯⎯⎯
    From   To
⎯⎯⎯⎯⎯⎯⎯⎯ Time Devoted Thereto ⎯⎯⎯

  (b) During such period have you handled any matters for any private client? ⎯⎯⎯. If the answer is "Yes" give the following information:

Date ⎯⎯⎯⎯ Nature of Matter ⎯⎯⎯⎯⎯⎯
Client ⎯⎯⎯⎯⎯⎯⎯⎯⎯⎯⎯⎯⎯⎯⎯
       Name   Address
Referred By ⎯⎯⎯⎯⎯⎯⎯⎯⎯⎯⎯⎯⎯⎯
       Name   Address
Amount of Fee ⎯⎯⎯⎯⎯
Nature of Your Participation ⎯⎯⎯⎯⎯⎯⎯
⎯⎯⎯⎯⎯⎯⎯⎯⎯ Time Devoted By You ⎯⎯⎯

(c) During such period have you referred any matters to other lawyers? _____. If the answer is "Yes" give the following information with respect to all such matters:

Date _____ Lawyer _____

                          Name   Address

Your Fee _____ Nature of Matter _____ _____ Time Devoted Thereto _____

15. List the following information concerning your income tax returns:

Year	Collector's Office in which Filed	Person Filing			
		Self	Wife	Joint	Member of Immediate Family
1947					
1948					
1949					
1950					
1951					

16. List any gifts exceeding $250 or any bequests or legacies exceeding $1,000 in value or amount received by you or any member of your immediate family during the past five years or during the period of your federal employment, if less than five years:

Date	Donor	Give Nature	Amount or Value

17. Have you now or at any time during the entire pe-

riod of your federal service had any personal, or private business relationship, other than in the course of the performance of your official duties, with any person known to you to have been convicted of a felony? _____. If the answer is "Yes" give the following information:

Period of Relationship		Name and Address of Such Convicted Felon		Nature of Relationship
From	To	Name	Address	

18. Have you won or lost any sums of money in excess of $500 per annum in any form of gambling during the past five years or during the period of your federal employment, if less than five years? _____. If the answer is "Yes" give the following information:

Date	Type of Wagering	Amount Won or Lost	With Whom Wagered

19. Have you or any member of your immediate family during the entire period of your federal employment received any gift or compensation or promise thereof from any person, firm or corporation for aiding or facilitating in any way dealings with any agency of the federal government? _____. If the answer is "Yes" give the following information:

Date	From Whom Received		Amount or Value	Explanation
	Name	Address		

20. Within the past five years or during the period of your federal employment, if less than five years, have you or any members of your immediate family had cash in excess of $500 at any one time in your pos-

session or under your control, other than in bank or savings accounts? _____. If the answer is "Yes" state full and complete details, including the amount, the manner of acquisition, the manner and place of holding, and the reason for holding:

21. During the past five years or during the period of your federal employment, if less than five years, has your name appeared on any office doors, or office stationery in connection with the practice of any profession or business other than in direct connection with your federal office and employment? _____. If the answer is "Yes" specify below:

Kind of Profession or Business	Where		Address if on Door
	On Door	On Stationery	

22. Have you, during the past five years, or during the period of your federal employment, if less than five years, ever received any brokerage fee or commission in connection with the sale of any chattel or realty? _____. If the answer is "Yes" specify fully below each instance and give complete details:

23. Have you during the past five years, or during the period of your federal employment, if less than five years, ever received compensation for the referral of a legal or business matter? _____. If the answer is "Yes" specify below the circumstances surrounding the transaction, the persons and the amounts involved:

24. List below all brokerage accounts held during the past five years or during the period of your federal employment, if less than five years, in your name, your wife's name, or the name of any member of your immediate family, or in a fictitious name, or in your behalf by any person, firm, or corporation, or through or by a nominee, trustee or escrow agent:

In Whose Name Carried _____

Nature of Your or Your Immediate Family's Interest __

_____

Broker _____

          Name   Address

State _____

           ss:

County of _____

   I, _____, being duly sworn, state that I have read and carefully considered all of the foregoing questions and answers and that the answers are true and complete to the best of my knowledge, information and belief.

Subscribed and sworn to before me

this _____ day _____, 1952

                          Signature

                                 (1)